NONVERBAL COMMUNICATION

Volume 139, Sage Library of Social Research

RECENT VOLUMES IN
SAGE LIBRARY OF SOCIAL RESEARCH

Nonverbal Communication
Survey, Theory, and Research

Daniel Druckman
Richard M. Rozelle
James C. Baxter

Volume 139
SAGE LIBRARY OF
SOCIAL RESEARCH

SAGE PUBLICATIONS
Beverly Hills / London / New Delhi

For information address:

SAGE Publications, Inc.
275 South Beverly Drive
Beverly Hills, California 90212

SAGE Publications India Pvt. Ltd.
C-236 Defence Colony
New Delhi 110 024, India

SAGE Publications Ltd
28 Banner Street
London EC1Y 8QE, England

Printed in the United States of America

Library of Congress Cataloging in Publication Data

Druckman, Daniel.
  Nonverbal communication.

  (Sage library of social research; v. 139)
  Bibliography: p.
  1. Nonverbal communications.   I. Rozelle, Richard M.
II. Baxter, James C. III. Title IV. Series.
P99.5D7   001.56   81-21309
ISBN 0-8039-1652-3   AACR2
ISBN 0-8039-1653-1 (pbk.)

SECOND PRINTING, 1983

CONTENTS

PREFACE

Nonverbal Communication is an attempt to provide a unique contribution to the literature. The volume combines breadth of coverage with analytical reach in experimentation. A broad sampling of concepts and processes are treated. These include channels of communication, impression formation and management, attributions of feelings and cause, information-processing stages, expression games, deception clues and leakage, and inference strategies. A variety of analytical techniques are used in the research. Interpretations are based on results from experiments conducted from the standpoint of the actor (encoding) and the observer (decoding). Both hypothesis-testing and predictive modeling are represented. The material covered should be of interest to social, cognitive, and political psychologists, as well as communications specialists and sociologists. In fact, there is something here for any professional or nonprofessional who is interested in a *technical* treatment of the subject.

Breadth of coverage is represented in Part I. Chapters 1 and 2, authored by Druckman, draw on work that preceded this volume. Five functions of nonverbal behavior are identified by the frameworks discussed in Chapter 1. Two of these functions, processing and persuasion (impression management), are used to organize the channel-by-channel review of Chapter 2. A third function, deception, is the focus of the research reported in Part II. Attempts are also made to seek linkages between nonverbal behavior and certain neurophysiological processes, and to explore the nonverbal aspects of political behavior. Chapter 3, co-authored by Rozelle and Baxter, provides an interlude between the survey of Chapter 2 and the experiments of Part II. The authors review their studies of police-citizen interactions, emphasizing the importance of roles and interpersonal distance in the attribution process.

Analytical reach is illustrated by the experiments and analyses of Part II. Focusing on the nonverbal aspects of deception, the research extends the literature in several directions. An analytically diverse approach yields a variety of insights and technical products. The research includes analyses both of nonverbal behaviors emitted by *subjects* and of nonverbal cues used by *observers* to infer intentions. Particularly noteworthy are the findings from baseline-data comparisons, the classification equations from discriminant analyses, the comparisons between expert judgments and computer predictions, and the intervening variables suggested by correlational results (Chapter 4). Moreover, an attempt is made in Chapter 5 to design cognitive aids for facilitating the task of using nonverbal cues to infer an actor's intentions. This is perhaps the first time that such a strategy has been used in the area of nonverbal communication. The modeling exercise of Chapter 6 shows how observers discount some factors and weight others preferentially in the process of judging intentions.

The research discussed in this volume and in its predecessors makes clear the value of treating nonverbal behavior as meaningful communication. While opportunities for application exist, more research is needed. Probes into the complex environments where actors engage in simultaneous encoding (presentation) and decoding (interpretation) would be useful. Guided by the concepts discussed in Chapter 8 and elsewhere, the investigator can explore processes involved in expression games played by negotiating partners or adversaries. Building on the results of the experiment described in Chapter 5, he or she can apply cognitive aids to other problems where inferences are required. The results of these additional investigations would further expand our understanding of the significance of nonverbal expressions and displays.

The following individuals are acknolwedged for their contributions.

At Mathematica, our colleague Robert Slater, a political scientist, has offered numerous suggestions and is engaged in a related study of nonverbal behavior in field settings; Robert Procelli provided programming support for the analyses reported in Chapter 6; and Emma Davis typed the entire manuscript through several versions, and has given us the essential support needed to bring the project to a successful conclusion. We are deeply indebted to each of these individuals.

In Houston, Steven Miller and Junifer Smith conducted the experiment reported in Chapter 4, performing the involved statistical analyses and offering many suggestions on research strategy and interpretation. Thanks also go to the secretarial staff of the Psychology Department for clerical help.

At Hurlburt Field Air Force Base, Colonel Richard A. Dutton, former Commandant of the USAF Special Operations School, invited us to participate in their training program; Carol E. Willett and Major John M. Allman, co-directors of the Cross-Cultural Communications course and Nonverbal Communications Laboratory, worked closely with us on both substantive and administrative details, and Lieutenants John Koren and Nancy Thomas aided in the collection of data and handled arrangements for our residence at the base. Of course, to all participants in the workshops we extend our sincere appreciation. These individuals made possible the studies reported in Chapters 5, 6, and 7.

At the Defense Advanced Research Projects Agency (DARPA), Judith Ayres Daly provided helpful advice and encouragement on many aspects of the work and, as monitor of the DARPA-sponsored project, made necessary administrative arrangements for data collection and dissemination of technical reports.

Thanks are due to the Defense Advanced Research Projects Agency for research support to develop nonverbal indicators of intentions and information-processing. Such support does not imply that this study reflects the views of the Department of

Defense. Finally, thanks are extended to our families, whose patience and good cheer facilitated the research.

—Bethesda, Maryland

Houston, Texas

INTRODUCTION

By virtue of a series of discoveries and conceptual departures in the social sciences, our understanding of the process of communication has been expanded. Where the emphasis in the study of communication was on the spoken or written word, there is now an emphasis on the nonverbal. In the words of Ashley Montagu and Matson (1979: xiii), "It is not merely a hidden dimension or a silent language that has been uncovered by the new wave of scientific explorers; it is more like a neglected universe of discourse and intercourse. We are becoming aware that the verbal domain is only the tip of the iceberg of communicative experience—that there is more, much more, to human dialog than meets the ear." The most recent of a score of popular and technical accounts, Ashley Montagu and Matson's *The Human Connection* makes evident the progress made to date.[1]

Results obtained in numerous experiments and naturalistic studies support the assumption that gestures, expressions, and other nonverbal behavior convey meaning. No longer must we rely on speculation about the versatility of the face for expressing emotions, the communicative value of "body language," the effects of gaze on arousal, the use of personal space for structuring social relationships, or the significance of implicit vocalizations for inferring psychological states. Ekman's work on facial expressions, Mehrabian's role-playing experiments on postural cues, work by Argyle, Ellsworth, and Exline on visual behavior, Sommer's studies on proxemics, and the detailed paralinguistic coding reported by Duncan and others suggest that nonverbal behavior has considerable psychological significance. These investigators have also defined a specialized field that cuts across traditional disciplinary boundaries.

By most signs the field has prospered. The appearance in recent years of literature reviews (for example, Harper et al., 1978) and books of readings (such as the one edited by Siegman and Feldstein, 1978) attests to the variety of aspects of nonverbal communication being explored. Broad theories that integrate these diverse specialties are beginning to surface, and, perhaps most significant, attention is being paid to applications. The nonverbal aspects of psychotherapy (Waxer, 1979), of communication between patients and medical practitioners (Friedman, 1979), of political behavior (Frank, 1977; Wiegele, 1978), of police-citizen encounters (Havis et al., 1981), and of city transit negotiations (Hermann, 1977) are a few of the recent attempts to apply the research to practical problems.

The study of nonverbal communication has roots in several intellectual traditions. Most notable, perhaps, are the orientations of symbolic interaction, behaviorism, and psychoanalytic theory. From symbolic interactionism we get a more complex, more total conceptualization of behaving man. Behavior is interpreted in a broader context defined by Goffman (1959), Berne (1964), and others: Gestures take on increasing significance as impressions "given off" unwittingly in everyday life; spatial manipulation is seen as a crucial factor in the negotiation of everyday encounters and relations in public space; and the importance of mutual looking in the initiation and maintenance of speech is made apparent. Together with other observations derived from naturalistic studies, these insights provide a basis for systematic work on the meaning of nonverbal behavior.

From behavioral psychology we get a focus on overt behavior. Measurable behavior may take the form of specific acts, streams of behavior, or behavioral programs (Scheflen, 1968). Once specified, the nonverbal behaviors can be related to accompanying verbal behavior or to the actions of another person. Such an empirical orientation has guided the conduct of numerous studies whose purpose is to discern a pattern from repeated observation of "streams" of behavior. It has also permitted cross-species comparisons that are part of a burgeoning literature on animal communication (Petrovich and Hess, 1978).

Psychoanalytically oriented investigators have also shown an interest in nonverbal behavior. Some have focused on the identification of particular moods or feelings from specific behaviors (Fromm-Reichmann, 1950). Others have explored nonverbal behaviors as a means of inferring a patient's "unacceptable" feelings: The consequences of repression or reaction formation provided an impetus for research on nonverbal behavior (Deutsch and Murphy, 1955). The psychoanalyst's interest in "deeper meaning" is represented in current research on nonverbal cues of psychological states. Together with symbolic interactionism and behaviorism, psychoanalytic theory provides a basis for investigating nonverbal behavior. A more total view of behavior, measurable acts, and a search for deeper meaning are the primary considerations of researchers in this area.

The study of nonverbal behavior may be dated from Darwin's (1872) account of the processes of emotional expression in animals and human beings. Freud (1938) was probably the first systematic investigator of the field, focusing on the hidden meaning of "accidental" behaviors. A number of German investigators pursued the dynamic significance of expressive behaviors in various abnormal groups, especially schizophrenics (Wolff, 1948). Allport and Vernon (1933) may be credited with both redirecting interest in the area to normal expressions and placing an emphasis on individual consistency in expression over extended periods in various settings.

However, Ray Birdwhistell (1952) has probably done more to revitalize the topic than any other recent investigator. He approached the subject of nonverbal behavior as a communicative act. His monograph, *Introduction to Kinesics,* sparked a great deal of interest. His major achievement, perhaps, was to suggest a multichannel model that portrays communication as a

continuous process "making use of all the sensory modalities—
not just the auditory-acoustic channel but also the kinesthetic-
visual channel, an 'odor-producing olfactory' channel, a tactile
channel, and so on" (Ashley Montagu and Matson, 1979: 47;
see also Birdwhistell, 1970).

Underlying Birdwhistell's approach is a linguistic-kinesic
analogy. Just as linguistic study can be divided into descriptive
and historical linguistics, kinesics can be broken down into
prekinesics (physiological determinants), microkinesics (units of
measurement), and social kinesics (patterns of movements in
terms of their social functions). The *kineme* is regarded as the
smallest set of body movements with differential meaning,
analogous to the linguistic unit referred to as the *phoneme*.
Along with both smaller and larger units, the kineme provides
the basis for extraordinarily detailed descriptions of each body
part in terms of its width and extent, or velocity. Not simply
content with measurement, however, Birdwhistell provided a
system for classifying types of nonverbal communication and a
vocabulary for discussing a wide variety of body movements.

Though recognized as a major contribution, Birdwhistell's
system has been criticized on several grounds, including
practical problems of measurement (Weitz, 1974), the weakness
of the kinesic behavior and language analogy (Dittmann, 1971),
and the lack of a guide for determining the relative significance
of different nonverbal behaviors (Mehrabian, 1972). Moreover,
the approach does not confront the issue of verification: One
cannot be certain that this is the best-fitting model or the
"correct" one (Weitz, 1974). Alerted to these problems, a more
recent generation of researchers have taken steps to solve them.
Birdwhistell's initial impact inspired a number of researchers to
look seriously at these channels of communication, and ushered
in the "nonverbal revolution."

Another of Birdwhistell's (1970) contributions was to point
out that no position, expression, or movement ever carries
meaning in and of itself. It must be understood in terms of a
broader context. Central to his concerns is the question of the
function of movement within the total communication situa-

tion. Other major contributors to the nonverbal communication literature (such as Hall, 1966) have also considered this question, and it is a primary concern of this project. Highlighted by this project is the role of nonverbal behavior in the context of international politics.

International politics is a context in which nonverbal behavior plays an important part. Nonverbal behavior influences those aspects of learning and communication that occur at the juncture where structural and psychological processes interact (Druckman, 1980). As such, it is an essential component of psychological analyses of political behavior. Its relevance to international politics is noted by Milburn (1977: 137):

> To function well together the superpowers need to be able to predict accurately the perceptions and responses of one another and, as a second-order perception, to understand that the messages that they as threat sources emit are thoroughly understood. Attention to the way the other perceives threats enables one to ascertain whether threats designed to inhibit violence are likely to provoke it.

Accurate prediction of responses and transmission of messages may well turn on the nonverbal cues that are "read" and presented.

Emphasized here is the dual role of political actors. Operating in a variety of settings, political actors are analysts and tacticians. As analysts they look for clues that may reveal another's objectives. As tacticians they attempt to elicit information and influence perceptions and evaluations. Nonverbal behavior can provide the clues and can be used tactically to produce certain effects. Results of experiments on stress and on deception illustrate how nonverbal behavior can provide clues to the presence of these psychological states or intentions. The work on persuasion and impression management demonstrates the way in which nonverbal behavior produces effects. Both types of experiments are reviewed below. Particularly noteworthy are the implications of this work for a conceptual framework that considers nonverbal communication in terms of both information-processing and impression management.

Implications for detection and impression management can also be derived at another level of analysis. Nonverbal behavior may reflect and affect certain physiological processes. For example, it has been argued that for each emotion there are particular patterns of neural firings and associated facial muscle movements, and that this proprioceptive feedback provides the basis for our experience of emotion (Tomkins, 1962). Such nonverbal behaviors as gazing and distancing have been shown to affect arousal as it is indexed by EEG readings (Gale et al., 1972) and by micturition time or duration (Middlemist et al., 1975). The results of these and other studies have practical implications: Nonverbal behaviors can substitute for or augment physiological indicators of psychological states. As such, the nonverbal variables can be employed in research programs on detection and control. They also may enter into considerations in the design of biocybernetic systems.

This volume is organized into two parts. Part I consists of three chapters. First, the meaning of nonverbal behavior is discussed in terms of concepts, functions, and frameworks. Then a state-of-the-art review is presented, including a consideration of special issues. The research is organized according to channel, although multiple-channel research is also considered. Four nonverbal channels are surveyed: paralanguage, facial expressions, kinesics, and visual behavior. Relationships between verbal and nonverbal behavior and the effects of cultural, situational, and personality variables are also discussed. Interwoven through the discussion are potential linkages between nonverbal behavior and neurophysiological processes, as well as nonverbal aspects of political behavior. The third chapter uses concepts developed in Chapters 1 and 2 to explain findings from studies on interpersonal distance, designed in the context of police-citizen interactions.

The four chapters of Part II report the results of experiments on nonverbal behaviors associated with deception. The experiment described in Chapter 4 deals with the nonverbal behaviors that distinguish among attempts to reveal, evade, or conceal information about policy-related issues. Highlighted are differences among the conditions in frequencies of nonverbal behaviors, correlation patterns, and correlates with psychological states. Chapter 5 is an experiment on decoding nonverbal clues to deception. Focusing on the observer, the experiment is an evaluation of the impact of alternative training regimens on accuracy of inferences about intentions. The modeling exercise of Chapter 6 is designed to separate components of perceived honesty, evasion, and deception; global impressions, attributed feelings, and nonverbal behaviors are compared. Finally, the impact of different portrayals (deceptive, evasive, honest) on perceptions is analyzed in Chapter 7. Illustrated by this research program is analytical diversity within the contours of a particular conceptual approach.

A final chapter presents a framework that distinguishes situations in terms of structural aspects; it is a first step toward linking nonverbal behaviors to features of the context in which they are displayed.

NOTE

1. Capturing the imagination are such popular titles as *How to Read a Person Like a Book* (Nierenberg, 1971), *Contact: The First Four Minutes* (Zunin and Zunin, 1972), *Body Language* (Fast, 1971), *Touching* (Ashley Montagu, 1971), and *The Hidden Persuaders* (Packard, 1957). More notable for their contribution to a lexicon than to a science of nonverbal communication, these treatments are not emphasized in this volume. Our approach is based on the growing technical literature, much of which is reviewed in the discussion to follow.

PART I:

SURVEY AND THEORY

The chapters of Part I consist of synthesis and theory. Chapter 1 is a discussion of the frameworks designed to provide a conceptual base for the study of nonverbal communication. These frameworks imply several functions served by nonverbal behavior. Five functions are distinguished: to indicate prearticulated feelings, to provide clues to information-processing activities, to serve as emphases in persuasive appeals, to facilitate deception or holding back information, and to convey subtle messages. Specific nonverbal behaviors are associated with each of these functions. Emphasized in the survey and in the research discussed in Part II are the processing, persuasion, and deception functions.

Implications for information-processing and impression management (persuasion) are highlighted in the state-of-the-art survey of Chapter 2. Each of the nonverbal channels reviewed provides indicators of information-processing activities. Such paralinguistic behaviors as unfilled pauses and verbal productivity may serve as signals of the completion of processing. Certain microfacial expressions are shown to index processes similar to those indicated by neurophysiological variables. Body movements play a role in the process of speech-encoding, an activity that occurs during the prearticulation stage of information-processing. In addition, such visual behavior as the pupillary response may be a useful indicator of those cognitive activities that precede decision-making.

Each of the nonverbal channels is also involved in impression-management activities. Such paralinguistic behaviors as speech volume and talking rate may facilitate or hinder attempts to convey desired impressions. Control over facial expressions enhances persuasiveness and facilitates the perpetration of deception: Its plasticity enables one to arrange one's appearance to "fit the occasion." Body movements can also be used effectively to convey impressions. Those body movements that lead to impressions of credibility, empathy, and attentiveness enhance a speaker's persuasiveness; those that suggest discomfort and anxiety may reveal deceptive intentions. The role played by eye contact in expression is illustrated by effects on the level of intimacy experienced in an interaction, as well as the influence of length of gaze on liking. However, as in the other nonverbal channels, the effects of eye contact are mediated by context. Different impressions seem to be conveyed in different situations.

A discussion of multiple-channel research concludes the state-of-the-art survey. Relationships among different types of nonverbal behaviors are illustrated by three types of findings: relative importance of different channels, interactive effects of different behaviors, and multiple indicators of intentions. Nonverbal behavior is shown to have a stronger impact on impressions than accompanying verbal statements; impressions conveyed by eye contact are shown to vary with distance between the interactants, and multiple nonverbal indicators provide a less ambiguous appraisal of psychological states than single-channel cues.

These findings have implications for information-processing and impression management. Each of three stages of processing activity is indexed by multi-channel behaviors. Impressions conveyed in one channel may be bolstered or offset by behavior displayed in another channel. For these reasons several types of nonverbal behaviors are assessed in the research program on detecting intentions and on managing impressions (Part II).

The use of personal space has received more attention in cross-cultural studies than other aspects of nonverbal communication. Several of these studies, conducted in the setting of police-citizen interactions, are reviewed in Chapter 3. Preferences for spatial arrangements, distance, postural arrangements, touching, and architectural design have been shown to vary from one culture to another. Different interpretations are placed on such behavior as standing too close, facing directly during conversations, touching members of the same sex, and placement of furniture.

Implications for communication effectiveness derive from these cultural differences. Certain seating arrangements, table placements and shapes, and postures during conversation can facilitate communication for members of one culture while hindering communication for members of another. Impression management can also be affected: Knowing a culture's spatial preferences increases the chances of creating a favorable impression; not knowing these preferences could lead to isolation and rejection.

1

CONCEPTS, FUNCTIONS,
AND FRAMEWORKS

Students of nonverbal behavior (NVB) have been aiming at what scientists everywhere strive for: meaning. Most of the research on this topic, has, however, been devoted to the refinement of that which precedes meaning: observation and description. While a large empirical literature has been developed, only a few attempts have been made to provide a solid conceptual base for the proliferating research. Whether this state is viewed as a serious disjunction or as a necessary first step, most agree that the field has reached the stage of integration. Efforts in this direction are discussed in this chapter.

Nonverbal behavior acquires meaning as part of a communication process. Recognizing this, several investigators have devised frameworks that construe NVB in terms of its communicative value. Most notable are the frameworks provided by Dittmann (1972), Ekman and Friesen (1969b), and Mehrabian (1972). Dittmann attempted to apply communication theory to the interpersonal communication of emotions. Ekman and Friesen provided the most elaborate system for classifying nonverbal behaviors in terms of origin, usage, and coding. Mehrabian construed nonverbal behavior in terms of social orientations. Together with the empirical literature, these schemes suggest certain basic functions of nonverbal communication (NVC). In what follows, each of the schemes and the various functions are summarized.

TABLE 1.1 ASPECTS OF MESSAGES

All messages may vary:

A. In terms of Sender or Encoder:

Message may vary in intentional control; how much control sender exercises in communicating message

B. In terms of Receiver or Decoder:

Awareness of message: message may be subliminal and not perceived, or perceived and repressed (kept out of awareness)

C. In terms of channel of communication:

Continuum of communicative specificity

Communicative . . . . Expressive
    Language   Facial expression   Vocalizations   Body movements

D. In terms of message information value:

    Language   Facial expression Vocalizations   Body movements

Discrete . . . . Continuous
Greatest channel capacity   Least channel capacity needed
needed (highest message   (lowest message information value
information value and most   and least decoder attention required)
decoder attention required)

SOURCE: Adapted from Dittmann, 1972.

Nonverbal Behavior as Nonverbal Communication

Drawing on communication theory, Dittmann (1972) provided a conceptualization of human communication that included both verbal and nonverbal behavior and dimensions within which such behavior can be categorized. Like verbal behavior, NVB can be construed in terms of sources and users, encoders and decoders, and channels. His structural characteristics of intentional control, awareness, communicative specificity, and channel capability are useful concepts for distinguishing between types of nonverbal messages. These dimensions are summarized in Table 1.1.

Intentional control refers to an encoding process whereby a communicator either allows his or her emotions to be expressed or controls them. *Level of awareness* concerns a decoding process whereby a message is transmitted with full consciousness, so weakly that it does not draw the receiver's attention (subliminal), or kept out of awareness entirely (repressed).

Communicative specificity refers to the information value of a message. A communication continuum might range from the most communicative message, language, at one end, to the least communicative expressive messages (for example, such body movements as self-manipulations), at the other. In between might be facial expressions and paralinguistic cues that convey less information than words but more than body movements.

Channels of communication refer to two overlapping dimensions: one ranging from discrete to continuous, the other from high to low capacity. Discrete messages (such as verbal statements) are more communicative, and continuous ones (like hand-rubbing) are more expressive; high-capacity channels (such as facial expressions) convey more information than do low-capacity channels (such as body movements).

Referred to also as indicative behavior (Dittmann, 1978), the continuous NVBs may be more difficult to interpret but are not less meaningful than language. Taking the form of stylistic cues, NVBs frame a communication in the sense of providing information about motives or intentions (Goffman, 1969). Such information can be understood as part of a metacommunication system where NVBs are "statements" about the relational aspects of an interaction (Exline and Fehr, 1978). It can also refer to "the basic state a person finds himself at any given time, from which all his behaviors derive" (Dittmann, 1978: 92). Both meanings contribute to an interpretation of the total message. Less clear, however, is the nature of this contribution: Which states are associated with which behaviors turns on the issue of the way in which the inference process works, a subject of the research to be reported below.

While most of Dittmann's concepts have been used frequently in the nonverbal literature, none is used more often than channels of communication (for example, auditory, visual, olfactory). Perhaps the most important implication of this term concerns message transmission. Discussed below, the issue of single- versus multiple-channel transmission is relevant to problems of accuracy: Messages sent through multiple channels can be either more or less accurate than those sent through single channels. Channel of communication is a key concept in organizing our treatment of NVC. It should be noted, however, that useful as Dittmann's concepts are, they have rarely been used to guide or interpret the research literature. Unfortunately, it appears that the research, in most instances, does not reflect the sophistication of this system.

An approach more closely linked to empirical work is the category system developed by Ekman and Friesen (1969b). Their unit of observation—referred to as the nonverbal act or position—is a clear movement observable to another person without the aid of special equipment. It has a distinct beginning and end. According to the authors, "the classificatory scheme is built directly from the acts and positions found in film records, rather than derived from a priori notions" (1968: 193-194). This being so, the labels used are more denotative than connotative. However, some of the categories reflect their primary interest, which is to detect psychological states, most notably those related to emotions. The system is summarized in Table 1.2.

The characteristics of NVB are construed in terms of usage, origin, and coding. Usage refers to the circumstances surrounding the occurrence of the act. The physical setting, role situation, and atmosphere are the external conditions that occur at the same time as the nonverbal act. The temporal relationship and meaning of co-occurring verbal behavior, the person's conscious or unconscious knowledge of the behavior being performed, and the feedback about that behavior received from others are other aspects of usage. Finally, important distinctions are made with respect to the type of information conveyed: informative, communicative, or interactive. Similar to Dittmann's (1972) concept of communicative specificity, this involves the extent to which the message is understood by others, is informative, and serves to influence or modify the behavior of another person or persons.

TABLE 1.2   EKMAN-FRIESEN CLASSIFICATION OF NONVERBAL BEHAVIOR

Types of Nonverbal Behaviors	Characteristics of Nonverbal Behaviors
1. Emblems: Movements that are communicative substitutes for words	
2. Illustrators: movements that accompany speech and accent, modify, punctuate it, etc.	
3. Regulators: movements that maintain or signal a change in listening/speaking role	
4. Affect displays: facial expressions	
5. Adaptors: Self- or object manipulations related to individual need or emotional state	
	1. Usage External conditions Relationship to verbal behavior Awareness/intentionality of person engaging in nonverbal act External feedback Type of information conveyed: idiosyncratic encoded meaning; informative; communicative; interactive
	2. Origin Innate response Species learned Culturally or socially learned
	3. Coding Extrinsically coded acts Arbitrarily coded acts Iconically coded acts Intrinsically coded acts

SOURCE: From Robert G. Harper, Arthur N. Wiens, and Joseph D. Matarazzo, *Nonverbal Communication: The State of the Art,* New York, John Wiley, 1978, p. 128. Reprinted by permission of the publisher.

Origin refers to the source of the nonverbal act. While some NVBs may be reflex actions and others are rooted in experience more-or-less common to a species, most are probably culture-specific, originating from instrumental tasks formally taught or learned by imitation in the course of social development.

Coding refers to how meaning is attached to nonverbal acts. The primary distinction is between extrinsically coded and intrinsically coded acts: The former signifies something else, while the latter "stands for itself." Extrinsically coded acts may bear no resemblance to their meaning, as when the forward movement of a fist conveys by itself no information on the intended meaning "to move the ball" (arbitrarily coded), or may resemble their meaning, as when a person makes a throat-cutting movement with his finger (iconically coded). Intrinsically coded acts contain the meaning of the act in the action itself, as in the good-bye wave or the "come to me" hand movement. Still finer distinctions are made by Ekman and Friesen in their seminal 1969 paper, "The Repertoire of Nonverbal Behavior."

Usage, origin, and coding form the basis for the category system proposed by Ekman and Friesen. Five general categories are distinguished in terms of the particulars of usage, origin, and coding. Emblems are movements that have a direct verbal translation and are easily understood. Examples include shaking a fist and waving as a greeting. Illustrators are directly related to speech and illustrate what is verbalized (rapping on the table to emphasize a point, for instance), while regulators are behaviors that maintain and regulate speaking and listening (such as head nods and small postural shifts). Affect displays consist primarily of facial expressions and are distinguished from illustrators and emblems in terms of the amount of information they convey about the emotional state of the subject. Finally, adaptors are self- or object manipulations. This category is important in terms of the meaning conveyed about individuals. It is divided into self-adaptors (head-scratching, picking at fingers), alter-adaptors (folding arms across body, upward leg movements), and object adaptors (smoking movements, fondling jewelry).

TABLE 1.3   MEHRABIAN'S DIMENSIONS OF NONVERBAL
             BEHAVIOR

Dimensions	Cues	Nonverbal indicators
Positiveness or Evaluation	Immediacy	Touching, distance, forward lean, eye contact, observation, orientation
Potency or Status	Relaxation	Arm-position asymmetry, sideways lean, leg-position asymmetry, hand relaxation, neck relaxation, reclining angle
Responsiveness	Activity	Facial activity, vocal activity, speech volume, speech rate

Further discussion of these categories is included with the research reviewed below. Some are also included in the system of analysis used in the research reported in Part II.

Another approach closely linked to empirical work is that of Mehrabian (1972). Using more categories than any other system, Mehrabian organized them economically in terms of three dimensions. The dimensions, referred to as basic social orientations (or referential dimensions), are positiveness or evaluation, potency or status, and responsiveness. Positiveness refers to evaluations of persons or objects that determine approach and avoidance tendencies. They are indexed by the "immediacy" cues of touching, distance, forward lean, eye contact, and orientation. Potency relates to social control and is indexed by such postural "relaxation" cues as arm- and leg-position asymmetry, sideways lean, hand and neck relaxation, and reclining angle. Responsiveness is regarded as the nonverbal counterpart of orienting behavior and indicates one's importance to another. Where immediacy and relaxation indicate variations in liking and status, respectively, activity communicates responsiveness. Such variables as facial and vocal activity, speech volume, and speech rate index this dimension.

Mehrabian's system is summarized in Table 1.3. Each of the dimensions and associated cues is involved in certain activities. Experimental findings obtained by Mehrabian suggest that the immediacy cues (positiveness dimension) are concomitants of deceitful and truthful communications. Relaxation cues (potency dimension) occur primarily in hierarchical situations where relative status is a salient categorization of the social environment. The activity cues (responsiveness dimension) seem to covary with intended and perceived persuasiveness.

Placing NVB in the context of social behavior, Mehrabian sought to capture fundamental interpersonal dimensions corresponding to the social motives of affiliation, power, and achievement (Terhune, 1968). By so doing, he provided a framework for identifying socially significant implicit (nonverbal) behaviors. Moreover, by reducing the problem to manageable proportions, he was able to generate important experiments on such topics as persuasion and deception. We will return to Mehrabian's work in our review and again in discussing our methodological approach. Some of his categories were adapted for use in the coding system presented in Part II.

Each of the systems described above contributes useful concepts and indicators to a conceptualization that links nonverbal communication to neurophysiological processes, on the one hand, and to political processes, on the other. From Dittmann's work is derived a focus on information-processing: channels, communicative specificity, and the encoding/decoding distinction are important features of the communication process. From Ekman and Friesen are derived distinctions among types of information conveyed, notably among messages that are informative, communicative, or interactive. Concentrating on persuasion and deception, Mehrabian contributes a focus on impression management. He also suggests the dimension of responsiveness, a concept that is central to our work on negotiation. More than these concepts, the systems also contribute nonverbal indicators that can be adapted to the study of political processes. Particularly useful are Ekman and Friesen's illustrators and adaptors, and Mehrabian's positions.

Together with the empirical work to be reviewed below, the systems imply several functions served by nonverbal behavior. Five functions in particular can be distinguished: NVBs are indicators of feelings difficult to articulate; they provide clues

TABLE 1.4 FUNCTIONS OF NONVERBAL COMMUNICATION

Functions	NVB Indicators and Channels
Pre-articulation	Postural shifts and other kinesic cues, speech disruption (omissions, filled pauses) and other paralinguistic cues
Information-processing	Filled and unfilled pauses, micromomentary changes in muscles, pupil dialation, eye blinks
Persuasive appeals	Level of activity indicated in facial and vocal behavior, timing of phrases
Deception	Gestures, eye contact, postural orientation, speech-error rate
Subtle messages	Paralinguistic cues, facial expressions, number of channels used

to the nature of information-processing activities; they serve as emphases in persuasive appeals; they are used in attempts to deceive or to withhold information; and they may be used to convey subtle messages, as in sarcasm. These functions assign communicative value to observed NVBs. Some indicators associated with each function are listed in Table 1.4. Particularly relevant are the processing, persuasion, and deception functions.

Conceptual Framework for Nonverbal Communication

Nonverbal communication is construed in terms of two processes: information-processing and impression management. The former refers to the decoding of messages for making inferences about another's intentions. The latter refers to the encoding of messages to influence another's intentions, evaluations, or perceptions. The one emphasizes interpretation; the other concerns impact. Interpretation is made from the standpoint of an *observer* who aspires to an "inside" view of his subject. Impact is treated from the standpoint of an *actor* who displays a repertoire to be viewed from the "outside." Placed in the context of international politics, this distinction is similar to that made between intelligence and policy execution.

Highlighted by this distinction are three functions of NVB: processing, persuasion, and deception (see Table 1.4). Processing is an analytical activity that links NVB to intentions and inner emotional states, including neurophysiological phenomena. Persuasion is a manipulative activity that can be enhanced by the deliberate performance of certain NVBs. Deception can be construed as an analytical and a manipulative activity, depending on whether one is interested in detecting or practicing deception. These distinctions and functions form the basis for the discussion to follow.

INFORMATION-PROCESSING

Information-processing refers to those intervening processes that link stimulus evaluation to decisions. Essential components of this process are interpretation and prediction. These components are aspects of strategy that can be distinguished from both intentions and response selection or execution. Together, these four aspects determine the direction in which the behaving organism moves—his or her strategy. This conception applies equally well to processes described at several levels of analysis: political, psychological, and neurophysiological.

Rather than drawing parallels between levels of analysis, however, it would seem more useful to create linkages among processes at the various levels. International politics provides the context for interpretation and prediction. Nonverbal behaviors and neurophysiological processes provide the indicators of these activities. The activities are viewed as a sequence of steps consisting of expectations, evaluations, and adjustments. Viewed in terms of an interpersonal encounter, these steps are as follows:

(1) Initial expectations are formed on the basis of information about the other's attitudes, beliefs, goals, and so on.
(2) The other's behavior is evaluated in terms of these initial expectations.
(3) Expectations are adjusted, if necessary, on the basis of the early evaluations.
(4) The adjusted expectations are evaluated again, later in the sequence, when the other's strategy becomes apparent.

(5) Expectations are readjusted, if necessary, on the basis of the later evaluation.

Placed in the context of international bargaining, this model has been applied to depict stages of cases where turning points or impasses could be identified (Snyder and Diesing, 1977: Ch. 4; Druckman, 1977a). These applications suggest another step:

(6) The readjusted expectations are compared to one's own negotiating pattern to ascertain the relative positions of the parties.

Important changes in one's own strategy seem to occur after step 4 and then again after step 6. The changes are indexed by reduced or increased concessions or by hardened or softened rhetoric. They may also be indexed by neurological processes, as illustrated by Donchin and his collaborators.

A series of experiments conducted in Donchin's (1979) laboratory illuminates the significance of a specific component of human electroencephalogram (EEG) event-related potentials (ERPs). This component is referred to as P300. It is defined in terms of amplitude, latency, scalp distribution, and cognitive receptive field (see Donchin, 1979, for details on measurement). Particularly relevant is the finding that this component seems to index cognitive activity associated with information-processing. It occurs reliably at what appears to be the completion of a process referred to as stimulus evaluation. It is evoked when a subject's expectations are disappointed: The more unpredictable the stimulus, the more likely it is to elicit a P300. However, in order for this to occur, the stimulus must engage the subject's attention—it must be relevant to the task being performed by a subject.

These findings are important. They suggest an indicator at the neurological level that relates to such psychological processes as evaluation, expectation, and attention. Evaluation and expectation are part of the information-processing model proposed above. Attention is similar to responsiveness, a concept that links processing to observed behavior (Druckman, 1977a). Here is the beginning of a conceptualization that creates possibilities for research that probes linkages among neurological, behavioral, and political variables.

The linkage approach does not assume high correlations between P300 and overt behavior. Along with Donchin, we contend that this component may precede, follow, or be largely independent of observed responses. On the basis of a number of studies showing low correlations between P300 and reaction time or decisions, Donchin and Isreal (1978) concluded that two processes are initiated by a stimulus: stimulus evaluation and response selection. However, this conclusion does not preclude the possibility of P300/overt response correlations: Responses that follow a stimulus-evaluation process should correlate with P300 magnitude.

These particular responses are of special interest insofar as they may reflect intentions. Many of them may be NVBs, including those micromomentary movements barely detectable without the aid of special equipment. By comparing these responses with those that do *not* correlate with P300, it should be possible to distinguish between intended and unintended NVBs.[1] Addressed again below, this is an empirical issue to be resolved by experimentation.

Results obtained in several experiments call attention to the role played by nonverbal behavior in information-processing activities. Frequent gazes (Foddy, 1978) and such paralinguistic behaviors as high duration of utterances, faster reaction-time latency, and speech interruptions (Matarazzo et al., 1961) seem to indicate *information-seeking* activities. Hesitations and unfilled pauses (Bruneau, 1973), head nods, frequent hand and feet movements, and postural shifts (Dittmann and Llewellyn, 1969), as well as pupil dilation (Simpson and Hale, 1969), seem to occur during the *processing* or *integrating* that precedes articulate speech. Such NVBs as facial muscle movements (Ekman, 1972; Schwartz, 1974), decreases in verbal productivity (Siegman, 1976), and increased eye contact are among those associated with *reactions* that follow stimulus-evaluation processes. Corresponding to information-processing stages, these behaviors are summarized in Table 1.5.

TABLE 1.5 INFORMATION-PROCESSING STAGES AND NONVERBAL BEHAVIORS

Information-seeking	Paralanguage	Higher duration of utterances, faster reaction-time latency, more speech interruptions
	Visual	More frequent gazes in the direction of the other actor
	Proxemic	Shorter spacial distance in standing or seating arrangement
Pre-articulation processing	Paralanguage	More frequent head nods and chin thrusts, more expansive hand and feet movements, larger postural shifts
	Visual	Larger pupil size, increased eye-blinking
Reactions/response selection	Paralanguage	Reduced verbalizations
	Facial	Raised brows, eyelids opened wider, dropped jaw
	Visual	Increased pupil size, change in eye contact

The results obtained in the earlier studies are speculative. None of the investigators assessed the validity of their interpretations of observed behavior. Such assessments require indicators of a subject's intentions, perceptions, and attitudes that are independent of the directly observable behaviors. One type of indicator is the P300 component. The expectation/ evaluation/adjustment cycles referred to above are similar to the stimulus-evaluation/response-selection processes indexed by that component. Both are represented in the processing stages shown in Table 1.5. These stages can be defined in a task that requires a subject to react to a programmed opponent's moves; simultaneous recording of the EEG record and NVBs is feasible, as will be shown in the section of Chapter 2 on facial expressions.

IMPRESSION MANAGEMENT

Impression management refers to behavioral displays designed to influence another's perceptions or behavior. Considered as the response selection or execution aspect of strategy, these displays are also referred to as interactive nonverbal behaviors. Such NVBs are described by Ekman and Friesen (1969b) as acts by one person that influence or modify the behavior of another person or persons. Impact turns on how the displays are interpreted, how well they are executed, and incentives that exist in the interaction. These variables illustrate, once again, the interplay between the political and psychological levels of analysis.

Interpretation is important from the standpoint of the impression manager. His or her messages or displays may be distorted by biases that receivers bring to the situation. Particularly salient is the attribution bias: the tendency on the part of receivers to attribute intentions to the sender of the message. Habitual patterns of selective attention, interpretation, and retention are problems for the impression manager (Lockhart, 1978).

Once the intent of the sender is established, his or her behavior may be interpreted in light of these intentions; changes in his or her intentions or strategy may go unnoticed as a result of this attribution process (Druckman, 1977b). Predictable in part from the context of interaction and shaped by experience, attributions may not reflect the sender's own intentions. Rather, they may reflect such aspects of the international system as the nature of the relationship between the sender's and the receiver's nations or the characteristics of those nations (Druckman, 1980). As such, the attributions are stereotypes. Sensitivity to these perceptions is necessary for effective impression management.

Effectiveness also depends on execution. Skilled impression managers are adept at controlling the images others form of them during social interaction. They must be empathetic—skilled at taking the role of the other—and be able to perform convincingly and naturally those verbal and nonverbal acts that will create the desired image. Referred to by Snyder as self-monitoring, these individuals seem "good at learning what is socially appropriate in new situations, have good self-control of their emotional expression, and can effectively use this ability to create the impressions they want" (1974: 536). Sensitive to situational and interpersonal specifications of appropriateness, they can communicate a wide variety of emotions in both the vocal and the facial channels of nonverbal behavior.

Although most of the research treats self-monitoring as an individual difference variable, its characteristics can be learned through role-playing experiences (see Danielian, 1967). By creating incentives for performance, these exercises encourage the acquisition of "appropriate" behaviors.

Incentives provide the motivation for displaying certain non-verbal behaviors. Manipulated in experiments, incentives are used to encourage those displays that have an impact. Enactment of these gestures and implicit cues is encouraged by the observation that the other is responsive to them. Such responsiveness renders attempts to persuade, bluff, or convey subtle messages more effective. It also facilitates adapting to new situations (Wrightsman, 1977: Ch. 4). Providing experiences for learning or practicing these displays is part of the art of environmental design, a problem that we have discussed elsewhere (see, for example, Druckman, 1971) and will address again below.

Nonverbal behavior plays an important role in the interpretive process. This process is illustrated in Figure 1.1. Psychological states mediate between intentions and observed behavior. Reacting to observed verbal and nonverbal behavior, decoders attribute psychological states to the actor. Determined largely on the basis of the nonverbal cues, these attributions affect the observer's perception of the actor's intentions: Intentions are inferred from the states or "qualities" assigned to the actor. For example, judgments (based on nonverbal cues) of confidence, relaxation, desire for affiliation, warmth, and empathy lead to impressions of credibility and intended persuasiveness. Cues that suggest anxiety, discomfort, and suspiciousness are used to identify a deceiver (Mehrabian, 1972). Research results, reported below, make evident the importance of states: Ignoring the intervening states, as when a decoder makes *direct* inferences of intentions, may lead to inaccurate judgments.

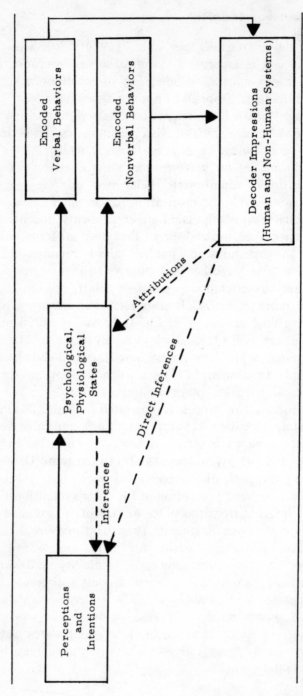

Figure 1.1 Process of Inferring Intentions and Perceptions from Behavior

38

But attributions are also based on the context in which the NVBs are displayed. The same nonverbal displays are likely to convey different messages in different situations. Impressions formed in the laboratory may not be the same as those formed in political environments. Consistent with our approach are arguments that emphasize the importance of context as a determinant of inferred motives or intentions (for example, Ellsworth and Carlsmith, 1968; Lewis and Fry, 1977). These arguments form a basis for the research effort discussed in Part II.

EXPRESSION GAMES

The processes discussed above are based on functionally differentiated roles, the observer and the subject. The focus of analysis is on the subject, who may be either an observer or an actor. Not considered by either perspective are those processes involved in interactions between the two roles. Interactions can take the form of competition, where one player attempts to outwit the other, or cooperation, where the players attempt to coordinate with each other. In both cases, there is a need to read the other's expressions and to ensure that one's own expressions are correctly (as intended) read. Such gamelike exchanges reveal subtle processes not identified by the functions discussed above; they require an expanded perspective on the communicative value of NVBs. These processes are considered briefly in this section.

Referred to by Goffman (1969) as expression games, observer-subject interactions consist of alternating moves, the one attempting to infer intent from the subject's style, while the other attempts to convey certain impressions. Unwitting moves taken by the naive subject can be exploited by the sophisticated observer; covering moves taken by the skilled subject can fool the naive observer. This is a complicated business: Just as an observer can catch a subject off guard, so too can a subject control his or her behavior to mislead the observer. Goffman's view is that of an extended process where exchanges are made in terms of a relationship that is not limited by time constraints. Even more subtle is the suggestion that each participant is in easy reach of both the observer and the subject roles. Reversed roles are a feature of the interaction that occurs as a result of mutual attempts to influence the other; the participant's sense of being more the subject or more the observer depends on whether he or she is persuading or analyzing during a particular episode (see Argyle et al., 1968).

Accurate reading of expressions is made difficult by the paradox that "the best evidence for [the assessor] is also the best evidence for the subject to tamper with" (Goffman, 1969: 63). The observer's challenge is to determine the significance of a cue when he knows that the subject is managing his expressions. He must anticipate what the subject expects him to look for and then focus his attention on other cues. The subject is challenged by the need to fool the observer when he knows that the observer is assessing his moves. He must anticipate the cues likely to be used by the observer and then control them. As Goffman (1969: 58) notes, "uncovering moves must eventually be countered by counter-uncovering moves." Both the observer and the subject are vulnerable. The objective for each is to minimize his vulnerability under difficult circumstances.

The assessment dilemma described above renders the expression game a highly sophisticated art form. Surely when the stakes are high it would seem prudent to defer to the professionals. Yet there is an element of common experience contained in the structure of such encounters. This is captured by Goffman's (1969: 81) observation:

> In every social situation we can find a sense in which one participant will be an observer with something to gain from assessing expressions, and another will be a subject with something to gain from manipulating the process. A single structure of contingencies can be found in this regard which renders agents a little like us all and all of us a little like agents.

It is this "structure of contingencies" that can be represented in a paradigm for research on the communicative value of nonverbal behavior.

The expression game provides a framework for analyzing the relationship between managing impressions (encoding) and processing information (decoding). The factors affecting the sender's nonverbal displays and the receiver's attentiveness to these displays can be varied systematically: physical aspects of the situation, means available for detection, players' technical knowledge, and the stakes for successful concealment or detection. Extended encounters consist of alternating moves and countermoves construed as nonverbal exchanges. These exchanges are the focus of analysis.

Similar features are associated with the two-person game tasks used for analysis of choice behavior. The differences are, however, instructive. Focusing on strategy, choice-behavior experiments attempt to discover factors affecting deliberate decisions; they illustrate the strategic value of alternative choice patterns in terms of monetary outcomes. Indeed, such NVBs as gaze (Foddy, 1978) and physical proximity (Lewis and Fry, 1977) have been shown to impinge on choices. Focusing on interaction process, expression games are assessment contests designed to conceal or convey information; they illustrate the diagnostic value of nonverbal behavior in terms of clues to unarticulated intentions. The "clues" are the essence of the game, not merely factors that affect other forms of behavior. Analysis concentrates on the ways in which they are managed and assessed. These are not unrelated activities: Interchangeable roles require that players use both skills in the course of an encounter. Whether these are *related skills,* however, is a subject for research. Of particular interest is the question whether improved sensitivity increases tactical proficiency.

But enthusiasm for the expression-game paradigm should be tempered by awareness of a possible dilemma. DePaulo et al. (1980) remind us that both encoders and decoders determine the outcome of the communication process. The problem is one of disentangling effects of senders and receivers. Accurate detection may be the result of encoding skill, decoding skill, or both. Consequently, we do not know whether detection is due to style of presentation or astute observation. One solution is to control part of the interaction, either the sender's enactments or the observer's clues. By so doing, however, we may lose the essential features of an *interactive* situation. This dilemma merits attention and will be raised again in conjunction with our experimentation. First, however, a selective review of single-channel and multiple-channel NVB research is presented. Implications for information-processing (decoding) and impression management (encoding) are highlighted in that discussion.

NOTE

1. Intentionality is defined by Ekman and Friesen (1969b) as the deliberate use of a nonverbal act to communicate a message to another interactant. These authors (1969b: 53-54) contend that "intentionality is a concept traditionally avoided by psychologists . . . on grounds that it is not possible to operationalize intentions, or that the investigator will become lost in questions of levels of intention or unconscious intention. We believe that there are some nonverbal behaviors which the sender usually consciously intends as communicative signals to convey messages, and that through naturalistic or experimental methods it is possible to differentiate these acts from other forms of nonverbal behavior. At the same time, we do admit that the intentionality of other nonverbal behavior is problematic, and it may not be possible to determine the intentionality of *every* instance of nonverbal behavior." Here is where P300 research would be useful. As an indicator of processing (stimulus evaluation), P300 may also signal intentionality of those NVBs that *follow* its occurrence. If this is the case, it should be possible to discriminate between intended and unintended behaviors.

2

THE STATE OF THE ART

The review to follow is organized by channel. Four channels are considered: vocal (paralanguage), facial, body (kinesics), and visual. This division is suggested by the observation that most NVC studies fall into these categories. Perhaps because of the time and effort involved in measuring many NVBs, most researchers have focused primarily on one nonverbal channel. Although communication is a multichannel phenomenon, a unichannel organization is convenient in reviewing the state of the art. Where feasible, however, we will note interrelationships among variables in two or more channels. Moreover, a separate section is devoted to a review of the smaller body of multi-channel studies.

The review presented in this chapter is selective. It is designed to accomplish two purposes: to reflect the state of the art, and to relate the research to the concepts developed in the previous chapter. The insights acquired from such an effort should make evident junctures where more basic research is needed and where extrapolations are warranted.

Paralanguage

Paralinguistic variables, referred to also as the implicit aspects of speech (Mehrabian, 1972), are the content-free vocalizations and pauses associated with speech. A popular focus for NVB research, the number of paralinguistic variables is an ever-expanding list. Included in this list are the vocal qualities of pitch, loudness, intensity, and amplitude; the speech-disturbance categories of stutter, omission, repetition, filled pauses (consisting of "ah" sounds and unnecessary serial repetition), and incoherent sounds; such temporal dimensions as duration of utterance, reaction-time latency, and percentage of interruptions; measures of verbal productivity such as speech rate and verbal quantity (time spent talking, number of words, number of clause units); silences as indexed by hesitations and unfilled pauses; and such conversational regulators as intonation changes, paralinguistic drawl, and drop in pitch or loudness. The ease with which many of these variables can be measured has made possible a wide variety of studies. Most of these studies are of two types: detecting emotional states, and the use and modification of paralinguistic cues in interactive situations.

DETECTION OF EMOTIONAL STATES

Results obtained in a number of studies substantiate the conclusion that vocal characteristics of speech communicate emotional states. Particularly easy to judge are the emotions of anger, nervousness, sadness, and happiness; somewhat more difficult to judge are fear, love, and surprise (Davitz and Davitz, 1959). The standard procedure used in these studies is to have an actor simulate an emotion by reading a neutral passage. Subjects then rate the presentation for peak tempo, pitch, and loudness. Constanzo et al. (1969) found correlations between vocal ratings and the portrayed emotions suggesting that voices rated highest in peak pitch were judged as love or grief, those rated highest for loudness were associated with anger and contempt, and peak tempo showed indifference. The authors hypothesized that these voice orientations might reflect modes of interpersonal orientation similar to those underlying Mehrabian's dimensions (see Table 1.3): "moving towards others" (peak pitch), "moving against others" (peak loudness), and "moving away from others" (peak tempo). More generally, Scherer et al. (1972: 282) noted "that the lower frequencies of the voice spectrum are sufficient to communicate the affective state of the speaker."

Anxiety or stress is the most frequently studied emotion. Experimentally manipulated anxiety has been related to measures of speech disturbance and verbal productivity. An example of the former is a study by Krause and Pilisuk (1961). These investigators found that "intrusive sounds" (laughs and sighs) were the best predictors of stressful interviews. Other studies investigating the anxiety-speech disturbance relationship are summarized in Table 2.1. The findings suggest a number of vocal indicators of anxiety. Results relating anxiety to verbal productivity are less clear. Summarized by Murray (1971), the results of several studies show an inverted-U relationship, where at low levels of stress, verbal productivity increases with stress, but as anxiety or stress increases, verbal productivity decreases.

One of the more inventive approaches to the study of anxiety is illustrated by Wiegele's (1978) work on voice stress. Voice stress is detected by vocal changes recorded by an electronic instrument referred to as a psychological stress evaluator. This instrument analyzes and displays graphic traces on a heat-sensitive moving strip. It was used in a study that examined U.S. presidents' addresses during international crises. By analyzing subtle changes in voice quality, Wiegele discovered aspects of situations that were particularly stressful. For example, when the North Koreans seized the *Pueblo,* Johnson's voice showed little stress in his announcement of the seizure but much stress when he discussed why the North Koreans had taken the ship. Equally intriguing results were obtained for each of the other presidents in times of crisis.

Speech errors, speech rate, and verbal quantity have also been found to relate to deception. Mehrabian (1971a) showed that interviewees, when encouraged to be deceitful, made more speech errors and had a shorter speech duration and a lower speech rate than those who were not so encouraged.[1] He suggested that these differences were the result of differences in the level of anxiety aroused by the conditions. These findings will be discussed again following consideration of other nonverbal indicators of deception.

Another paralinguistic measure shown to distinguish between deceivers and truth tellers is tone of voice. Several studies reviewed by DePaulo et al. (1980) found that when subjects

TABLE 2.1   SUMMARY OF ANXIETY-SPEECH DISTURBANCE
             RESEARCH

Study	Procedure	Findings
Mahl (1956)	Compared defensive versus conflicted speech of patients	Speech disturbance ("ahs" and "non-ahs") more frequent with conflicted (anxiety-arousing) speech segments
Panek and Martin (1959)	Compared patients' GSR fluctuations with speech disturbances	Speech disturbances ("ahs" and repetitions) were associated with increased GSR fluctuations
Boomer (1963)	Nonpurposive body movements employed as index of anxiety	"Non-ah" ratio correlated .42 with body movement measure
Krause and Pilisuk (1961)	Subjects described their probable reaction to stressful and nonstressful situations	Intrusive sounds more frequent during stressful interviews
Kasl and Mahl (1965)	Discussion of stressful topics	Increase in "non-ah" ratio during discussion of anxiety-arousing topics
Siegman and Pope (1965)	Low- and high-anxiety-arousing topics discussed	"Non-ah" speech disturbances increased with anxiety-arousing topics
Pope, Siegman, and Blass (1970)	Discussion of anxious and nonanxious interview topics	"Non-ah" ratio failed to decrease during anxiety-arousing interview compared to neutral interview
Pope, Blass, Siegman, and Raher (1970)	Examined high- and low-anxiety monologues of patients	High-anxiety monologues had more "non-ah" disturbances
Siegman and Pope (1972)	Interview behavior of psychiatric patients on anxious and nonanxious days	Patients evidenced more "non-ah" speech disturbances on nonanxious days

SOURCE: From Robert G. Harper, Arthur N. Wiens, and Joseph D. Matarazzo, *Nonverbal Communication: The State of the Art,* New York, John Wiley, 1978, p. 45. Reprinted by permission of the publisher.

were told to pay particular attention to tone-of-voice clues they tended to be more accurate at detecting deception than when they were told to attend to words or visual clues or when they were given no attentional instructions. Moreover, subjects who expected more deception (compared to those who expected less) were relatively more influenced by tone-of-voice cues than by facial cues. If, in fact, tone-of-voice cues are leakier than other modalities, then the strategy of attending to them is appropriate to the extent that the sender is not aware of the salience of that modality. Results of a recent study by Streeter et al. (1977) indicate that this may be the case.

These investigators examined changes in voice pitch during attempted deception. A first experiment showed that the average voice's fundamental frequency tended to be higher when lying than when telling the truth, and that this difference was somewhat greater when the deceiver was aroused or under stress. In a second study, it was found that raters used pitch variation as a cue to deception more when the semantic content of the message was unintelligible. Noting that "there is nothing in our results to suggest that it is advisable to ignore the content of an utterance," the authors (1977: 349) concluded that "speech does contain a measure of useful information apart from its semantic content." This conclusion is supported also by the DePaulo team (1980: 150), who emphasize "verbal superiority" while noting that "[such] superiority was not nearly so striking in communications involving deception as it was in communications involving no deceptive intents." Whether tonal clues are predictive of deception or stress in a variety of situations remains to be determined. Clearly, more focused attention to these and to such other paralinguistic indicators as response latency and speech duration (Harrison et al., 1978) is warranted.

REGULATION OF CONVERSATIONAL BEHAVIOR

Paralinguistic cues play an important role in the process of coordinating social communication. Timing of speech and "turn-taking signals" have received special attention. Research on timing demonstrates the extent to which interactants can influence each other's nonverbal behavior. Rather clear tendencies to imitate the other were observed for duration of utterances, reaction-time latency, and percentage of interruptions (Matarazzo and Wiens, 1972). Such responsiveness renders effective attempts to modify another's speech pattern: Increases and decreases in each of the indices have been shown to co-occur as synchronous patterns in both laboratory (see Allen et al., 1965) and naturalistic (see Matarazzo et al., 1968) dyadic interactions.

Perhaps the most detailed research on NVB is Duncan's work on turn-taking signals. On the basis of meticulous analyses of speech and body-motion behavior during two taped 19-minute conversations, Duncan (1972, 1974; see also Duncan and Fiske, 1979) identified three paralinguistic signals that indicate a speaker is ready to yield to a listener: (1) intonation changes—a rising or falling in pitch level at the terminal juncture of a phonemic clause, (2) paralinguistic drawl on the last syllable or stressed syllable in a clause, and (3) drop in paralinguistic pitch or loudness in association with a commonly used statement such as "you know."

Duncan (1974) also described those cues that are feedback to the speaker that a listener is following the conversation. More interesting, perhaps, than the specific findings obtained by Duncan is his approach. His work focuses on the coordinated actions of both interactants, or, as he states, it is a "continuing, active negotiation between speaker and auditor concerning the immediate course of the interaction" (Duncan and Fiske, 1979: 95). This focus links the work to Mehrabian's concept of responsiveness, a dimension also indexed by vocal cues (see Table 1.3). A key concept for understanding negotiating behavior, responsiveness is probed by Duncan at the micro-level of dyadic communication.

The studies reviewed above, and those discussed below, make evident the importance of paralinguistic variables. These variables are implicated in each of the NVB functions presented in Table 1.4 (Chapter 1). Omissions, filled pauses, and speech dysfluencies occur when feelings or intentions are difficult to *articulate* (see Mahl, 1956). Hesitations, including filled and unfilled pauses, reflect the *information-processing* that occurs during the encoding and decoding of speech (see Bruneau, 1973). While the timing of phrases seems to affect the impact of *persuasive* messages (Chapple and Arensberg, 1940), speech-error rate may be a useful indicator of *deception* (Mehrabian, 1971a). Used effectively, pitch, loudness, and vocal amplitude can convey *subtle messages,* as in sarcasm (Mehrabian, 1972). Relevant also to the distinction between information-processing and impression management, paralinguistic variables provide a basis for interpretation and tools for creating impact.

SILENCE AND VERBAL PRODUCTIVITY: INFORMATION-PROCESSING

Just as P300 seems to be an indicator of the completion of information-processing (stimulus evaluation), so might paralinguistic variables serve this function. Hesitations, unfilled pauses, and reduced verbal productivity may signal processing activity. Bruneau (1973) described one kind of silence as "psycholinguistic"—hesitations related to the encoding and decoding of speech. Such hesitations enable the encoder to process thought into proper words and grammatical form to be spoken. When hesitations occur and their duration suggest the way in which information-processing may operate: Boomer (1965: 155) found that pauses occurred most frequently at the beginnings of phonemic clauses, suggesting "that speech encoding at a grammatical level operates with units larger than the word." Goldman-Eisler (1967) reported that longer hesitations were followed by longer or more complex periods of speech, suggesting a "cognitive rhythm" consisting of a regular structure of speech and silence durations.

Less clear in the research on hesitations is whether processing is occurring during the periods of silence. Processing activity is inferred from observed behavior. It may also be attributed to a client in the context of a professional relationship. Fischer and Apostal (1975) found that counselor-client sessions were judged high in self-disclosure when there were more unfilled pauses. Unfilled pauses presumably signaled processing activity. In their words, "The presence of unfilled pauses over that of filled pauses and minimum pauses indicates to a counselor that the message which ensues is revealing more about the counselee and that the counselee is more willing to disclose the material" (1975: 95). Assessed during these unfilled pauses, P300 may provide evidence that some form of processing is indeed occurring.

Neurophysiological indicators may also correlate with measures of verbal productivity. Elicited as a result of disconfirmed expectations, P300 may precede responses that indicate reduced verbal productivity (speaking time). Siegman (1976) found that male subjects' expectancies interacted with the interviewer's behavior in affecting productivity. Those subjects expecting a warm interviewer but interacting with a cold one were the least verbally productive, whereas those expecting a cold interview but receiving a warm one were less productive than those expecting and receiving a warm interview. Disappointed expectations inhibited verbal productivity. These results suggest another linkage between P300 and a paralinguistic variable: Correlations obtained between these variables would bolster the case for using the one *or* the other as an indicator of processing.

ATTRIBUTIONS AND INTERPERSONAL INFLUENCE: IMPRESSION MANAGEMENT

Attributions based on paralinguistic "performances" suggest how one can use these variables to affect another's perceptions. Results obtained in several studies demonstrate relationships between paralinguistic variables and perceptions. Most interesting, perhaps, are the studies on persuasiveness. Mehrabian and Williams (1969) obtained significant correlations between each of three paralinguistic variables and ratings of persuasiveness: The higher the speech volume, the more the vocal activity, and the higher the speech rate, the more persuasive the speaker.[2] Packwood (1974) examined the relationship between loudness and persuasiveness. Comparing the statements rated highest and lowest in persuasiveness, he found a difference in the relative sound levels. The more persuasive statements were louder than the less persuasive statements, but not so loud as to be interpreted as hostility. An attribute related to persuasiveness is perceived credibility. Addington (1971) found that the vocal characteristics judged least credible included throaty, "denasal," tense, nasal, monotone, and breathy.

Other aspects of social behavior have also been shown to relate to voice characteristics. For example, subjects preferred to affiliate with a confederate who made more statements per minute, more declarative statements per minute, and had a higher-percentage duration of speech relative to the subject (Mehrabian, 1972). Similar kinds of relationships were obtained for ingratiation (Mehrabian and Ksionzky, 1972) and for responsiveness to other (Mehrabian, 1971b).

A number of studies have examined relationships between vocal variables and perceived qualities. Stang (1973) found that subjects with the highest talking rate in three-person groups were judged most positively on leadership qualities, while those exhibiting medium amounts of talking were rated highest on a measure of liking. In a more recent extension of this research, Kleinke et al (1976) discovered that persons talking 80 percent of the time were viewed as outgoing and domineering as well as impolite, inattentive, and inconsiderate. The 50 percent talkers were seen as less dominant and most liked, while the 20 percent talkers were viewed as submissive and were only moderately liked. Based on their findings on the quantity and quality of verbal interaction, Sorrentino and Boutiller (1975) concluded that quantity is perceived as a motivational factor (one's investment in the group) and that in the absence of verbal quantity, a person who is competent will not be perceived as a socioemotional leader. Finally, research by Addington (1968) demonstrated a number of relationships between various vocal characteristics and inferred personality traits (such as speaking rate and "extraversion").

The research reviewed in this section demonstrates that reliable inferences are made on the basis of paralinguistic cues. This conclusion has implications for prediction and control. Knowing how a particular performance is likely to be perceived renders one capable of shaping the other's perceptions.[3] Informed by the research, a person responsible for policy execution should be an effective impression manager.

Facial Expressions

Although interest in facial expressions dates back to Darwin's *The Expression of the Emotions in Man and Animals* (1872), the research on this topic has been dominated by one contemporary team of investigators. In numerous experiments, Ekman and his associates have demonstrated the communicative value of facial expressions. Shown to convey rather specific information in a short period of time, the face is an important nonverbal channel for the communication of emotions or attitudes. Like the research on paralinguistic variables, the central concern of this work has been detection: Which emotions are conveyed by different expressions? However, facial expression in interpersonal interaction has not been a focus of investigation. Nor have interrelationships between the face and voice been examined. For these reasons the review to follow emphasizes the problem of detection. Implications for information-processing and impression management are also discussed in conjunction with the issue of universal versus culture-specific origins of behavior.

DETECTING EMOTIONS

Research to date demonstrates that facial expressions reliably communicate emotional states. Three procedures have been used to assess accuracy: (1) verbal descriptions of situations depicted in candid photographs (Ekman et al., 1972); (2) posed or enacted expressions depicted in still photographs or in motion pictures (for example, see Thompson and Meltzer, 1964; Levitt, 1964; Zuckerman et al., 1975), and (3) samples of spontaneous behavior obtained through experimental manipulation (Ekman, 1965; Howell and Jorgensen, 1970).

While accuracy varied somewhat for different emotions, most studies obtained above-chance accuracy for recognition of most emotions: The positive emotions of happiness, love, surprise, and interest are usually easier to judge than the negative emotions of fear, sadness, anger, and disgust. Sex differences have also been obtained for enactment, with females usually tending to be better expressers or communicators of emotions than males (Zuckerman et al., 1975; Gitter et al., 1972).

Using New Guineans as subjects, Ekman and Friesen (1971) demonstrated agreement across cultures in assigning categories to depicted emotions. High percentages of agreement between the New Guineans and the Westerners were obtained for happiness, sadness, anger, disgust, and fear. Unlike the Westerners, however, the New Guineans had some trouble distinguishing fear from surprise. High levels of agreement have also been observed for members of different Western societies. Choosing one of six emotion words for each photograph, observers from the United States, Japan, Chile, Argentina, and Brazil showed similar percentages of agreements: Most photographs were depicted similarly by more than 90 percent of the observers in each culture, reaching a high of 100 percent for Japanese observers on happiness and surprise (Ekman, 1972; Ekman et al., 1969). Taken together, the results of these and other studies led Ekman (1978: 105) to conclude that "the appearance of the face for each of the primary emotions is common to all peoples." However, events that elicit and conventions that control expressions may vary from one culture to another.

Having demonstrated agreement on the meaning of particular facial expressions, investigators attempted to identify the fewest essential variables needed to define emotions. These studies, employing what is referred to as the "dimensional approach," attempt to isolate dimensions from factor analyses of rating judgments. While there is little agreement on the exact number of labels for dimensions, three dimensions appear common to most studies: pleasant-unpleasant, attentional activity, and intensity-control (Ekman et al., 1972). Plausibly construed, these dimensions parallel Mehrabian's fundamental dimensions of NVB: pleasant-unpleasant is like positiveness; attentional activity is similar to responsiveness; and intensity-control parallels the potency or status dimension. They are also similar to the Osgood (1966) verbal factors—evaluation, potency, and activity—obtained from his semantic-differential work.

Another approach to defining the fewest essential variables is to determine a set of basic emotions. Using the category approach, a number of investigators have followed Woodworth's (1938) lead in identifying primary emotions from correlations between the poser's intended expression and observer judgment. Despite variations in procedural details, considerable agreement across studies has been obtained. Summarizing these studies, Ekman et al. (1972) proposed seven primary categories: happiness, surprise, fear, sadness, anger, disgust-contempt, and interest. These categories formed the basis for studies designed to isolate aspects of the face involved in expressions corresponding to each emotion. The studies are part of the larger effort to ascertain the determinants of judged emotions.

In most real-life situations, facial expressions are observed in the context of particular experiences. Provoked by this observation, several investigators have attempted to determine whether the expression or the situation is a more important source of information. Using various combinations of expressions and situation descriptions—some consistent, others inconsistent—these investigators showed that the facial cues were more important than the situation in determining judgments (Frijda, 1969; Thayer and Schiff, 1969). Taking into account a possible source of ambiguity in the earlier studies—that is, ambiguity in facial and contextual cues—Watson (1972) also found facial expressions to be more salient in the judgment process. Noting other methodological problems, Ekman et al. (1972) suggested that the results of these studies should not be regarded as definitive. Rather, they observed that it is important "to investigate the nature of those occasions when the face provides more information . . . [and] when the context provides more information . . . [and] the particular cognitive mechanisms employed to resolve discrepant information between the face and context"

(1972: 150). Nonetheless, the results obtained to date make evident the importance of facial cues. Given this, then, the next task is to determine the relative importance of different facial cues in the expression of different emotions.

Results obtained in Ekman's laboratory provide convincing evidence for the differential importance of facial areas in expressing emotions. Using the Facial Affect Scoring Technique (FAST), these investigators carefully evaluated both photographed and videotaped expressions. This technique yields scores for each of the seven emotion categories and three facial areas: the brows/forehead area, the eyes/lids, and the lower face.

Frequent co-occurrences between the categories and facial areas provided evidence for predictability. For example, happiness was best identified from the cheeks/mouth (98 percent correct judgments) and eyes/eyelids with cheeks/mouth (99 percent); surprise was best judged from all three areas together (brow/forehead, 79 percent; eyes/lids, 63 percent; eyes/lids, 63 percent; and cheeks/mouth, 52 percent). These results, obtained by Boucher and Ekman (1975), derived from a procedure in which subjects rated each facial area on all emotion categories, giving an intensity value for each. A facial area was considered to contribute to an accurate judgment if the subject rated that emotion highest in intensity. Interestingly, these judgments of facial areas are comparable to agreement obtained for photographs of the entire face (Harper et al., 1978).

Based on experiments using the FAST atlas photographs, Ekman and Friesen developed a manual for detecting emotions from facial areas. *Unmasking the Face* (Ekman and Friesen, 1975) provides the reader with illustrations of the distinctive signs associated with each of the primary emotion categories. For example, Ekman and Friesen's (1975: 45) distinctive clues to *surprise* are:

- The brows are raised, so that they are curved and high.
- The skin below the brow is stretched.
- Horizontal wrinkles go across the forehead.

- The eyelids are opened; the upper lid is raised and the lower lid drawn down; the white of the eye shows above the iris, and often below as well.

- The jaw drops open so that the lips and teeth are parted, but there is no tension or stretching of the mouth.

And, for *disgust* (1975: 76):

- The upper lip is raised.

- The lower lip is also raised and pushed up to the upper lip, or is lowered and slightly protruding.

- The nose is wrinkled.

- The cheeks are raised.

- Lines show below the lower lid, and the lid is pushed up but not tense.

- The brow is lowered, lowering the upper lid.

Each of the emotions varies in intensity, and the face reflects these differences by slight changes in the patterns of clues. Of course the accuracy of these characterizations depends on the validity of the atlas on which they are based. The authors summarize experiments that attempted to demonstrate validity "by showing that measurements of the face with the Atlas corresponded with other evidence of the subjective emotional experience of the persons whose faces were measured" (1975: 29).[4]

More recently, Ekman and his collaborators developed a more sophisticated coding system for recording facial affect. Referred to as the Facial Affect Coding System (FACS), the system describes visibly distinctive facial actions in terms of muscle activity; for example, a smiling appearance can be produced by the action of zygomatic major, zygomatic minor, buccinator, risorious, or caninus muscles. Ekman et al. (1980) correlated these actions to rather specific aspects of emotional experience, such as felt intensity of a pleasant or unpleasant emotion. Facial actions were associated with differences in reported happiness, in the intensity of negative feelings, and in the experience of disgust. The pattern of correlations supported the general hypothesis that particular facial actions are related to the subjective experience of certain primary emotions. These findings suggest that the face is a rich source of information about emotion and have implications for theories of differentiated response systems.

Often, however, confusions occur in judging primary emotions. One source of confusion is affect blends. These are expressions that result from combinations of primary affects. One area of the face may show one emotion while another shows a second emotion. Blends may occur when a stimulus elicits more than one emotion, as when winning at roulette produces both surprise and happiness. Because of their complexity, blends are often difficult to judge and may be subject to more cultural variability than are the primary emotions.[5] Taking them into account is necessary if we are to understand the host of complex facial expressions. They also have implications for the cognitive processing that occurs prior to the activation of an expression, a topic to which we now turn.

NEURAL PROGRAMS, SURPRISE, AND MICRO-EXPRESSIONS: INFORMATION-PROCESSING

Cognitive processing is likely to occur between an eliciting event and the activation of a facial affect program. The more complex the eliciting events, generally, the more processing is involved (Harper et al., 1978). Whether the processing occurs before reaction to an external event or in conjuction with intentional encoding, it plays a role in determining the display of a facial expression. The link between processing and expressions is mediated by the activation of neural programs or socially learned display rules.

Tomkins (1962) contended that for each emotion there are particular patterns of neural firings and associated facial muscle movements, and that this feedback is the basis for our experience of emotion. Izard's (1971) theory posits three interrelated components of emotion: neural activity, striate muscle or facial-postural activity, and subjective experience. Building on these sources, Ekman (1972) developed a neurocultural theory of emotion that emphasized universals in the relationship between distinctive facial muscle movements and particular primary emotions. Some support for this theory is provided by the results obtained by Schwartz (1974). Using electromyographic (EMG) measurement of facial muscles, this investigator found relationships between muscle patterns and the subjective experience of such emotions as happiness and sadness (see also Schwartz et al., 1975; Ekman et al., 1980). While these findings suggest a close association between the face and the experience of emotion, they do not bear on the third link in the theory: neurological processes. If, as Tomkins suggested, there are specific neural firings associated with facial movements, then such linkages should also be demonstrated.

One type of "neural firing" associated with information-processing is the P300 component. Regularly observed to occur when expectations are disappointed (Donchin and Isreal, 1978), this component may be hypothesized to precede those facial muscle movements associated with "surprise." These movements include those documented by Ekman and Friesen (1975), listed previously (raised brows, stretched skin below brows, opened eyelids, and so on), as well as facial expressions that are so short-lived that they seem to be quicker than the eye (micromomentary expressions). Recordings of micro-expressions (MMEs) are particularly valuable, since they occur in a time frame closer to the duration of the P300 onset and termination.

Micro-expressions are detectable with the aid of special equipment. These rapid expressions can be seen when motion picture films are run at a fraction of their normal speed. Noting the large difference between expressions observed at slow and normal speeds, Haggard and Isaacs (1966) found that MMEs tend to occur in the context of conflict and may serve as indicators of therapeutic change. Implied by these findings is the notion that MMEs are indicators of intrapsychic processes that are sensitive to changes in events. If this is the case, it would seem plausible to consider MMEs as indicators of such changes as disappointed expectations.

Assessment of MMEs provides several advantages. Occurring in a time frame comparable to the P300 component, MMEs can be evaluated as *contemporaneous* correlates of neurological processes. Being closer to the operation of specific muscle patterns, they may reflect more directly the neurological activity that controls those patterns. The variety of expressions observed as MMEs is similar to the range seen at normal speed; smiles, frowns, furrows, and squints can be seen at both levels of analysis (compare Ekman and Friesen, 1975, with Ekman et al., 1980). Such variety is represented in measuring procedures designed for an investigation in progress.[6]

Changes in facial expressions were assessed from still photographs taken from videotaped subject performances. This approach differs from that taken by Haggard and Isaacs (1966) and by Schwartz (1974). The former measured MMEs as judgments of facial expression change from slow-motion films; the latter used electromyographic (EMG) procedures to record electrical activity of facial muscles. Judgments entail assessments of interjudge reliability; the average reliability coefficient obtained by Haggard and Isaacs for MMEs was .50, which, while statistically significant, is not impressive. EMG assessment requires placing electrodes on several facial locations; such intrusion is likely to constrain the range of expressions shown by a subject, as well as call attention to the focus of the investigation. Neither reliability nor intrusion was a problem in the current study. Intercoder agreement was assured by precise measurement from preestablished reference points. Moreover, subjects were unaware of our specific interest in facial expressions.

Expressions were assessed from changes in positions measured on 11 variables. Listed in Table 2.2, these variables include width of eye opening, distance from edge of eye to pupil, head angle, head position as nod and as turn, brow-to-nose measurement, brow elevation, cheek measurement, width of mouth, length of mouth, and jaw reset. Each variable was measured on frames shot at two per second in the context of a bargaining task, a total of eight frames per concession/counterconcession sequence. Measurements were made by two coders working independently, each coding separate subjects.

The variables are positions of aspects of the face measured at one point in time. Differences in measured position from one frame to the next define changes in expression. As shown in Table 2.2, changes occur more often for some variables than for others, most notably for width of eye opening, head angle, and head position (up or down). For other variables, very little change occurs. Whether the variation is associated with certain types of computer concessions is the research issue. More expression changes were predicted to follow *surprising* events, such as a sudden change of strategy (for example, from a hard to a soft pattern) than after other (expected) concessions. Of interest also is whether the predicted changes are limited to certain variables, or whether reactions to strategy shifts are reflected in particular combinations of variables.

Results obtained to date are encouraging. Discriminant analysis results showed that two variables, head angle and brow-to-nose measurement, distinguished among the conditions. A significantly larger change in head angle occurred following an unexpected strategy shift than when no shift occurred; significantly less change in nose-furrowing was observed following a shift than at other times during the course of bargaining. Eighty-six percent of the cases were classified correctly by condition when only information on these variables was known.

Similarly, the amplitude of the P300 component was shown to be influenced by strategy shifts. A companion study conducted by the investigators was designed to assess changes on P300 amplitude in response to changes in bargaining strategy. P300 amplitude was significantly larger for trials when the computer changed its strategy than when it did not. A next step consists of computing correlations between changes in P300 amplitude and the measured MMEs. Results to date suggest that high correlations would be obtained. Such evidence would support theories that posit linkages between behavioral and neurological variables (see Tomkins, 1962).

TABLE 2.2 DESCRIPTIONS OF MICROMOMENTARY
EXPRESSIONS

Variable	Description	Measurement Range[a]	Amount of Variation[b]
Width of eye opening	Distance from top to bottom of right eyeball	00-04 mm	High
Pupil/eye position	Distance from side edge of eye to pupil	00-06 mm	Low
Head angle	Distance between a point midway between the eyebrows and the 90° angle created by the midpoint of a protractor	01-42°	High
Head position up or down (nod)	Size of neck from midpoint of chin to base of photo, or distance from top of head to top of forehead	08-52 mm	High
Head position side to side (turn)	Difference between width of right and left nostrils, each measured from the center tip of the nose	00-05 mm difference	Low
Brow to nose	Distance from center tip of nose to the center of the brow line, a point equidistant between the brows	14-21 mm	Moderate
Brow elevation	Distance from outside corner of right eye to outside edge of right eyebrow	03-06 mm	Moderate
Cheek length	Distance from the top corner of the lip to the center of the eye lid	13-24 mm	Moderate
Width of mouth	Distance between center top of upper lip to center bottom of lower lip	01-09 mm	Moderate

(Continued on p. 62)

TABLE 2.2   Continued

Variable	Description	Measurement Range[a]	Amount of Variation[b]
Length of mouth	Distance from a point at one side to a point at the other side of the mouth	09-24 mm	Moderate
Jaw reset, up and down	Distance between the center tip of the nose to the center point at the bottom of the chin	09-24 mm	Moderate

a. The range is from the smallest to the largest measurement across five subjects; measurements were made in millimeters or degrees.

b. Judgment by coders based on observed frequency of changes in measurement; high, moderate or low variation is defined in terms of a scale going from relatively frequent to infrequent changes in measured values.

This research also has implications for a system of movement representation. Recordings of multiple MME positions can be used to develop a system similar to the notation and animation systems developed by Badler and Smoliar (1979). Extracted from the data are sets of coordinated movements that may change over time and situations. The coordinated movements are "display package concepts" that can be represented in animated graphic displays. Illuminated by such displays are expression differences within subjects responding to different events (strategy shift versus no shift). These displays turn on the issue, How are feelings evoked by different situations represented in facial expression?

Facial affect programs are also regulated by culturally learned "display rules." Display rules serve to modify facial expressions in keeping with the social situation. Learned usually during childhood, these rules also reflect the cognitive processing that precedes the observed expression.

While the distinctive appearance of the face may be universal, the particular expression that appears in certain circumstances varies with culture (see Ekman, 1978, for a review of the experiements). One function served by such rules is to mask the appearance of an expression. Masking an emotion with a different one may be dictated by the culture or situation, as when the

Japanese mask their unpleasant feelings or when a benched football player is supposed to show happiness for his substitute's successful performance.

Elicited by clearly defined stimuli, masking is the result of information-processing cycles involving expectations, evaluations, and adjustments (see earlier discussion). It also consists of controlling emotions, a process involved in impression management.

DECEIVING WITH THE FACE: IMPRESSION MANAGEMENT

Masking consists of concealing a felt emotion with the appearance of another emotion. It is one of several techniques that can be used to falsify a facial expression. Simulating and neutralizing are two others. When one simulates, one attempts to show a feeling when one has none. Neutralizing, on the other hand, consists of appearing as though one feels nothing when in fact one does have a particular feeling. By systematically varying appearances, each of these techniques is used to affect observer inferences about one's feelings or intentions. They are facial management techniques designed to convey certain impressions.

The face is a valuable channel for impression management. Its plasticity is noted by Ekman et al. (1972: 1), who point out that "although there are only a few words to describe different facial behaviors, man's facial muscles are sufficiently complex to allow more than a thousand different facial appearances; and . . . these could all be shown in less than a few hours time." This protean quality of the face enables one to arrange one's appearance so that it befits the occasion. Regulated by learned display rules, these adjustments may involve qualifying an expression, intensifying or deintensifying it, or falsifying the expressed emotion (Ekman and Friesen, 1975). While the primary dimension of difference in "adjustments" is culture, variation has also been found for individuals within the same culture: Individuals are likely to differ in their sensitivity to social norms, in some cases showing rather extreme deviation (Ekman, 1978: 111-114).

Dittmann's (1972) classification scheme places facial expressions toward the communicative end of the scale (see Table 1.1, Chapter 1). Because of its visibility, close attention is paid to the face and, perhaps, "next to human speech, it is the primary source of giving information" (Knapp, 1972: 69). The information communicated is specific and, as the studies reviewed above suggest, usually decoded accurately. Facilitating impression management, these qualities bolster the probability that messages sent are received as intended. They also render effective attempts to deceive. Ekman and Friesen (1974a) found that when deceptive behavior was judged, more accurate judgments were made from the body than from the face. Moreover, in perpetrating the deception, subjects claimed that they controlled the face more than the body.

The primary obstacle to detection, control of facial muscles enables one to communicate directly one's misleading or falsified message. Control of expressions also enhances persuasiveness, a quality of considerable value in political settings. In spite of such control, deception clues or leakages can often be discerned. These detection problems will be treated below in conjunction with the discussion of multiple-channel research.

Kinesics

More popularly known as "body language," kinesics includes gestures, postural shifts, and movements of the hands, head, feet, and legs. The subject of several classification systems, kinesics has been defined in a variety of ways. Whether defined in terms of Birdwhistell's (1970) kinemes, kinemorphs, and allokines, Ekman's emblems, illustrators, regulators, and adaptors (see Table 1.2), or Mehrabian's (1972) forward/ sideways lean, arm or leg position asymmetry, trunk swivel movements, and gesticulations, the system is designed to assign meaning to movements and to provide a framework for research. These systems have indeed been heuristic: Going from conceptual categories to coding rules, each of these investigators has produced results that enhance our understanding of the role of kinesics in communication. Some of these experiments are discussed in this section.

Unlike facial expressions, kinesic behavior falls at the expressive end of Dittmann's continuum of communicative specificity (see Table 1.1). Providing less specific information than other channels, body movements tend to be diffuse in meaning, indicating broad "psychological states" rather than specific emotions or intentions. Along with the observers in Ekman and Friesen's (1974a) experiment, we might note the importance of body cues in identifying deception: Subjects engaging in deception displayed more hand-shrug emblems, fewer illustrators, and more face-play adaptors, each of which suggests discomfort or anxiety. Conveying gross affective states, body movements can serve as deception clues (indication that deception is occurring) but not leakage (the message being withheld). Compared to the other channels, body movements are continuous (lowest message information value and least decorder attention required) rather than discrete (high message information value and most decoder attention required).

These characteristics do not however reduce the importance of body movements in the communication process. Kinesic behaviors serve various functions in relation to speech, including repeating, contradicting, substituting, complementing, accenting, relating, and regulating interpersonal communication (Harper et al., 1978). Much of the research on kinesics has been done in conversational situations. Some of these studies will be reviewed below, and the role of body cues in coordinating the interaction will be highlighted.

Related to conversational behavior is the role played by body movements in information-processing. Such movements often anticipate later verbalizations, occurring early in the process of speech-encoding (Dittmann and Llewellyn, 1969). Referred to below as prearticulation behavior, these movements may serve as clues to reactions and intentions. But the role of body movements is not limited to conversational behavior. They also can be used to manage impressions. Evidence indicating that observers attach consistent meaning to gestures implies that those gestures can be used to influence perceptions (Gitin, 1970). Indeed, work on persuasiveness and perceived empathy, discussed below, demonstrates the impact of body movements.

BODY MOVEMENTS IN CONVERSATION

Experiments in conversation synchrony suggest that "interpersonal communication is not a matter of 'isolated entities sending discrete messages' back and forth but a process of mutual participation in a common structure of rhythmic patterns shared by all members of the culture" (Ashley Montagu and Matson, 1979: 153). Synchronous EEG recordings for two individuals engaged in direct conversation led Condon and Sander (1974) to conclude that interaction within a culture is governed by "body synthesizers" set in motion soon after birth.

Similarly, a rhythmic tempo of kinesic and speech behavior seems evident. On the basis of Condon's earlier work, Condon and Ogston (1966: 339) observed that "kinesic segmentation in general seems to coincide with etic segmentations of speech," that is, physical aspects of the articulation process. On the basis of his studies of "interactional synchrony," Kendon (1970: 164) observed that body movements in listening are coordinated with the cognitive processes that occur with these activities: "The coordination of the listener's movements with the behavior of the speaker is brought about through the listener's response to the stream of speech." Observations such as these provided a foundation for Duncan's meticulous research on turn-taking signals in conversation.

As discussed earlier, in this chapter's section on paralanguage, Duncan (1972, 1974; Duncan and Fiske, 1979) examined NVBs involved in minute-to-minute conversational interactions. Focusing primarily on turn-taking signals, Duncan observed that a number of body cues (gesticulations, head nods, head turns) have an important function in this activity (see Table 2.3). Used to signal a shift in roles, body movements serve to coordinate the structure of the interaction. They communicate speaker and listener intentions to move the conversation along, facilitating the flow of the discourse. Though often subconscious, monitor-

TABLE 2.3   HYPOTHESIZED SIGNALS USED IN CONVERSATION BY THE SPEAKER AND AUDITOR

Signal	Constituent cues	Effect in Conversation Pattern
Speaker turn	Intonation-marked clause Sociocentric sequence Grammatical completeness Paralinguistic drawl Decrease in pitch and/or loudness on sociocentric sequence End of gesticulation	Auditor may attempt to take turn
Speaker gesticulation	Gesticulation Tensed hand position	Speaker suppresses auditor's attempts to take turn
Speaker state	Turning head away from partner Begin gesticulation	New turn begins
Speaker within turn	Grammatical completeness Turning head toward auditor	Auditor may respond in back channel; speaker retains turn
Between-unit auditor back channel	Five different types, both audible and visible	Auditor provides feedback; speaker retains turn
Early auditor back channel	Same as between-unit auditor back channel	Auditor provides feedback; speaker retains turn
Speaker continuation	Turning head away from auditor	New within-turn unit begins

Source: From S. D. Duncan, Jr., and D. W. Fiske, "Dynamic Patterning in Conversation," *American Scientist*, 1979, vol. 67, p. 94. Reprinted by permission of the publisher.

ing these cues is essential to achieving the ostensible goals of the interaction.

As illustrated in Table 2.3, a number of body cues have effects on conversation patterns: the end of hand gesticulations is a signal to the listener that he or she can speak; illustrators maintain the floor for the speaker; shift in head direction and initiation of gesticulation signal to the listener that he or she is to become the speaker. Moreover, head nods, head shakes, and head turns toward or away from the listener are used to signal various behaviors between the speaker and listener during a turn. More than this, Duncan (1972) found such subtle cues as relaxation of the foot from a marked dorsal flexion to indicate speaker floor-yielding.

More broadly, interrelationships obtained among the cues suggest that these NVBs are elements in a system that serves to regulate conversations. One example is that speaker within-turn signals were strongly correlated with speaker continuation signals just as the next speech unit began (Duncan, 1974). Another example is that listener turn-taking increased as a function of speaker-yielding cues, while head turns away from the listener assumed that he or she would remain silent (Duncan, 1972). Such relationships illustrate one property of a social system: interdependence.

Another property, equilibrium, is illustrated by the effects of inattentiveness (failure to monitor) and poor synchronization of verbal and nonverbal behaviors (lack of coordination) on the quality of the conversation. Conversation impasses are deviations from a "steady state" (equilibrium). Relevant to a variety of face-to-face interactions (such as negotiations), this property of conversations remains to be explored.

Other work further illustrates the role of body movements in conversation. Some of the findings include the following: hand and feet movements conformed more closely to speech rhythm than head movements (Dittmann and Llewellyn, 1969); more hand movements occurred with more cognitive activity, especially when this activity was ideational, as in making up a story (Wolff and Gutstein, 1972); object-focused movements were associated with expressions of hostility, usually preceding such expressions (Freedman et al., 1973); more illustrator activity occurred in face-to-face communication compared with communication over an intercom (Cohen and Harrison, 1973), and leave-taking regularly consists of such movements as left positioning, forward lean, and head-nodding, timed appropriately (Knapp et al., 1973). Performed in harmony, these NVBs ensure synchronous patterns of interaction. Just as interesting is the significance of these movements for information-processing.

The movement-speech rhythm relationship also has implications for the process of speech-encoding, to be explored below.

BODY MOVEMENTS AND INFORMATION-PROCESSING

Head nods, hand and feet movements, and postural shifts have been found to be related to cognitive activity. Reflecting the tension that often precedes vocalizations, these movements have been found to occur at the start of a phonemic clause (Dittmann and Llewellyn, 1969). Indicating increased cognitive activity, more hand movements were found to be associated with increased ideation and fluency (Hoffman, 1969) as well as with the content of the stories presented (Wolff and Gutstein, 1972). Influencing memory, postures were shown to contribute to the early stages of recall (Rand and Wapner, 1967).

Together with the results of other studies, these findings suggest that body language plays an important role in the process of speech-encoding. As Rand and Wapner (1967: 271) note, "When . . . one examines the individual at an early stage in the learning process, i.e., where the 'work' of language and/or memory is 'in progress,' the contribution of these (kinesic) variables becomes more apparent." Of relevance also to neurological processes, the prearticulation stage may be the juncture at which body movement and the P300 component intersect.

Hypothesized linkages between body movements and P300 are based on the inference that both are indicators of processing activity. Unlike other nonverbal channels, however, there are dimensions of difference between these types of variables that may militate against such linkages. Most notable, perhaps, are the differences on Dittmann's dimensions of communicative specificity and message information value (see Table 1.1, Chapter 1): Where body movements are relatively diffuse, P300 is specific; where body movements have relatively low information value, P300 has rather high information density. Moreover, these variables operate in different time frames: seconds versus milliseconds. These differences do not preclude correlations between body cues and P300. They do, however, suggest consideration of alternative research strategies for exploring such relationships.

Body movements may be delayed manifestations of earlier processes indexed by the P300 component: lagged correlations might reveal that certain hand movements and postural shifts follow reliably the elicitation of P300. On the other hand, short-duration muscle movements, detected by miniature accelerometers, may coincide with the neurological processes (see Dittmann, 1978: 87). Detected by contemporaneous correlations, these movement/neural firings linkages may be seen to precede the gross body movements more frequently discussed in the kinesics literature. Perhaps, alternatively, body movements can serve as indicators of emotional states that co-occur with the processing activity. Already shown to correlate with tension, discomfort, and anxiety (Mehrabian, 1972), hand-gesture frequency and posture shifts may change during the prearticulation stage referred to above.

Having explored these possibilities, it may become evident that body movements reflect an aspect of information-processing not indexed by the P300 component. This too is useful information. It suggests that body movements and P300 are independent measures of different processes, the one construed as the *encoding* that precedes speech, the other referring to the *decoding* involved in stimulus evaluation. As such, the two types of variables are largely independent, co-occurring only when a "surprise" reaction is translated into verbalizations.

These conjectures form the basis for yet another hypothesis: P300 reflects the completion of an interpretive (decoding) process, while body movements reflect the formation of thoughts into words (encoding). The plausibility of this hypothesis depends on the outcome of experiments designed to arbitrate among the alternatives presented above.

ATTRIBUTIONS BASED ON BODY MOVEMENTS: IMPRESSION MANAGEMENT

Like the other nonverbal channels, body movements play an important role in impression formation. Though low in communicative specificity, body cues contribute to observer attributions concerning qualities or intentions. Attaching consistent meaning to gestures (see Gitin, 1970), observers are often confident in their judgments of persuasiveness, empathy, warmth, enthusiasm, and deceit. Particularly notable is Mehrabian's (1972) finding on the relation between intended and perceived persuasiveness: The same body movements used by an actor to convey an attitude were used by observers to infer that attitude. Providing impression managers an advantage, such communicative accuracy enables them to shape perceptions in keeping with their intentions.

Several studies by Mehrabian and Williams (1969) demonstrated that the enactment of certain NVBs enhanced perceived persuasiveness. Increased facial activity and gesticulations, reduced reclining angles, increased head-nodding, and reduced self-manipulation were related to intended and perceived persuasiveness. The facial activity seemed to convey an increase in the communicator's responsiveness to the target, while the body cues conveyed liking. Moreover, for male communicators, relaxed postures were judged more persuasive than slightly tensed postures—for female communicators tenseness of posture had little effect. Using a clinical interview situation, LaCrosse (1975) found that smiles and gesticulations were the primary cues used in ratings of counselor persuasiveness.

Carrying this research a step further, studies by London (1973) and by McGinley et al. (1975) demonstrated effects of body cues on attitude change. The London results showed that the more confidence conveyed by a communicator through body movements, the more agreement with the communicator's positions was expressed by the target of the communication. The McGinley et al. study showed a significant shift in target attitudes when the communicator assumed a body-open (limbs-outward) as opposed to a body-closed (limbs-inward) position. The body-open position conveyed the impressions of being more active, liked, and potent.

Even more dramatic are the results obtained by Rosenfeld (1966) and by Dabbs (1969). Rosenfeld found that gestures by one subject tended to be reciprocated by the other. Dabbs found that mimicked subjects reported that they were more similar to the actor. However, if they perceived initially that they were similar to the actor and he or she enacted contrary movements, that actor was rated especially low on liking. The latter finding confirms other demonstrations of the impact of a disappointment in expectations (see Druckman and Bonoma, 1976). Taken together, these studies suggest that body language can be used to enhance (or decrease) interpersonal influence.

Body movements are used also as clues to other qualities. Haase and Tepper (1972) found that forward trunk lean was important in judgments of interviewer empathy, while D'Augelli (1974) observed that frequent head nods conveyed understanding and warmth. Strong et al. (1971) compared ratings of counselors who exhibited many body movements with those who showed little movement. The former were rated as warm, casual, agreeable, and energetic, while the latter were seen as logical, cold, and analytic. Finally, Washburn and Hakel (1973) showed that high-gesturing interviewers were perceived as liking their jobs, more enthusiastic, easily approached, and considerate. Taken together, these studies suggest that more expressive subjects are seen as more attractive and are liked more than their less expressive counterparts.

Useful advice for the impression manager is suggested by the results of Ekman and Friesen's (1974a) experiment on detecting deception. These investigators found that subjects more accurately identified deception from body cues than from face cues. Specifically, deceptive communicators enacted more hand-shrug emblems, fewer illustrators, and more face-play adaptors (see Table 1.2, Chapter 1) than did the honest communicators. Similar findings obtained by Mehrabian (1972) show that these movements seem to indicate discomfort or anxiety. Knowing this, skillful impression managers might attend to their body language when they engage in deceptive communications.

Finally, attention should be given to the context in which the nonverbal behaviors are enacted. As pointed out by Ellsworth and Carlsmith (1968), the context of a relationship is likely to be important in determining the interpretation and impact of nonverbal behavior. For example, Mehrabian's "immediacy" behaviors (forward lean, orientation) may be interpreted differently in competitive and in cooperative situations: In a competitive situation they may be interpreted as attempts to intimidate or to dominate the relationship; alternatively, the same behavior may be viewed as a sign of friendship and liking in a cooperative context. Similarly, the meaning of Mehrabian's "relaxation" dimension (arm-position asymmetry, sideways lean, neck relaxation, reclining angle) may depend on situational norms or expectations: Postures and positions may be interpreted differently in a formal situation where status differences among colleagues are acknowledged from the way they are interpreted in a casual social gathering among friends.

Context refers also to prior associations and experiences, as well as to the particular combination of nonverbal channels enacted. Rarely are interpretations made *de novo*. Previous encounters are familiarization experiences that provide "baseline data" against which to compare current displays. Body movements are seldom interpreted in isolation. As demonstrated by Mehrabian (1972), observers base their attributions on the "display package": For example, communicators who were perceived as more persuasive displayed higher head-nodding rates, lower rates of self-manipulation, higher rates of gesticulation, more facial activity, higher speech rate and volume, and more eye contact. If they are isolated from the other cues, the body movements may not convey the communicator's intent to be persuasive. Addressed again below, these issues are considered in relation to research designs. Now we turn to a consideration of another channel of nonverbal communication: visual behavior.

Visual Behavior

An icy glance, a seductive or a pleading stare, an inquisitive look, shifty eyes—all are inferences made from observations of another's visual behavior. Whether intended for effect or the result of observer attributions, these are impressions often conveyed by "that certain look." Illustrating the impact of this nonverbal channel, these impressions are substantiated by results of studies on such functions of visual behavior as arousal, expression, and monitoring. When it comes to seeking information or expressing desires, clearly, the eyes have it.

The significance of the eyes is noted by Heron (1970: 244) in his philosophical essay on the gaze: "The most fundamental primary mode of interpersonal encounter is the interaction between two pairs of eyes and what is mediated by this interaction. For it is mainly here, throughout the wide ranges of social encounter, that people actually meet." A popular topic for research, visual behavior has been assessed as both independent and dependent variables, in a variety of situations, including those that are politically relevant (such as negotiations), and as indicators of information-processing.

Construed usually as direct gaze, visual behavior has a high probability of being noticed, quickly attracts another's attention, and engages his or her concern. As stated by Ellsworth (1975), the three characteristics of gaze are saliency, arousal, and involvement. The acknowledged significance of this nonverbal channel has resulted in widespread agreement with respect to its functions. Less agreement obtains, however, on a classification terminology and on measurement procedures.

There is more to a gaze than meets the eye! Its meaning can be defined in terms of several functions, including the regulation of conversation, the seeking of information, the expression of feelings, and the attempt to influence another's behavior. Its measurement can be defined in terms of various aspects, including a one-sided look, a face gaze, an eye gaze, a mutual look, eye contact, gaze avoidance, and gaze omission (von Cranach, 1971: see Table 2.4). The one is a question of validity, the other a matter of reliability: Meaning can be inferred from the context of interaction; measurement is accurate to the extent that observers can agree on what they see.

Whether a particular gaze is used to express feelings or to seek information is one issue that has received attention in the literature. Another is just how gaze is used to coordinate speech patterns. A third relates to the way situational or contextual variables qualify relationships between "looking" and "liking." What does gaze indicate? What functions are performed in

TABLE 2.4 DEFINITIONS OF VISUAL BEHAVIOR

Term	Definition
One-sided look	Gaze by one person in direction of another's face.
Face gaze	Directing of one person's gaze at another's face.
Eye gaze	Directing of one person's gaze at another's face.
Mutual look	Two persons gaze at each other's face.
Eye contact	Two persons look into each other's eyes and are aware of each other's eye gaze.
Gaze avoidance	Avoidance of another's eye gaze.
Gaze omission	Failure to look at another without intention to avoid eye contact.

Source: Adapted from M. von Cranach, "The Role of Orienting Behavior in Human Interaction," in A. H. Esser (ed.), *Behavior and Environment,* New York, Plenum Press, 1971. Adapted by permission.

interactive situations? Answers to these questions have implications for intentions. They also highlight the role of gaze in information-processing and impression management.

But inferences about the meaning of gaze must be tempered by the extent to which assessments are accurate. Observer judgments contribute to the quality of inferences. How accurate are the observers? On the basis of real-time observations, Exline and his collaborators (Exline, 1963; Exline et al., 1965) demonstrated interobserver reliabilities in excess of .90 for total gaze and number of looks. The coefficients are even higher when ratings are made from videotaped slow-motion recordings (Harper et al., 1978). Similarly, ratings of gaze direction are reasonably accurate, though observers have been found to be less accurate than receivers in judging this variable (von Cranach, 1971). Generally, reliabilities vary somewhat with distance between the sender and observer, position of the observer, sender head orientation (for gaze direction), sender-receiver axis, eye and head movements, and observer training. Judgment errors may result from ratings made at large distances when the sender's head and eyes are not aligned in the direction of the observer. Yet even under these conditions judgments are reasonably accurate. Interobserver agreement is high even when observers rate gaze in spontaneous social interactions. Vine

(1971) found remarkable acuity for observers (92 percent agreement) who were rating moving actors in a filmed natural situation. Bolstering our confidence in the rating of gaze, the reliability studies suggest that assessments can be compared for diverse interactions, including those that take place in the laboratory and *in situ.*

Contributing also to the quality of inferences is participant awareness. To what extent are participants aware, aroused, and involved? Ellsworth and Ludwig (1972: 383) noted that "subjects in social interactions may not be able to describe the other's visual behavior accurately, even when it can be demonstrated that this behavior has had an effect on their behavior." Self-reports may not be good indicators of awareness. Like other subjective variables, awareness is an issue that can be resolved experimentally.

Observed impacts on gaze of experimental conditions can be explained in terms of differences in awareness: So conceived, awareness is a construct used to explain observed differences in visual behavior. It could also be inferred from formulas devised to assess deviations from expected or chance looking (see Argyle and Ingham, 1972). These issues are considered again below in conjunction with research on arousal.

GAZE: REGULATING INTERACTION AND EXPRESSING AFFECT

Effects of gaze can be construed in terms of the regulatory and expressive functions of visual behavior (Kendon, 1967). Visual behavior provides information and feedback essential to the regulation of speech. It also communicates interpersonal sentiments. Much of the research on this channel has focused on these two functions. Findings, issues, and implications are summarized in this section.

Part of the rhythm of conversation, visual behavior is used to synchronize speech. Looking decreases considerably when there is no need to synchronize communication with a listener (Argyle et al., 1973). Direct gazes signal a readiness to communicate. From that point on, the eyes perform a number of functions: Direction of gaze serves as a turn-taking signal

(Duncan, 1972); amount of looking distinguishes between the listener and speaker (Argyle and Ingham, 1972); looking away enables a speaker to maintain the floor while looking toward is an attention signal (Kendon, 1967); and while long looks without speaking convey the need for a listener response, gaze aversion can be used to cut off the communication entirely (Kendon, 1967). "Breaking eye contact" is part of an elaborate ritual designed to terminate a conversation, although in the case of close friends more mutual looking may occur at the end of their interaction (Knapp et al., 1973).

The importance of visual behavior in conversation management is illustrated by the effects of lack of eye contact during communication. Wiener et al. (1972) found that discomfort, interruptions, and dysfluencies occurred when vision was obscured. Varying patterns of speech-eye coordination for dyads of different cultures can cause problems in cross-cultural communication. Commenting on an implication derived from results obtained in their interracial communication study, Mayo and LaFrance (1973: 7) note: "When Blacks and Whites interact ... these differences may give rise to communicational breakdowns. The White may feel he is not being listened to while the Black may feel he is being unduly scrutinized. Further, exchanges of the listener-speaker roles become disjunctive, leading to generalized discomfort in the encounter." These investigators found that black-black dyads reversed the speaker-listener eye contact patterns obtained for all-white dyads. Such disjunctures might have implications for interactions among representatives of different nations. They may account for the impasses that occur often in international negotiations.

The expressive function of visual behavior is illustrated by experiments on the "liking-looking" relationship, findings on the use of eye contact in serving affiliative needs, and the use of gaze to communicate intentions in cooperative situations. Considerable evidence supports a strong relationship between looking and interpersonal attraction. Mehrabian reports five studies that support this relationship: Males engaged in more looking toward a liked than a disliked person (Mehrabian, 1968a); gaze decreased with degree of unfamiliarity and with dislike

(Mehrabian, 1968b); gaze was related to the communication of a positive attitude (Mehrabian and Friar, 1969); amount of looking was related to an affiliative behavior factor (Mehrabian, 1971b); and subjects looked more at a confederate who reacted positively to them (Mehrabian and Ksionzky, 1972).

This relationship, found also in other studies (Gatton, 1970; Pellegrini et al., 1970), may be qualified by other variables. Such contextual variables as accompanying verbal statements (Ellsworth and Carlsmith, 1968), quality of arguments presented (Burroughs et al., 1973), game-playing orientation of the gazer (Kleinke and Pohlen, 1971), and, perhaps most interesting, whether looking followed a period of not looking (positive ratings) or preceded a period of not looking (negative ratings; Breed and Porter, 1972).[7] These results suggest that looking signals liking under certain conditions; whether it precedes, coincides with, or is a consequence of liking is less clear. Under other conditions looking is likely to be used for information-seeking, regulating, or influencing.

Eye contact is one of several NVBs that affect the level of intimacy experienced in an interaction. Argyle and Dean (1965) proposed that eye contact operates to establish an equilibrium level of intimacy in an encounter. Support for this theory comes from findings on the relationship between eye contact and physical distance: Increased gazing occurs at greater distances (Argyle and Dean, 1965; Goldberg et al., 1969; see also Patterson's 1973a review of the evidence).

According to the theory, looking compensates for closeness when interactants are far apart. However, further research has introduced qualifications to the theory. Important variables are sex, social context, and kind of intimacy. For males, looking increases linearly with distance; for females there is a curvilinear relationship (Aiello, 1972). Quantity of speech may operate as a way of reducing intimacy at close distances (McDowell, 1973), and intrusions on personal space cause increasing glances that reflect the degree of dislike toward the intruder (Mehrabian, 1968b; Patterson et al., 1971). As is the case with the looking-liking relationship, the distance-contact relationship operates under certain conditions. Even so, it appears that the eye plays an important role in expressions of intimacy or affiliation in social encounters.

Yet, as noted above, looking may not serve an expressive function. It may be used for seeking information. Inferring intentions turns on an ability to make this distinction. Of particular relevance to this issue is a recent study by Foddy (1978). Consistent with her predictions, Foddy found different patterns of visual behavior for cooperators and competitors. Average length of gaze and mutual gaze were greater for cooperators, while frequency of gaze and mutual gaze were the same in both conditions.

Reflecting differences in intentions between cooperators and competitors, these indices distinguish between the expressive and monitoring functions of gaze. Cooperators engaged in both functions while competitors used gaze primarily for monitoring: Cooperators showed a large amount of gaze to signal trust, liking, and honesty, and gazed frequently to aid coordination; competitors used frequent, short gazes to estimate the other's intentions while not giving away their own. These results have implications for information-processing, which we discuss next.

GAZE, PUPIL DILATION, AND INFORMATION-PROCESSING

Foddy's (1978) results support the hypothesis that frequency of gaze is an index of information-seeking or -monitoring. Short, frequent gazes characterize the individual who needs information about another but needs to control information about himself or herself. Frequent sustained looks seem to be used by the individual who seeks information from another and discloses personal information. Construed as tactics, these patterns of visual behavior may be effective in eliciting the desired information. Several studies show that gaze can have an effect on a subject's verbal behavior: Increasing interviewer gaze resulted in subjects making more self-references (Snow, 1972); continuous or contingent interviewer eye contact led to more intimate interviewee speech (Ellsworth and Ross, 1976); increasing face gazes by a child confederate produced more positive verbal expressions and a higher work rate from teacher subjects (Bates, 1975); and gaze-averting interviewers were disliked more by subjects but increased their talkativeness, including the length of their replies (Sodikoff et al., 1974). These results suggest that patterns of gaze can affect the amount and content of information disclosed.

The relationship between gaze and verbal behavior may be mediated by arousal. A number of studies reported direct effects of gazing on indices of emotional arousal, including galvanic skin response (Nichols and Champness, 1971), "transoccipital EEGs" (Gale et al., 1972), and heart rates (Kleinke and Pohlen, 1971). In all cases gazing or staring increased the frequency and amplitude of the physiological measures. Provoked by the gazer, subjects may feel more involved in the interaction. Feeling more involved, they are likely to disclose more information about themselves. Whether the information disclosed is revealing is the next issue to consider. Here, too, visual behavior may be useful when combined with data generated by physiological measures.

An aspect of visual behavior that has significant implications for information-processing is pupil dilation. Convergent research findings on pupil dilation and on P300 suggest that these are functionally equivalent indicators of processing. Like P300, variations in pupillary behavior have been found to reflect attention, processing a stimulus input, apprehension of the experimental situation, and task relevance (see Hess and Petrovich, 1978). Linked more closely with cognitive processing than with emotions, increased dilation occurs with increasing information-processing load (Simpson and Hale, 1969; Beatty and Kahneman, 1966) and with political interests (Hess, 1965). Particularly interesting is Janisse's (1976) conclusion that dilation may occur following an unexpected stimulus. Taken together with findings that show pupillary response to stimuli as a function of their attention value (Libby et al., 1968; Janisse, 1973), this finding suggests the hypothesis that P300 is correlated with pupil dilation. Nor are these simply different measures of similar processes. Pupillary behavior may derive from neurological activity, as suggested by Lowenstein and Loewenfeld (1970): "The pupil size depends on more than sympathetic and parasympathetic innervation and is profoundly influenced by states of consciousness and various neurological activities such as those involving changes in the cortico-diencephalic and reticular systems" (cited in Hess and Petrovich, 1978: 171). Clearly a candidate for NVB/neurophysiological correlations, pupillary behavior can be investigated in the context of the "Donchin paradigm" (Donchin, 1979).

There is much yet to be learned about pupillary behavior. Further clarification of its role in signaling intentions is needed. Following the leads of observers who suggest that pupillary behavior is a measure of arousal and interest, pupil size changes could complement other indicators of "stress" during the course of a political speech (see Wiegele, 1978, for paralinguistic indicators). Following Leyhausen's (1967) observation that pupil constriction is an indication of an animal's intention to attack, this variable can be assessed before, during, and after the onset of aggressive political behavior. Based on Clark's (1975) interesting finding that pupillary response can be used to detect deception, pupil size can be compared for deceptive and honest messages presented in a laboratory situation.[8] Yet with all these potential sources of pupillary variation, the number of variables that could confound the interpretation of obtained correlations also increases. Alerted to these concerns, Hess and Petrovich (1978) suggest solutions based on carefully controlled experimentation and precise measurement.[9] These efforts are producing a research literature that can underwrite extrapolations to political contexts.

ATTRIBUTED ATTRACTION, EFFECTIVENESS, AND CREDIBILITY: IMPRESSION MANAGEMENT

Visual behavior is another source of attributions concerning characteristics and motives. Observer agreement on the interpretation of gaze has been obtained in a number of studies. Impressions based on high eye contact (more time spent looking) include attraction (Wiener and Mehrabian, 1968; Kleck and

Nuessle, 1968), situational intimacy (Ellsworth and Ross, 1976), skilled, informed, and experienced (Beebe, 1974), affiliative (LaCrosse, 1975), self-confident (LeCompte and Rosenfeld, 1971; Kleck and Nuessle, 1968), and empathic (Haase and Tepper, 1972). Combined with ratings of dominance (Thayer, 1969), these positive attributions may be responsible for the finding that those being looked at by the gazer are regarded by others as more powerful.

When accompanied by sustained eye contact, a presentation may be viewed as more authentic and the speaker judged to be more confident (Exline and Eldridge, 1967). Gaze aversion, on the other hand, has been shown to elicit suspicions. Hemsley and Doob (1975) found that when gaze aversion was used as a cue, a confederate witness in a simulated courtroom testimony was judged as less credible, and the defendant more likely to be guilty. Similarly, Baxter and Rozelle (1975) found that gaze-averting subjects were judged by policemen as more suspect, intentionally withholding or misrepresenting information.

Speculating on the implications of these attributions, Baxter and Rozelle note that they are likely to be false. Gaze aversion was found to occur more often at closer distances. Since police-citizen interactions usually occur in close proximity, the observed aversion may be a function of distance rather than intentions. Highlighting the interplay between nonverbal channels, this finding is discussed again in the section on multiple-channel research.

The attributions elicited in the studies reviewed above should aid impression managers. Equipped with this information, they should be able to control their presentations to elicit desired effects. However, they must also be aware of qualifying conditions. Involvement, sex of observed, culture, and context may affect the impact of gaze. Holstein et al. (1971) report that gazing was more salient to their participant observers (inter-actants) than to their outside observer. Kleinke et al. (1976) found significant sex differences in the interpretation of gaze: Males rated females as being more attractive when told they (the females) had given them low levels of gaze, whereas females rated their male partners as most attractive when told they (the males) gazed at a high level. Moreover, females have been found to look more than men (Kleinke et al., 1976). Watson (1970) found patterns of gaze behavior for Arabs, Latin Americans, and southern Europeans (direct focus on eyes or face) different from those of Asians, Indian-Pakistanis, and northern Europeans (peripheral gaze or no gaze at all). These patterns are probably also desired when members of these cultures are recipients of others' gazes: Deviations from a direct focus may make Latins suspect the gazer's intentions, while deviations from a peripheral focus may make Asians uncomfortable.

Like the other NVB channels, gaze effects may be a function of the context of a relationship. Sustained gazing may be interpreted as a sign of positive regard and friendship (see research reviewed above) or as an attempt to dominate or intimidate (Ellsworth and Carlsmith, 1968). Consistent with this reasoning are the results of two experiments on bargaining.

More lengthy gazes and mutual gazes were found for Foddy's (1978) "cooperators" than for her "competitors." The cooperators also produced quicker and better agreements. Frequent gazing by individualistic bargainers (instructed to get the best agreement for themselves) promoted a distributive strategy (tactics used to elicit unilateral concessions) and reduced the likelihood of a satisfactory agreement in the Lewis and Fry (1977) experiment. Perceptual data indicated that the more often an opponent gazed at a subject, the more the subject evaluated his behavior as hostile and cold. Lewis and Fry's competitive bargainers may have based their attributions on the impression that their opponents were focusing on the interpersonal aspects of the relationship rather than on the problem (see Mehrabian, 1972). In contrast, Foddy's cooperative bargainers seemed to infer trust and liking from the other's gaze, leading them to coordinate effectively toward a problem solution.

Expanding upon the implications of the research reviewed above, it would be appropriate to explore the effects of gaze in a variety of political situations. Two situations in particular provide compelling scenarios for research designs: negotiations and conference diplomacy. Sensitive to the effects of sustained gazing and gaze aversion, a negotiator can control his or her visual behavior to make a verbal bid more convincing as well as to bluff more effectively. Alerted to the interplay between distance and gaze, a diplomat can arrange a conference situation to create the impression of credibility and competence. The importance of situational engineering is illustrated by the work done on proxemics.[10]

Multiple-Channel Research

A channel-by-channel view of nonverbal behavior may overlook the fact that interpersonal communication is a multiple-channel phenomenon. Emotional expression, cognitive states, and social interaction involve facial, body, and eye movements as well as vocal and verbal behavior occurring together. While our organization of the literature was dictated by the predominant research focus of most investigators, it is now appropriate to note interrelationships among the channels. Certain relationships suggested by the previous discussion can be highlighted in this final section of the state-of-the-art survey.

Multiple-channel research can be considered in terms of three types of relationships: relative importance of different channels, interactive effects of two or more types of NVB, and the synergistic effects of multiple cues. Contributing most of the information about each of these relationships is Mehrabian's work, summarized in his 1972 volume, *Nonverbal Communication*. His multiple-channel approach extends also to a consideration of relationships between verbal and nonverbal behavior. The examples to follow are drawn largely, though not exclusively, from his work.

RELATIVE IMPORTANCE OF CHANNELS

The separate effects of verbal, vocal, and facial components of attitude were assessed by Mehrabian and Wiener (1967) and by Mehrabian and Ferris (1967). Taken together, the results of these studies suggest that the combined effect of these variables is a weighted sum of their independent effects expressed in terms of the following equation:

$$A_{total} = .07\ A_{verbal} + .38\ A_{vocal} + .55\ A_{facial}$$

where A_{total} is the attitude inferred on a degree-of-liking scale from the three-channel communication, A_{verbal} is the attitude communicated in the verbal component only on the same scale, and so on. This linear model suggests that the nonverbal component dominates in determining one's attitude based on a multichannel communication. Of the two nonverbal components, the facial aspect accounted for more variance than the vocal (paralinguistic) component.

Citing other experiments, Mehrabian (1972: 108) concluded that "when there is inconsistency between verbally and implicitly [nonverbal] expressed attitude, the implicit portion will dominate in determining the [impact of] the total message." Implicit cues include position and postural movements as well as vocal and facial behavior. Though he states that this is only a "first-order approximation," as there may be interaction effects, this is strong evidence for the importance of NVC in conveying impressions.

Another assessment of the relative importance of verbal and nonverbal cues was made by Havis et al. (1981). Various combinations of positive (conveying positive affect) and standard (impartial, impersonal) verbal and nonverbal behaviors were enacted by police officers during a police-citizen encounter. The interviewer's (police officer's) nonverbal behavior accounted for more variance in interviewee (citizen) impressions than did the verbal aspects of his behavior. Few interaction effects were obtained. Particularly significant were the contributions of the enacted nonverbal display to ratings of courtesy, friendliness, good-naturedness versus irritability, and mild versus headstrong attitude. These results provide further support for Mehrabian's model and bolster the contention that NVC is effective in conveying impressions.

A third example of relative importance is Ekman and Friesen's (1969a) experiment on the nonverbal betrayal of affect. These investigators hypothesized that the body would provide more accurate cues of deception than would the face. Being less subject to awareness and voluntary inhibition, body movements are a more likely source of "leakage" than are facial expressions. Indeed, observers used body cues significantly more than facial cues in judging deception. Moreover, deceivers claimed that they attempted to disguise the face more than the body while perpetrating the deception. The cues provided by the body included decreased use of hand illustrators, increased use of self-adaptors, and more postural shifts.[11] While not analyzed, leg and foot movements were considered the most likely sources of leakage. This evidence indicates that one nonverbal channel is likely to be more important than another in diagnosing attempts to dissimulate intentions.

Finally, paralinguistic variables have been found to be useful indicators of deceptive intentions. As noted earlier, DePaulo et al. (1980) present evidence suggesting that tone-of-voice clues are more revealing than face or body cues. Judges were told to pay particular attention either to tone of voice, to words, or to the visual cues, or were given no particular attentional set. They were most successful at detecting deception when told to attend to the tone, and least successful when told to attend to visual clues. Although this evidence is from studies designed from the perspective of the decoder (judge), other findings highlight the importance of voice cues from the standpoint of the encoder (sender). Streeter et al. (1977) obtained significant differences in measured voice pitch between a deceiver and a truth teller. More definitive resolution of the issue of relative importance of different channels awaits results of a study where the modality in which senders are instructed to communicate is varied systematically.

INTERACTIVE EFFECTS OF DIFFERENT CHANNELS

Interactive effects are illustrated by the results of Mehrabian's (1972) experiments on inconsistent messages. Positive and negative verbal messages were combined with positive and negative vocalizations. The impact of the verbal message depended on the type of vocalization with which it was paired. Inconsistent negative communications contained a negative vocal and a positive verbal component, producing an overall negative effect (for example, "That's just great" communicated in a tone that conveys sarcasm). Inconsistent positive communications contained a positive vocal component combined with a negative verbal component, producing an overall positive effect (for example, "You are simply incorrigible," communicated with humor conveyed by vocal and facial expressions).

Interactive effects derived from different targets for the different channels: Where the verbal portion conveyed attitudes toward the addressee's actions, the nonverbal portion conveyed attitudes toward the addressee himself. These effects, discussed previously, are construed as one of the functions of NVC—to convey subtle messages (see Table 1.4).

Other examples of interactive effects are relationships between distance and various nonverbal and verbal behaviors. As already mentioned, Argyle and Dean (1965) demonstrated that as distance decreased, so did mutual gazing, in compensatory fashion. Replicated in a number of studies, the relationship between distance and looking seems to reflect perceived intimacy: As intimacy increases (closer proximity), such compensatory behaviors as reduced eye contact may occur to reduce the arousal to an appropriate level.

In addition to eye contact, changes in body orientations as a function of distance have been found to occur. Watson and Graves (1966) reported that as physical distance decreased, body orientations between American and Arab dyads became less direct. This relationship, found also in several other experiments (see Aiello and Jones, 1971), appears to be stable over time and occurs even when experimental instructions discourage this approach (Patterson, 1973b).

Finally, interaction distances have been found to have implications for verbal communication: Stone and Morden (1976) found a greater discussion of personal topics at an intermediate (five-foot) distance, compared to close (two-foot) and far (nine-foot) distances. Cultural norms would seem to regulate "appropriate" interaction distances for various types of verbal communications.

The Lewis and Fry (1977) study presents another example of interaction effects. Gaze and seating distance were related to the types of verbal arguments made by bargaining opponents: The more often members of a dyad gazed at their opponents' faces, the more often they used irrelevant arguments to support a demand; the closer members sat to each other, the more often they engaged in irrelevant arguments. Fewer agreements were achieved for dyads whose members engaged in high levels of gaze and who sat closer to one another. An apparent function of hostility, the high gaze at closer distances served to arouse bargainers to a level that seemed to interfere with attaining agreements. Just as speech dysfluencies have been found to accompany anxiety (Mahl, 1956), Lewis and Fry's observed irrelevant arguments were probably symptoms of arousal incurred by the "looking-distance" relationship (Argyle and Dean, 1965). These findings demonstrate, once again, the impact of NVB on verbal communication and its implications for political behavior.

MULTIPLE INDICATORS OF INTENTIONS

Implied in much of the preceding review is the contention that certain intentions can be indexed by multiple nonverbal cues. This contention is supported by the results of Mehrabian's (1972) experiments on persuasion and deception. His combined encoding/decoding research designs identified the *set* of nonverbal behaviors indicative of these states. For persuaders, he found more activity and more positive responsiveness indicated by the NVBs: increased facial activity and gesticulations, reduced reclining angles, increased head-nodding, and reduced self-manipulations.

For deceivers, he found more negative affect and less activity being expressed in the nonverbal repertoire: less nodding, fewer gestures, fewer leg and foot movements, less talking, slower speech rates, more speech errors, and more smiling. Fewer gestures, referred to as illustrators, were also found for Ekman and Friesen's (1974a) deceivers. Moreover, the latter investigators found more self-manipulations and more postural shifts for their deceivers as compared with the honest subjects (see also McClintock and Hunt, 1975).

Like intentions, general psychological states can be indexed by multiple NVBs. Anxiety, comfort/discomfort, confidence, guilt, and approval-seeking are some of the states that have received attention. Typical findings are those produced by correlations between self-report measures and observed NVBs. Preliminary work in our laboratory suggests, for example, more frequent postural shifts, less eye contact, faster speech rates, and more speech errors for anxiety; more postural shifts, more self-manipulations, more overall movement, and faster speech rates for discomfort; more eye contact, fewer self-manipulations, and slower speech rates for confidence; and less gesturing, more self- and object manipulations, and less overall talking for guilt related to deception. In addition, for approval seekers, more head nods, smiles, and gesticulations were observed (Rosenfeld, 1966).

In addition to providing a more encompassing portrait of self-presentations, multiple nonverbal cues are useful to political analysts. While a single indicator may be an ambiguous symptom of a psychological state, several indicators are likely to bolster the analysts' confidence in their own judgment. Moreover, by alerting analysts to rely on a variety of indicators, premature inferences may be avoided. Multiple assessments are an integral part of the research designs presented in the next part of this volume.

INFORMATION-PROCESSING AND IMPRESSION MANAGEMENT

Multiple-channel NVBs can be used to index the information-processing and impression-management functions. As noted in Table 1.4 above, for example, paralinguistic, kinesic, and visual behaviors serve as indicators of processing, while facial and vocal cues facilitate persuasion. Within each of these channels specific behaviors corresponding to a finer breakdown of the two functions can be listed.

Three aspects of information-processing, suggested by the discussion above are (1) information-seeking, (2) prearticulation processing activity, and (3) reactions following stimulus evaluation (see Table 1.5). Micro- and macro-NVBs are involved in each of these activities. Frequency of gaze (Foddy, 1978), spatial distance between interactants (Stone and Morden, 1976), and such temporal speech characteristics as duration of utterances, reaction-time latency, and speech interruptions (see Matarazzo et al., 1961) seem to indicate information-seeking activities. Hesitations and unfilled pauses (Bruneau, 1973; Boomer, 1965), head nods, hand/feet movements, and postural shifts (Dittmann and Llewellyn, 1969), and pupil dilation (Simpson and Hale, 1969) occur often during the processing phase.[12] Such NVBs as facial movements associated with surprise (raised brows, open eyelids; see Ekman and Friesen, 1975), decreases in verbal productivity (Siegman, 1976), and pupil dilation (Hess, 1965) are among those associated with the reactions that follow processing activities. Each of these NVBs can be measured reliably. Each can be used in research designs, either as an indicator of processing *in situ* or as a correlate of other behaviors in the laboratory.

Impressions conveyed in one nonverbal channel can be bolstered or offset by behavior displayed in another channel. Mehrabian's (1972) research, reviewed above, illustrates the bolstering effects of multiple NVBs on perceived persuasiveness: speech volume, activity, and rate, increased facial activity, more head-nodding, gestures, eye contact, and fewer self-manipulations combine to convey impressions of liking, competence, and confidence. Ekman and Friesen's (1974a, 1975) work, also reviewed above, illustrates the offsetting effects of face and body cues in attempting to be deceitful. Control over the configuration, timing, and location of facial expressions enables an actor to falsify, modulate, or qualify an emotion. Without similar control over those body movements that suggest discomfort (such as hand-shrug emblems, illustrators, and adaptors), however, the "true" feelings may be leaked.

Other impressions may also be more effectively conveyed through multiple channels. For example, forward trunk lean (Haase and Tepper, 1972), frequent head nods (D'Augelli, 1974), and more time spent looking (Foddy, 1978) contribute to judgments of empathy. Sustained gazing at short distances (Hemsley and Doob, 1975; Baxter and Rozelle, 1975) combined with relaxed vocalizations (Addington, 1971) convey credibility. Liking or affiliative desires are likely to be evoked by the speaker who gestures frequently (Washburn and Hakel, 1973), engages in lengthy gazes and mutual gazes (Foddy, 1978), and makes more declarative statements per minute in a message that accounts for about half of the total conversation (Mehrabian, 1972; Kleinke et al., 1976). These impression-management tactics will be explored further in the chapters of Part II on experiments. Our elucidation of them concludes our survey of the state of the art.

NOTES

1. In another study he found speech rate to increase, leading him to postulate a U-shaped relationship between anxiety level and speech rate.

2. The correlations were .46 for speech volume, .51 for vocal activity, and .41 for speech rate.

3. Paralinguistic performances are particularly important in situations where communicators can be heard but not seen. In face-to-face situations, paralinguistic cues are likely to combine with facial, body, visual, and distance cues to create an impression.

4. The validity issue is treated in some detail by Ekman and Friesen (1975). These investigators were also sensitive to other methodological issues in this area of research. They note, *inter alia*, that careful specification of the decoding task is important, representative sampling of both encoders and decoders is desirable, and still photographs provide a stable but unnatural stimulus while films provide a natural but complex, changing stimulus (see also Ekman et al., 1972).

5. The New Guinean subjects studied by Ekman and Friesen (1971) found it more difficult to distinguish between fear and surprise than did their Western counterparts.

6. This study is being done in collaboration with E. Donchin and associates at the University of Illinois. A preliminary report is available and may be obtained from the senior author (DD).

7. The Breed and Porter (1972) finding reflects the effects of contrasts or changes in status. It is similar to the difference in affect accorded to a "convert to the

cause" (positive ratings) as compared to a renegade (negative ratings; see Druckman, 1968b).

8. Clark's (1975) procedure consisted of having subjects role play a "secret agent" who memorized a code to which they were subsequently exposed during a lie-detection session. Significantly more pupil dilation occurred following presentation of the secret code number than to neutral codes. Combined with Galvanic Skin Response measurement, the pupil dilation measure yielded 95 percent accuracy in detecting deception.

9. Differences between blue-eyed and brown-eyed subjects were found by Hess (1975). Pupil size was easier to assess in blue eyes than in brown eyes, and the blue-eyed subjects manifested a greater range of pupillary responses. Moreover, blue-eyed subjects discriminated better the relationship between stimulus attributes and pupil size. Thus, while blue-eyed negotiating opponents may be better objects for assessment of pupil change, they may also be better at assessing one's own pupillary behavior.

10. A detailed review of the work on proxemics can be found in Harper et al. (1978: Ch. 6). This channel is also discussed in Chapter 3, where studies of interpersonal distance are reviewed.

11. More illustrators also characterized Mehrabian's (1972) deceivers, while increased self-adaptors and postural shifts were also found for the deceiving respondents in the McClintock and Hunt (1975) interview study.

12. Recall the distinction made earlier between the decoding involved in stimulus evaluation and the encoding that precedes speech. Each of these aspects of processing may be reflected in particular NVBs. One hypothesis is that pupil activity and micromomentary facial expressions occur during stimulus evaluation, while changes in paralinguistic and body indicators are observed during attempts to formulate thoughts into words.

3

IMPRESSIONS, ATTRIBUTIONS, AND
INTERPERSONAL DISTANCE

Much of the research on nonverbal communication has focused on the discovery of universal expressions of emotional states and intentions. Less attention has been directed to role and situational constraints as causes of behavior (see Chapter 2). However, role relationships and specific conditions of interaction may have substantial influences on nonverbal behavior.

An analysis of the strategic features of many types of interaction is identified by Goffman's (1969) treatment of expression games. His analysis encourages a search for types of encounters suitable to study the complexity of participant roles and the constraints on actor behavior (see Chapter 1). While a number of examples of such interactions could be found, the police-citizen encounter appears to represent a type of interaction wherein strategic nonverbal behaviors occur and may be studied systematically. Such encounters are an important social form: The structure of interaction is flexible and the outcomes are sufficiently varied to permit meaningful research (Banton, 1964; Primeau et al., 1975; Skolnick, 1967). Therefore, a series of studies was undertaken in order to examine some of the processes of impression formation and management under these conditions. The studies are discussed in terms of four themes: attribution biases, interpersonal distance, verbal versus nonverbal behavior, and cross-cultural interactions.

Attribution Biases

Although not dealing exclusively with nonverbal behavior, an early study by Rozelle and Baxter (1975) illustrates an attempt to investigate factors involved in interpreting behavior in a particular, role-defined situation. The study dealt with the process of danger recognition in police officers. Of particular interest was the existence of any differences in the focus of attention on dispositional, behavioral, or situational cues when comparing dangerous and nondangerous encounters with citizens.

The procedure consisted of interviewing a sample of police officers in the Houston Police Department. The officers were asked to indicate the "traits, characteristics, and features they look for when interacting with a citizen while in the role of a police officer." They were also asked to indicate the cues they utilized in forming their impressions of the citizen. The officers were to describe a critical incident of a dangerous face-to-face encounter with a citizen and to identify the cues used in forming impressions under these circumstances.

Results showed that the perceptual scan employed by the officers was greater under conditions of danger than when they interacted with a citizen in a nondangerous situation (that is, when obtaining information from a witness to a crime or accident). More general behavioral cues, within the context of the situation, were used under conditions of danger. Under less stressful conditions, the officers indicated more use of specific facial and vocal cues, eye contact, arm and hand movement, dress, and behavioral sequences such as posture and body orientation. From these cues, a preponderance of dispositional, as opposed to situational, attributions were made in explaining the citizens' behavior.

These results illustrate two points about impression-formation processes. First, under conditions of danger, the perceptual scan and the integration of complex and varied information was increased by the police officer. This finding is inconsistent with a number of studies that have demonstrated a general constriction of cognitive functioning under stress (Janis and Leventhal, 1968; Lazarus, 1966). Perhaps for reasons of training and experience, the police officer engaged in different decoding activities, resulting in impression-formation processes more functional to his or her specific role. Second, when engaging in a more typical, nondangerous professional role with a citizen, the police officer concentrated on a number of specific nonverbal behaviors with little regard for possible situational causes of those behaviors. This narrowed focus of attention could lead to systematic misinterpretation of behavior, particularly since police officers themselves play an important role in such situations, potentially contributing causal elements related to the observed behavior.

An important aspect of role- and situation-related analyses of impression-formation and -management processes has been attributed to differences arising from different participants' perspectives (Jones and Nisbett, 1972). It has been proposed that observers tend to overemphasize dispositional qualities of actors in inferring the causes of their behavior, while overlooking more immediate situational factors contributing to performance. Actors, on the other hand, often overemphasize situational factors as causal determinants of their behavior, while underemphasizing dispositional qualities as causal agents. Several studies have provided empirical support for such an analysis (Nisbett et al., 1973; Storms, 1973). Other investigators have established qualifications for the actor-observer biases, in which such factors as empathy training have modified or reversed the attributional biases (Monson and Snyder, 1977; Gould and Sigall, 1977; Zuckerman, 1979).

In the context of police-citizen interaction, it is unlikely that participants have undergone any specific attributional training; as a result, the original actor-observer biases are most likely operating. The face-to-face interaction setting is complicated by the consideration that the participants assume the role of both actor and observer in the course of expressing themselves and observing the other participants.

Of particular interest are the potential attributional biases of the police officer. A general conclusion drawn from the Rozelle and Baxter (1975) study is that, in the described situation, police officers see themselves as observers, judging various qualities of the citizen with whom they are interacting. In response to a citizen's behavior, a police officer attributes dispositional qualities to that citizen. The police officer is perhaps unaware of the contributions of his or her own behavior, which is a causal factor regarding the citizen's actions. Since the police officer's behavior is an immediate, situational variable, the observer bias of attributing behavior to "dispositions" is maintained, while situational factors (such as the police officer's behavior) are ignored or underestimated as contributing to the citizen's behavior. This misinterpretation of behavior should be evaluated to the degree that the "observer" has minimal information regarding the "actor" and must make immediate decisions regarding action taken as a result of the interpretation of the actor's behavior. The police-citizen interaction is a good example of such conditions.

Interpersonal Distance

Perhaps one of the more important elements in direct face-to-face interactions is proxemics, or interpersonal spacing. Hall (1966) has elaborated on the interplay of type and amount of perceptual information available as they depend on the physical distance separating interactants. It is proposed that sensory shifts occur as interpersonal distance changes and rules defining territoriality are established.

Much research has been conducted on this topic (Stone and Morden, 1976; Argyle and Dean, 1965; Lewis and Fry, 1977) with somewhat confusing results, particularly when cross-cultural factors are considered. Most of the work has focused on task variables; there has been little concentration on role-defined situations. If research on proxemics were categorized by context and role, within and between cultural settings, perhaps more meaningful results would be obtained. The next study, by Baxter and Rozelle (1975), was an attempt to investigate specifically the effects of interpersonal distance between a police officer and a citizen on the nonverbal behavior of the citizen.

A simulated interview was conducted between each of 29 white undergraduate male student-subjects and an interviewer playing the role of a police officer. The interview consisted of four phases during which the distance between the officer and citizen was varied. Subjects were told that the purpose of the study was to investigate police-interviewing techniques and were unaware of the experimental manipulation. They were randomly assigned to an experimental (severely crowded) or a control (mildly crowded) group.

The interview was divided into four two-minute periods and consisted of the police interviewer asking the subject about various items in his wallet. For the experimental and control groups, the interviewer maintained a four-foot distance from the subject during the first two-minute phase of the interview. Precisely at the beginning of the second two-minute phase of the interview, the interviewer casually moved within two feet of the subject for both groups. The severe-crowding manipulation occurred during the third two-minute phase, which involved the police interviewer moving to an eight-inch nose-to-nose distance from the subject in the experimental group, and remaining at the two-foot distance in the control condition. The police interviewer then moved back to the two-foot distance for the fourth two-minute phase in the experimental condition, while the two-foot distance was simply maintained for the control group. The police interviewer was instructed to maintain eye contact throughout all phases of the interview. The subject was positioned at a point one foot from a wall to prevent escape from the interviewer during the crowding conditions. The prescribed distances between police interviewer and subject were designed to coincide with Hall's (1966) categories of interaction distances: social consultation (four to seven feet), personal (one and one-half to four feet), and intimate (six to eighteen inches).

Forty-six nonverbal behaviors were rated directly from the videotapes. The categories were similar to those used in Birdwhistell's (1970) structural nonverbal-language system (see our introduction). For this reason, the study provides a test of the utility of his system for recording NVBs under conditions of crowding.

Results revealed consistent reactions to severe crowding. As the subject was increasingly crowded by the police interviewer, his speech time and frequency became disrupted and dis-organized, with an uneven, staccato pattern developing. An increase in eye movements and gaze aversion occurred, while few other facial reactions were evident. Small, discrete head movements were seen, and head rotation/elevation movements tended to increase. Subjects adopted positions to place their arms and hands between themselves and the interviewers, and there was a substantial increase in hands-at-crotch positioning. Brief rotating movements tended to increase, while foot move-ments decreased.

A striking similarity exists between these behaviors, resulting from crowding, and the behaviors identified by police officers as indices of dispositional attributions of guilt, deception, or honesty during real interviews with citizens (Rozelle and Baxter, 1975). In the earlier study, officers placed an emphasis on facial and vocal cues, arm and hand behavior, posture, body orientation, and related acts on the part of the citizen. It should be emphasized that the interviews recalled by the police officers were usually brief encounters with a minimum of verbal ex-change.

As noted above, the study also provided a test of the useful-ness of Birdwhistell's (1970) nonverbal-language system. Of the 46 categories coded, only 11 showed reliable differences as a result of the experimental manipulation. Because of the exten-sive and detailed rating procedures developed in this study, the utility and validity of this hypothesized separate language system must be questioned. Although the study did not attempt to relate specific nonverbal behaviors to emotional or inten-tional states, the results underscore the heuristic value of role prescriptions and situational constraints in investigating the area.

Rozelle and Baxter (1978) conducted an encoding study to determine if nonverbal behaviors caused by situational crowding are *interpreted* by observers as caused by dispositions. The specific behavioral responses obtained as a result of spatial intrusion in the Baxter and Rozelle (1975) study were pro-grammed into a videotaped, simulated police-citizen interview.

In the experimental condition, the citizen encoded these spatial-intrusion responses while being interviewed by a police officer. The camera angle was a frontal view of the citizen over the left shoulder of the officer, making the actual distance between them ambiguous. Conditions were identical for the control group, except that the citizen did not display the spatial-intrusion responses. Separate groups of randomly assigned observers were shown the video portion (without audio) of the nine-minute interviews and rated the citizens and the officers on a number of scales, including impressions, attributed feelings, and confidence in these ratings.

A high degree of consensus in both conditions indicated that observers formed a coherent impression of the citizen. Further-more, the spatial-intrusion behaviors were judged to be significant indicators of deception, guilt, anxiety, suspicion, and generally negative qualities on the part of the citizen. However, only one-third of the impression ratings that produced significant differences between the experimental and control conditions showed significantly greater confidence ratings in the experimental condition. It was expected that with physical proximity held constant and ambiguous, the more expressive (and atypical) spatial-intrusion behaviors would result in more confident ratings. Perhaps the observers did consider proximity as a factor causing the citizen's behavior. This possibility is supported by observers' estimates of physical distance: They estimated distance as significantly less for the experimental than for the control condition.

A clarification of these results was sought in a second study, in which the physical proximity between the police officer and citizen was made explicit during their interaction. This manipulation would allow the observer to discount the situational factor of physical distance more adequately in explaining the citizen's behavior, particularly where the spatial-intrusion behaviors were inappropriate for the distance between the inter-actants in either the experimental or the control condition (see Kelley, 1972).

The presence or absence of spatial-intrusion behaviors was made orthogonal to two conditions of physical proximity: the one-foot distance (nose-to-nose) and the four-foot distance. This was also reproduced from the Baxter and Rozelle (1975) study. Thus, two "appropriate" conditions were created involving spatial-intrusion behavior present in close proximity and absent in distant proximity. Likewise, two "inappropriate" behavioral conditions were created, in which spatial-intrusion cues were present when interactants were spatially distant and absent when they were close. In all conditions, the interactants were viewed from the side; therefore the physical distance between them was clearly visible. As was the case in the first study, separate groups of randomly assigned observers viewed the four conditions, the number of observers ranging from 11 to 13 for each condition.

Results of this study replicated those obtained from the first study in that, regardless of physical proximity, spatial-intrusion behaviors produced a coherent impression of the citizen as deceptive and having generally negative attributes. However, attribution-theory predictions were confirmed on a number of confidence ratings for impressions formed: Greater confidence was indicated in the behaviorally "inappropriate" conditions. Thus, in the spatial-intrusion behavior *present/distant*-proximity and the spatial-intrusion behavior *absent/close*-proximity conditions, the situational factor of proximity was discounted and the atypical behavior was emphasized in forming an impression of the citizen. Less confidence was revealed for impressions formed in the behaviorally "appropriate" conditions, indicating that observers may have considered both situational and dispositional factors to contribute to the citizen's nonverbal behavior. However, it would appear that the contribution of physical proximity was significantly underestimated, since organized impressions were formed on the basis of empirically determined intrusion behaviors and were misinterpreted as indications of deceptive, suspicious, and generally negative attributes.

Verbal Versus Nonverbal Behavior

Another study in the police-role research program was designed to measure impressions formed as a result of police-behavior encoding, and to examine the relative effects of verbal and nonverbal behavior exhibited by the police officer (Havis et al., 1981). An important feature of this study is that both the encoder and decoder were active participants in an ongoing, face-to-face interaction. This contrasts with the procedure used in most studies, which is to assess impressions made by passive observers. Both procedures have advantages: While the former is realistic, allowing both parties to encode and decode messages, the latter avoids the problem of lack of control over the specific content contributed by the subject.

Encoding scripts were developed for the police-officer role in consultation with police-training authorities and relevant research literature. "Positive" and "standard" presentations of verbal and nonverbal behavior were produced and compared, resulting in four experimental conditions: positive nonverbal-positive verbal; positive nonverbal-standard verbal; standard nonverbal-positive verbal; and standard nonverbal-standard verbal. Standard police behavior was intended to represent the more typical or "proper" presentation of this role, as reflected in training protocols. Generally, the police officer is expected to be properly presented by the use of objective, impartial, and impersonal behaviors. In the experiment, standard nonverbal behaviors included erect posture and nonsmiling facial expressions without illustrators or head nods, while maintaining eye contact for 80 percent of the interview period. The officer also faced the citizen directly (180 degree angle) and held a clipboard in front of himself, to serve as a barrier between him and the citizen. Standard verbal behaviors were represented by formal questioning techniques and a neutral-to-authoritative tone of voice.

The positive police style was generally more relaxed and expressive than the standard style, but was judged to be within an appropriate and acceptable range by the police consultants. Positive nonverbal behavior included relaxed posture, friendly facial expressions, and use of head nods to reinforce responses to questions while maintaining a moderate amount of eye contact (60 percent of the interview period). For the positive condition, the officer faced the citizen at a 120 degree angle and held his clipboard to the side, not using it as a barrier between himself and the citizen. Positive verbal behaviors involved the use of a relaxed and expressive tone of voice, supportive verbal reinforcers, and informal-nonaggressive questioning techniques.

Two campus police officers were trained to express appropriate verbal and nonverbal behaviors in each of the four conditions. The citizen-participants were 70 male students randomly assigned to one of the four conditions. The interview was five minutes in length and consisted of the citizen being questioned about controversial topics such as alcohol consumption and the use of marijuana. In all interviews, the interactants stood approximately three feet apart. The interviews were monitored carefully and only those exhibiting criterion-level performance by the police officer were included in the analyses. This procedure yielded 16 acceptable interviews per condition. Dependent measures were obtained by administering an "impressions" questionnaire to the citizen-participant at the conclusion of the interview.

Results supported predictions that positive verbal and nonverbal encoding conditions would lead to more favorable ratings on interpersonal and job-related qualities of the police officer than would be the case for the standard presentation. In addition, nonverbal behaviors accounted for a greater proportion of the variance in the obtained ratings than did verbal behaviors. For example, officers displaying positive behaviors were rated more favorably on dimensions of courtesy and respectfulness, and citizen comfort was enhanced by these behaviors. The importance of nonverbal behaviors is demonstrated by the finding that officers were evaluated with decreasing favorability— from positive nonverbal-positive verbal to positive nonverbal-standard verbal, standard nonverbal-positive verbal, and standard nonverbal-standard verbal conditions—indicating a slight yet preponderant effect of nonverbal over verbal behavior. (See the section in Chapter 2 on the relative importance of channels.) Nonverbal and verbal positive behaviors contributed to higher ratings of such job-related items as the ability to provide security, dependability, and success in dealing with campus problems.

Cross-Cultural Interactions

The studies reported thus far have demonstrated the impact of nonverbal behavior and interpersonal spacing on impression management and formation in the police-citizen situation. An important extension of these studies, particularly involving unintended interpretation and/or attribution of behavior, is to the area of cross-cultural communications. Much of the literature on this topic has been based on nonintrusive observation and has provided suggestions regarding possible aspects of misinterpretation of observed and enacted behavior (Hall, 1963a, 1963b, 1964). However, little research has involved experimental intervention based on recorded observations. A notable exception is the work of Watson and Graves (1966) and subsequently that of Collette (1971).

Watson and Graves reported reliable nonverbal behaviors that distinguished Arab student interaction dyads. Collette programmed these behaviors into encoding conditions in which English students were trained to interact with Arab students, with the former displaying either Arabic or English nonverbal behaviors and distancing variables. Findings revealed that when English students displayed Arabic behaviors, they were judged to be socially and professionally preferable by the Arab students to a significant degree.

A similar approach has been used in a few studies dealing with cross-cultural factors involved in the police-citizen interaction situation. The (sub)cultural differences concerned Black-American and Anglo-American nonverbal behaviors and spacing practices. Several observational studies have shown reliable differences among these groups (Baxter, 1970; Thompson and Baxter, 1973; Willis, 1966). Generally, adult Blacks prefer to interact with others at greater physical distances than do Anglo-Americans. In addition, the Black subjects used body orientation and gaze-aversion techniques to achieve these preferred interaction distances.

Garratt et al. (1981) trained Anglo-American police officers to engage in empirically determined "Black nonverbal behavior characteristics" during an interview with Black citizens. Each of 30 Black male undergraduate subjects was interviewed, in random order, by two Anglo police officers approximately 30 years of age, one of whom produced "Black-oriented" behavior and spatial positioning, with the other engaging in nonverbal behaviors and positioning more typical of "Anglo interactions." The participants stood four and one-half feet from each other during the Anglo-American interview and six feet apart during the Black-American interview.

Instructions for the police officer in the two interview conditions were as follows:

Anglo-American Interviews

(1) Open the door moderately wide, step through, continue facing and looking at the subject (S), and close the door behind you.
(2) Approach the S quickly while continuing to look at him.
(3) Stand four and one-half feet away from the S while asking for his identification.
(4) Approach the S quickly and directly to receive the identification card, and stand directly facing him while close to him, perusing the card.
(5) Position yourself four and one-half feet away from the S again after returning the card.
(6) Upon leaving, turn and walk quickly away to the door, open the door moderately wide, step through, and close the door behind you.

Black-American Interviews

(1) Open the door widely when entering the room, swing completely around and close the door slowly with your back to the S.
(2) Approach the S slowly and deliberately while averting your gaze.
(3) Stand six feet away from the S while asking for identification.
(4) Approach the S slowly to receive the identification card and stand at right angles to the S while close to him, perusing the card.

(5) Position yourself six feet away from the S again after returning the card.

(6) Upon leaving, turn and walk slowly away, open the door widely, step back, turn, and then walk out, closing the door.

The officer was also instructed to maintain minimal eye contact during the Black-American interview. The verbal content of the interviews was similar, with topic and order of questions strictly prescribed. The officers were trained and rehearsed in each interview style and closely monitored during the five-minute interviews. The Black subjects were administered a questionnaire at the completion of the second interview. Subjects indicated their preference for one of the two officers on items dealing with personal, social, and professional competence.

Results revealed a significant preference for the officer behaving in the Black-American interview style with the most substantial preference shown for personal competencies and, to a lesser extent, for social and professional areas of competence. An interesting observation by the experimenter was that those Black subjects whose manner and appearance was more similar to the "Anglo-American style" responded more favorably to the Anglo-American interview, while the subjects, whose manner and appearance reflected a stronger "Black-American style," responded more favorably to that interview style.

Although a more thorough set of comparisons would entail including Anglo subjects and Black police officers, the results of this study are compelling, particularly in light of the empirical bases used to construct the protocols. With verbal content held constant, nonverbal behaviors and spatial conditions substantially influenced the impressions formed during this interethnic, police-citizen communication. These results have implications for proper training in nonverbal encoding to achieve optimal impression management.

Conclusion

The police-citizen studies reviewed above grew out of an interest in examining complex interactions with strategic features. Each participant is concerned with gathering information and forming impressions while, at the same time, recognizing that he is sending signals that contribute to the other's impressions. Such interdependencies have a strategic quality. It is often to the actor's advantage to present certain appearances in order to invite interpretations from the other that conform to the actor's purposes. A tacit feature of the interaction is the recognition that the other is also staging his presentations.

The processes involved in revealing and concealing information in this context merit further attention. The police-citizen encounter is a ubiquitous form of interaction, having social-psychological implications. But other formats may be more conducive to experimentation that varies the conditions affecting processes of information exchange. One possibility, providing for theoretical interpretation consistent with previous work, is a televised interview with a diplomatic representative.

The diplomatic interview provides several advantages. While preserving the strategic role-prescribed qualities of the police-citizen interview, it allows for incorporation of a greater variety of relationships and roles. It also provides the opportunity for examining complex positions, extensively elaborated and presented in a longer time frame. Moreover, the format allows for the natural inclusion of technical equipment, necessary for investigation of nonverbal behavior. These are some of the reasons subsequent work has been done in this venue. Other reasons are discussed in the next chapter.

Finally, the results presented in this chapter illustrate the influence of certain factors on attributions of cause and impressions. Highlighted were the effects of role, interpersonal distance, and culture. Attributions are an important element in the process of inferring intentions from observed behavior. This is *indicated* in the model shown in Figure 1.1 (Chapter 1). It is *demonstrated* by the results obtained in the experiments reported in the next part of this volume.

PART II:

EXPERIMENTS

In Part II we report the results of experiments on the non-verbal aspects of deception. These studies are part of a research program that focuses both on the NVBs emitted by *subjects* during the course of role performances and on the nonverbal clues used by *observers* to infer intentions. Focusing on the subject, the experiment described in Chapter 4 is an attempt to isolate the veridical cues to deception. An analytically diverse approach yields a variety of findings, extending the literature in several directions. Particularly notable is the idea that NVBs can serve several analytical functions, distinguishing conditions (deception, evasion, honesty) in terms of relative frequencies, correlation patterns, and correlates of psychological states. The results suggest that specific NVBs reflect feelings that are aroused by the role or intention, and they have implications for the model shown in Figure 1.1 (Chapter 1).

The related studies presented in Chapters 5, 6, and 7 are probes of observer perceptions. Topics addressed include cognitive aids for improving judgments of intentions (Chapter 5), the relative importance of different factors that combine to produce a decision about intentions (Chapter 6), and the impact of alternative portrayals (displays) on impressions (Chapter 7). The results of these studies are pertinent to both information-processing and impression management. The experimental findings of Chapter 5 underscore the contention that processing aids are essential tools for inferring intentions from nonverbal behavior. How observers discount some factors and weight others preferentially in the process of judging intentions is elucidated by the modeling exercises of Chapter 6. Finally, the analyses of Chapter 7 show the impact of different nonverbal displays on observer perceptions. Regarded as largely heuristic, the results reported here suggest ways nonverbal cues can be used to increase analytical sensitivity. They provide a basis for further exploration.

4

REVEALING AND
CONCEALING INFORMATION
Nonverbal Indicators of Deception

Intention assessments turn on the human tendency to acquire, reveal, and conceal information. When the information sought is strategic, the situation is a conflict of interest between an observer and a subject: The observer attends to cues that may be revealing; the subject attempts to control his or her presentation so as to reveal certain information while keeping other information hidden. Construed as contests, the gamelike features of such interactions consist of moves that alternate between a subject's impression-management tactics and an observer's attempts at assessment. The sequence of moves and countermoves highlights stylistic cues. A focus on these cues renders the interaction an expression game.

Expression games are prototypes for situations in which there are two protagonists, an observer and a subject. Rarely do we discover social situations in which an observer has little to gain from assessing expressions and another has little to gain from manipulating this process. The ubiquity of the phenomenon makes this a general model that, as Goffman (1969) notes, contains a "single structure of contingencies" to be found in contexts as diverse as intelligence networks and informal social gatherings. That structure frames a communication process in which meaning is stylized and patterned from information that has an expressive and semantic character. Knowing what to attend to and knowing what is *being* attended to are the key challenges for assessing intentions and shaping perceptions about them.

The observer-subject model assumes functionally differentiated roles, one focusing on assessment mechanics, the other on
control of information. The model suggests two analytical
questions: What are the varieties of assessment devices used by
an observer? and What is the range of possible actions taken by
a subject? Answers to these questions derive from an understanding of the physical aspects of the situation, the players' technical knowledge of detection and/or concealment, and the
nature of the stakes that are contingent on the outcomes. These
variables impinge on game-playing behavior. When that behavior
is nonverbal, the *context* stylizes what is elicited and how it is
interpreted.

Of primary concern are the features of expression games
found in a particular context. Following from a general methodological approach, discussed below and elsewhere (Mahoney and
Druckman, 1975), is the assertion that behavior derives its
meaning from the setting in which it is embedded. The
"context-relevant clues" are those associated with certain kinds
of information, conveyed by certain kinds of actors, who
address a type of receiver in particular situations. Such a tax-
onomic approach suggests categories for analysis, some of which
also include general features of expression games (see DePaulo
and Rosenthal, 1979).

Categories for analysis are suggested by the focal setting for
this project, which is international politics. Information consists
of policy-relevant intentions that may be revealed or concealed
by official representatives. The actors (subjects) are diplomatic
representatives who make public appearances and/or are
assigned to negotiating delegations. Receivers (observers) include diplomatic representatives from other nations, foreign
audiences, or government analysts who make assessments of
intentions. Public interviews, conferences, and private meetings
or negotiations provide the settings for those strategic exchanges that render the interaction an expression game. The
ease with which intentions can be "read" depends on the
dimensions of these situations, just as the likelihood of deception clues turns on the incentives for hiding or revealing infor-

mation. Considered in terms of its parts, the problem consists of attempts by the subject to reveal or conceal information during a presentation, clues provided the observer by the subject's behavior, and a situation depicted in terms of certain dimensions.

Playing a central role in expression games, nonverbal behavior may provide clues that information is being withheld. Referred to by Ekman and Friesen (1974a) as "deception clues," these indicators have been shown to consist of such body movements as self-manipulations and postural shifts (McClintock and Hunt, 1975). In broader terms, it is the "negative-affect indicating cues" discussed by Mehrabian (1972), which may also include distancing, smiling, speech duration, and speech-error rate, that are likely to be affected by conscious attempts to manipulate the presentation of information. Suggested here is an approach that integrates each behavior into an ongoing stream of other behaviors, especially those concerned with postures, gestures, gazing, and paralinguistic cues (see Exline and Fehr, 1978). While several previous studies measured elicited NVBs, none has generated a purview of nonverbal communication as an integrated set of deception clues. Nor has any study attempted to reproduce the situations of concern to political analysts.

Other differences exist between the previous work and this study. These differences, however, should be evaluated in terms of a particular approach to the study of deception. The psychological literature on deception can be divided into three approaches (see DePaulo and Rosenthal, 1979). One focuses on the ability to detect lies and to deceive successfully. Another line of inquiry examines accuracy of lie detection as a function of differential access to different channels, such as the face, tone of voice, and words. A third approach is concerned with identifying particular cues that distinguish deceptive from nondeceptive responses. This experiment is in the tradition represented by the third approach.

Six previous studies have examined responses associated with deceptive versus honest enactments. While they have focused on a comparison between "deceivers" and "truth tellers," they differ on the kind and range of cues examined. Five of the six studies concentrated measurement on a small number of behaviors, usually in one of two modalities: Ekman et al. (1976) measured only hand movements and voice pitch; Harrison et al. (1978) focused on response duration and latency; McClintock and Hunt (1975) examined eye contact, smiles, hand movements, and posture shifts; Streeter et al. (1977) only measured voice pitch; and Fugita et al. (1980) examined such facial behaviors as glances, smiles, facial manipulations, and eye blinks. Only the Mehrabian (1972) experiment has covered a range of nonverbal behaviors comparable to those assessed in this study.

Commenting on the importance of context, DePaulo and Rosenthal (1979) note that the question, "What are the clues to deception?" is probably too broad. Instead we should ask, "What are the clues to which kinds of deceit by which kinds of deceivers to which kinds of receivers in which kinds of situations?" An attempt was made in this experiment to capture subtleties and carefully formulated ambiguities in diplomatic styles of discourse (Axelrod and Zimmerman, 1979). Taking the form of indirect deception or "evasion," this form of communication contrasts with the narrower constructionist or legalistic definitions of "lying" used in the earlier studies. For this reason, *comparisons* of results are limited to conditions defined as direct lies as opposed to truths.

The "display rules" for nonverbal behaviors are likely to be different from one setting to another. Our diplomatic context requires subjects to be detached, rational, and circumspect in dealing with the issues. Results from postinterview questions showed that subjects regarded themselves to be effective, confident, serious, in control, and calm while performing their roles. None of the earlier studies encouraged subjects to adopt this approach. Rather, each required strong personal identification with the issues. Moreover, in three of these studies, type of affect (unpleasant or pleasant) was confounded with condition (deceiving or telling the truth). Acknowledging this, several of the investigators concluded that it is not clear whether the deceptive displays reflected negative affect or deception per se

(McClintock and Hunt, 1975; Ekman et al., 1976; Mehrabian, 1972).

Each of the arguments introduced above, and related points, can be stated in summary form.

(1) The exchange of strategic information is an expression game in which an observer can gain from assessing another's intentions while a subject can gain from controlling his or her presentation.

(2) Of particular interest are features of expression games played in the setting of international politics. Policy-relevant intentions are conveyed or concealed by diplomatic representatives to various foreign audiences in such situations as interviews, conferences, and negotiations.

(3) Deception clues are likely to be provided from nonverbal behavior. Patricularly relevant may be the negative-affect cues of smiling, speech duration, and speech-error rate, as well as the body-language cues of self-manipulations and posture shifts. However, an assessment of a wide variety of NVBs, representing each of the communication channels outlined by Dittmann (1972), is needed.

(4) Styles of diplomatic discourse suggest a broader conception of deception and honesty than that used in previous research. Diplomatic fictions, carefully formulated ambiguities, evasions, and misdirection are some of the forms taken by statements.

(5) Detection of nonverbal deception clues is a function of a subject's demeanor control and visibility. Affected by various aspects of the political environment, these variables determine the extent to which nonverbal cues provide useful indicators of psychological states associated with deception or honesty.

These points suggest elements of a research program on nonverbal communication. We plan to examine the interactive dynamics of expression games as they unfold in the arena of international politics. This approach implies a two-party perspective that may be cumbersome for analysis, especially when players alternate between the two roles. Moreover, players may be contesting several items of information, and each is likely to be involved in several games. For purposes of analysis, it is convenient to restrict the experimental situation to nonalternating roles and to a limited number of items.

Approach

The experimental design incorporates features of a more general research strategy referred to as a context-relevant approach. This approach is based on the assumption that behavior derives its meaning from the broad context in which it is displayed. It has guided our earlier work on collective bargaining (Druckman, 1967, 1968a), international alliance behavior (Druckman, 1968b), political decision-making (Druckman and Zechmeister, 1973; Zechmeister and Druckman, 1973), inter-religious council decision-making (Druckman et al., 1974, 1977), and international negotiations (Druckman, 1977b).

The context-relevant approach is a methodological innovation for research on nonverbal communication. It bridges the gap between the two predominant approaches to the topic, structural and external variable. The contrasting approaches emphasize naturalistic observation, on one hand, and laboratory manipulation, on the other. Employed primarily by Birdwhistell (1970), the structural approach focuses on the communication process per se and is guided by an explicit theoretical model. Represented by Ekman's work, the external variable approach focuses on specific psychological states and develops theory from empirical findings. Our strategy is a synthesis of these approaches. By moving between field and laboratory, it serves to link naturalistic and experimental observations. By examining multiple NVBs as part of a communication process and as indicators of psychological states, it provides a more encompassing view of the role of nonverbal communication.

Applied to this particular research program, the approach consists of interfacing laboratory and selected political environments. This is done by conducting a limited number of experiments and by making selected probes in various real-world contexts. The experiments suggest dimensions that can be used in analyses of field material; the real-world probes suggest variables that can be manipulated in experiments (Ackoff and Emery, 1972; Druckman, 1977b). Linking the findings obtained in both settings is a general model developed from concepts suggested by the state of the art and modified on the basis of the research experience.

This project represents one of the ways experimentation is brought into closer contact with relevant nonlaboratory settings. Aspects of the real world are brought into the laboratory. These aspects consist of current issues in Soviet-U.S. relations, dimensions of a real interview situation, and certain obligations associated with the role of ambassador. Here, context is regarded as the background within which an experimental design is embedded. Referred to by Mahoney and Druckman (1975) as a Type II design, this experiment is a step toward more sophisticated designs. Encompassing rather subtle aspects of critical real-world environments, the "sophisticated" designs manipulate contextual variables and incorporate them in the analysis. Examples are a simulation of the decision-making process as it unfolds in the Politburo and an experimental comparison of several U.N. committees operating *in situ.*

Focusing on decoding, this experiment is designed to elucidate an interpretive process used for making inferences about another's intentions and perceptions. The clues provided by the results should enhance an analyst's sensitivity to the meaning of nonverbal communication. But this is only one part of the research program. Other projects will focus on encoding—the process of influencing another's perceptions by controlling one's performance. The postures made evident by encoding are tactics that can be used to produce certain effects. The shifting foci of these different methods are captured by an approach that interweaves aspects of both in research designs. Particularly notable is research designed to explore the relationship between decoding and encoding skills.

The research, developed in stages, will build toward complexity by considering, first, the interaction between an actor and an observer from the standpoint of the actor (this chapter). Second, we will focus on the observer's inferences and impressions (Chapters 5 and 6). Third, we expect to examine an exchange between an actor and an observer. Ultimately, the analyses performed for these tasks will enable us to uncover clues from NVBs displayed by political actors *in situ.* For each of these tasks we are concerned primarily with the meaning of nonverbal behavior.

The results obtained to date make clear the value of a multiple-channel approach to NVB measurement. Different

NVBs serve different functions in the interpretation of intentions. Some behaviors distinguish among intentions in terms of relative frequencies. Other behaviors acquire meaning as part of a pattern of intercorrelated NVBs that distinguishes among the intentions. Still other behaviors are important as correlates of psychological states that are elicited by the conditions. Each of these functions is illustrated in terms of statistical findings. Of particular interest is the observation that a number of the NVBs serve several functions. The findings also have implications for an observational strategy: Rather than reduce intentions to a few behavioral indicators, we should attempt to assess a large number of behaviors. Such a strategy was followed in this experiment.

The analytical approach of this experiment differs in certain respects from that taken in the earlier studies. Concentrating exclusively on an evaluation of condition differences, those experiments neither attempted to develop a model for prediction nor examined interdependencies among the nonverbal behaviors. Some of our most interesting results derive from those analyses.

Notable also are differences in analysis procedures. New results derive from analyses of time-period effects and baseline differences. None of the earlier studies examined condition by time-period interactions. Moreover, there was no attempt to collect baseline data. These variables provide additional information about condition differences: More subtle effects are those that occur in particular time periods or manifest themselves as a difference from a subject's "normal" or relaxed behavior. Such effects were obtained and will be presented later in a discussion of results.

Procedures

The situation was a hypothetical *Meet the Press* interview with the Soviet ambassador to the United States. Subjects were assigned the role of the Soviet ambassador, "Mr. Trienko." The 15-minute interview consisted of questions directed to the ambassador about three current events: the Soviet invasion of

Afghanistan, Soviet military activities in Cuba, and Soviet troops in Europe. Background material was prepared for each of these issues, and subjects were given time to study the material.

The situation created was designed to reflect essential aspects of a real interview. It was somewhat more rehearsed than spontaneous, more public than private, more normative than ambiguous in terms of expectations, and more role-defined. Each of these aspects was represented as follows: Subjects were given time to prepare positions on the three issues; they were made aware of the camera and were told that the tapes would be viewed by others to develop training exercises; they were told to follow the instructions of their "governments"; and they were made aware that concealing, evading, or revealing information about government policy was an expected diplomatic posture.

Systematic variation of these dimensions, a long-term research goal, is hypothesized to affect observed nonverbal displays. Each is likely to increase (decrease) the subject's sensitivity to control over his demeanor, an important element in the game of revealing and detecting deception clues. Interpreted in terms of these dimensions, the results of this experiment will be compared to those obtained in situations that are less rehearsed, more private, less role-defined, and more ambiguous in terms of expectations (such as informal conversations).

Concealing, evading, or revealing information were postures assumed by subjects who were assigned to one of three experimental conditions: strategic deception, evasion, and honesty. Deceptive subjects were given the following instructions: "Misrepresent your nation's actual policy.... On all three issues you are to present arguments that reflect a compelling yet false interpretation of the actions of your government." Evasive subjects were told, "Do not speak directly to the issue about your nation's actual policy.... On all issues you are to present statements that are compelling but do not directly answer the questions being asked." Instructions to honest subjects were, "Honestly express your nation's actual policy as communicated to you.... On all three issues you are to present statements that are compelling, honest, and direct in terms of official

policy given to you by your superiors." Deceptive and evasive
subjects were rewarded for fooling the interviewer. Honest
subjects were given credit for leading him to make the correct
guess. In all conditions, they were given information that would
help them in preparing arguments. The issue of Soviet activities
in Cuba for the deception condition provides an example:

> Your task, as ordered by the Kremlin, is to successfully deceive the
> U.S. into accepting the Soviet's reasons for its activities in Cuba.
> Essentially, the U.S. considers the Soviet involvement as military,
> whereas the Soviet defense has been that it is providing technical
> assistance to Cuba for purposes of development. Such assistance,
> according to the Soviets, is in keeping with a bilateral treaty between
> the two countries. *In reality,* the Soviet activities are directed toward
> the construction of a military base equipped with modern weapons
> and aircraft. The actual Soviet policy is to establish a base in Cuba
> from which strikes could be launched if necessary. This activity is
> justified by citing the presence of U.S. bases in countries close to the
> Soviet mainland.
>
> In speaking with the U.S. press, you must *not* reveal the actual
> Soviet policy, but must convince the U.S. that Soviet policy is based
> on the following points.
>
> (1) The Soviet Union does not want to risk a nuclear confronta-
>   tion. It is against their interests to escalate tensions in the
>   North American continent.
> (2) It is clear that the facilities being constructed are to be used
>   for industrial development.
> (3) Presence of advisers is justified by the terms of the bilateral
>   treaty with Cuba. To reject requests for assistance would be a
>   violation of the intent of the treaty.
>
> These points should aid you in successfully deceiving the audi-
> ence. It should provide them with an understanding of the situation
> at variance with their current accusations.

Subjects were 30 advanced male graduate students recruited
from the political science and psychology departments at the
University of Houston. Considerable attention was given to the
subjects' understanding of current international developments,
notably those concerned with U.S.-Soviet relations. Interviews
formed the basis for selection of subjects. Told of the time

requirements and the $5 payment, each prospective subject was scheduled for an appointment at the studio. Upon arrival he was assigned randomly to a condition, a procedure used until 10 subjects were assigned to each condition.

An important procedural decision was the separation of experimenter and interviewer roles. The interviewer was uninformed about the subject's condition assignment. Not knowing the subject's condition would prevent the possibility of an interviewer bias. The experimenter's role consisted of introducing the situation, informing subjects of the experiment's purpose and incentives, presenting them with condition instructions, introducing the issues, and presiding over the preparation period. Upon completion of this phase, each subject was escorted to an adjoining room where the interviewer was seen sitting at a table with a nameplate reading "Mr. Spivak."

General introductions were followed by turning on the video recorder and aligning the 25mm-lens camera. The interviewer was responsible for guiding the interview, maintaining the conversation with a standard set of queries. An effort was made to ensure that his presentation did not vary noticeably from one interview to another. The interview began with an introduction of the ambassador, who was described as "particularly skillful in dealing with sensitive issues in United States–Soviet relations." Raising the first topic, the interviewer announced, "Let us begin our questions with the issue of Soviet troop strength in Europe. According to current information, there is a discrepancy between the number of Soviet troops in Europe as reported by the U.S. and your country's official count. You can see in our table that this discrepancy is roughly 150,000 troops. . . . How do you explain this discrepancy? What's the truth here?" A standard set of questions was used to maintain the conversation. Having dealt adequately with the first topic, or after five minutes had expired, the interviewer introduced the next topic and so on until the three issues were covered. When more time was needed to bring the interview to 15 minutes, the interviewer attempted to link the issues with general questions.

In order to obtain baseline data, a postinterview discussion was held. This was introduced as follows: "I would like you now to step out of your role as ambassador and talk informally for a few minutes. . . . We would like to discuss a few general topics related to your activities at the university." The ostensible purpose for this discussion was to provide additional material for a training regimen that would include role-playing exercises. The discussion lasted for about seven minutes, and was conducted in a relaxed, casual manner. Upon completion, subjects filled out a self-report questionnaire and were paid and debriefed.

In summary, the essential features of the experiment are as follows:

- The scenario was a "televised" interview modeled after *Meet the Press*, with subjects assigned the role of the Soviet ambassador to the United States.
- Three issues in current U.S.-Soviet relations were addressed: the Soviet invasion of Afghanistan, troops in Europe, and activities in Cuba.
- Subjects were unaware that the purpose of the experiment was to assess nonverbal behaviors.
- The interviewer was unaware of the interviewee's condition, his role being separated from that of experimenter.
- The interview consisted of three five-minute time periods followed by a seven-minute postinterview informal discussion.
- A between-subjects design was defined by assigning subjects randomly to one of three conditions: deception, evasion, and honesty.
- Ten subjects were assigned to each condition; each subject maintained the same posture across the three issues.

These design features permitted us to determine the extent to which selected NVBs distinguish among intentions. We turn now to a discussion of those behaviors.

As shown in Table 4.1, 26 nonverbal behaviors, arranged in 10 categories, were assessed. This set of behaviors met the following criteria:

(1) They had multiple-channel coverage, including paralinguistic, visual, facial, body, and head/arm movements.
(2) They were likely to provide deception clues, such as fidgeting, leg/foot movements, position shifts, and speech errors.

TABLE 4.1 DESCRIPTION OF NONVERBAL BEHAVIORS

Variable	Description
1. Speech	
A. Speaking time	Connected meaningful utterances, including
B. Speaking frequency	single-word responses but not including interruption attempts
C. Speech errors	Number of noticeable breaks in speaking indicated by stuttering, repetition of phrases, broken phrases, or the insertion of nonsubstantive phrases
2. Gaze Time	
A. Camera	Fraction of the duration of interaction when
B. Interviewer	addressee is looking at the source.
3. Gaze Frequency	
A. Camera	Number of times that addressee is looking at the
B. Interviewer	source
C. Notes	
D. Other	
4. Gestures	
A. Illustrator gestures	Movements that are used for emphasis and expression of ideas
B. Object adaptors	Movements that use an instrument, object, or tool for purposes other than that for which it is intended
C. Self-adaptors	Movements that are directed toward one part of the body by another, with the hand frequently employed
D. Facial displays	Number of smiles, frowns, glares, or stares
5. Fidgeting	
A. Object	Motion of a part of the body with the action primarily on an object not used to mediate stimulation of the communicator's body
B. Self	Motion of a part of the body in contact with another either directly manipulated or mediated by an instrument
6. Position Shifts	
A. Trunk swivel	Number of times the body is moved from side to side
B. Rocking movements	Number of times the body is moved backward and forward at least $10°$
7. Leg and Foot Activity	
A. Leg movements	Number of leg movements at the knee
B. Foot movements	Number of foot movements or rotations of the ankle

TABLE 4.1   Continued

Variable	Description
8. Eye Blinks	Number of times the eye is blinked
9. Head and Shoulder Movements	
A. Nodding	Head movements at the neck in a vertical direction
B. Shaking	Head movements at the neck in a side to side motion
C. Shoulder-shrugging	Brief upward and forward movements of the shoulders
10. Arm Movements	
A. Head support	Support of the head with the arm
B. Arms crossed	Number of times both arms are crossed at the chest
C. Hands crossed	Hands clasped in front of the body or resting in the lap

(3) They had been measured reliably in earlier studies, most notably those by Mehrabian (1972), Ekman and Freisen (1974a), Baxter and Rozelle (1975), and in our pilot work.

(4) They were linked together by a concept such as negative-affect cues, immediacy, relaxation, or activity (Mehrabian, 1972).

One goal of this study is to isolate a subset of behaviors that discriminate among the conditions. As discussed above, "discrimination among conditions" has several meanings, including relative frequencies, correlational patterns, and relation to psychological states. In order to capture these various meanings, broad coverage is desirable. Moreover, broad coverage enables us to detect interrelationships among the variables. Such relationships may emerge as postures that characterize deceivers, evaders, and honest role players.

This project recognizes the distinction, raised by Dittmann (1978), between communicative and indicative behaviors: The former are rather specific messages under the voluntary, conscious control of the sender; the latter are more expressive, of lower information value, and usually involuntary in the sense that they are not designed to communicate specific messages (see Chapter 1). Focusing on indicative behavior, the project seeks to understand its meaning in terms of a broader process of political communication. The experiment reported here is a first step toward such understanding.

The set of NVBs shown in Table 4.1 were coded directly from the videotapes. An efficient coding procedure enabled us to complete the coding of all tapes in about three weeks. This was done by creating channel specialists: Some 200 student volunteers worked in groups that ranged in size from 12 to 24; each group rated a subset of NVBs for selected interviews, a task that took about two hours. The taped interviews were shown simultaneously in two rooms, one with sound, one without. A research assistant maintained control over the two video monitors and the pacing of the two coding groups by means of an audio communication system.

The coding task consisted of recording either time or frequency of occurrence for the assigned NVBs. All measures were taken during successive one-minute segments of the interview, including the postinterview session. No indication was given of the purpose of the experiment or the types of postures assumed by the subjects. Following instructions and questions about the procedures, the coders assigned to the paralinguistic and illustrator gesture variables were taken to the viewing room so that they could both see and hear the interviews. After rating the 15-minute interview, coders were asked to record their impressions on adjective checklists and to indicate whether they thought the interviewee was being honest, deceptive, or evasive. This information formed the basis for an analysis of the extent to which specific NVBs provide clues to intentions. All entries on the recording sheets were transferred to a computer tape for analysis.

Overview of Findings

The findings obtained for each NVB are organized by analytical function: relative frequencies, correlation patterns, or correlates of psychological states. Interestingly, with only one exception (arms crossed), each of the NVBs is involved in at least one of these types of relationships. Several NVBs serve more than one fuction, as is the case, for example, with leg movements, gaze time at interviewer, and hand-crossing. Particularly notable are those NVBs that show strong effects or are involved in patterns obtained for two or more conditions. (A tabular presentation of the findings may be obtained from the senior author, DD.)

Six variables showed strong condition effects on relative frequencies. These included main effects (gaze time at interviewer, gaze elsewhere, leg movements), interactions with time period (gaze time at interviewer, object-fidgeting, gaze frequency at interviewer), and differences from the baseline period (speech errors, gaze time at interviewer). Bolstering these effects are the results of the discriminant analyses: The top three variables emerging from these analyses were leg movements, object-fidgeting, and gaze time at interviewer. These particular variables are useful as components of prediction equations, which are presented later.

Other variables, not shown to discriminate among the conditions in terms of frequencies, were shown to be useful in terms of correlation patterns. Nine variables were part of patterns found to result from at least two of the conditions. Speaking time was the basis for patterns that characterized evaders and honest subjects; rocking movements and crossed hands were found to be part of a pattern for each of the three conditions; and clusters of body-head and coordinated hand movements distinguished the deceivers from the evaders and honest subjects. *Covarying* behaviors constitute one pattern that discriminates among the conditions. Another pattern is that of *co-occurring* behaviors. These patterns are also summarized in the discussion below.

Of considerable interest is the large number of relationships between NVBs and psychological states. Most of the variables correlated with at least one subjective rating for one of the conditions. Ten variables correlated with states for two or more conditions; particularly notable are the many relationships obtained for trunk swivels and crossed hands. Special significance is attached to those correlations that can be used to explain condition differences in frequencies or patterns: Each of the top three discriminating variables correlated significantly with certain states; several of the variables that were part of condition patterns correlated also with certain subjective feelings. Often the meaning of particular NVBs differ for the different conditions.

The results have implications for our conceptual framework. First, the findings support the argument that intentions are indexed by multiple nonverbal cues: Leg movements, object-fidgeting, gazing at the interviewer, and speech errors are likely to be more useful in combination than in isolation. Second, the concept of the display package is useful: Covarying behaviors, such as body-head movements or coordinated hand movements, distinguished deceptive from evasive and honest intentions. Third, psychological states served as intervening variables for certain NVBs: The averted gazes shown by evaders indicated involvement and tension, whereas the same behavior by deceivers seemed to indicate a calm, pleasant, and trusting disposition; trunk swivels had opposite meanings for honest as opposed to evasive and deceptive intentions; and the intercorrelated cluster of body-head movements for deceivers indicated confidence and certainty in conveying their positions. Each of these implications is explored in the sections to follow.

Relative Frequencies as a
Function of Condition

Results for differences in mean frequencies/time are presented in this section. These findings are evaluated in terms of the relatively unique design and analysis features of this study. The three (conditions) by four (time periods) design developed for the study provides more information about the problem than currently exists in the literature. This information includes an evaluation of evasion effects, time-period interactions, baseline effects, and multiple nonverbal assessments.

EVASION EFFECTS

Following from our context-relevant approach, an attempt was made to capture such forms as diplomatic fictions, carefully formulated ambiguities, evasions, and misdirection (see Axelrod and Zimmerman, 1979). These styles were represented by a condition referred to as indirect deception, or evasion. Included for the first time in a research design, evasive postures were shown to produce a number of interesting effects. Most notable, perhaps, was the effect on leg movements. Evasive subjects made significantly more leg movements in each of the interview time periods than did their deceptive and honest counterparts (F = 3.2, p < .057; see Figure 4.1). The differences no longer appeared in the postinterview period as subjects in each condition showed about the same amount of leg-movement activity. Even more dramatic is the effect obtained for the combination of leg and foot movements. This combination produced the strongest *main effect*, evasive subjects displaying a large amount of activity in this area compared to those in the deceptive and honest conditions (F = 3.7, p < .036).

Other evasion effects included frequency of gazes elsewhere, head-shaking, rocking movements, and self-fidgeting. More frequent gazes elsewhere by evasive subjects (as opposed to deceivers and honest subjects) suggest a nonverbal indicator of evasion with intent to mislead: While attempting to mislead the interviewer verbally by evading his questions, subjects avoided focusing their attention on the salient objects in the room (interviewer, camera, notes). The size of the difference between evasion and the other conditions increased through the successive time periods, reaching a maximum level during the third period and decreasing in the postinterview session (see Figure 4.2; F = 1.9, p < .09 for interaction between condition and time). Another nonverbal indicator of evasion is head-shaking. Significantly more head-shaking by evaders during the first time period suggests that this may be an evasive gesture that is manifest early in the interaction, compared to gazing elsewhere, the strongest difference occurring during the third time period (F = 3.1, p < .02; see Figure 4.3). The decreasing trend for

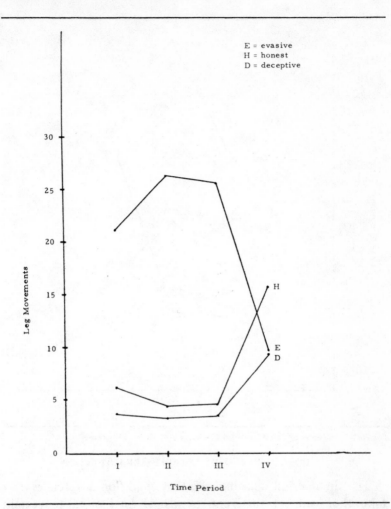

Figure 4.1 Effects of Conditions on Leg Movements

rocking movements combined with a dramatic increase in the postinterview period suggests that evasive subjects suppressed this behavior during the interview (F = 1.9, p < .096 for interaction). An increasing trend of self-fidgeting for evaders indicated that, similar to gazing elsewhere, these subjects showed considerable fidgeting after the halfway point in the interview (F = 2.4, p < .06). The evasion effects reported here suggest that these nonverbal behaviors are indicators of evasive intentions.

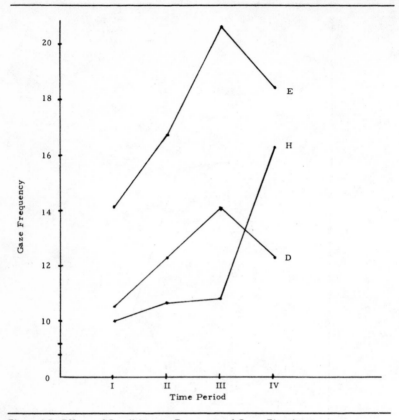

Figure 4.2   Effects of Conditions on Frequency of Gazes Elsewhere

CONDITION BY TIME-PERIOD INTERACTIONS

The time-period data indicate that condition differences may take the form of different trends or be limited to certain junctures of the interview. These results suggest the importance of distinguishing between early, middle, and late displays shown for certain variables. They also make evident limitations in earlier studies. Six NVBs produced interactions between time period and conditions: gaze frequency elsewhere, gaze time at interviewer, self-fidgeting, object-fidgeting, head-shaking, and rocking movements. Five of these are similar to variables measured in Mehrabian's (1972) study; two are similar to behaviors assessed by McClintock and Hunt (1975), and two resemble

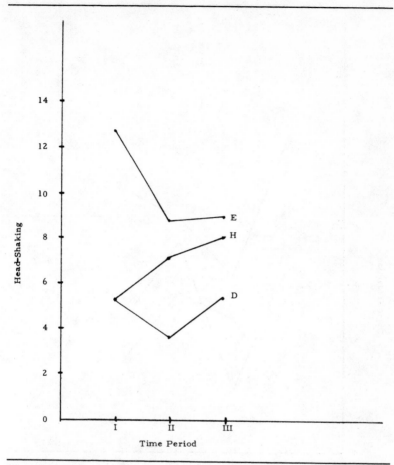

Figure 4.3 Head-Shaking as a Function of Condition

variables examined by Ekman et al. (1976). None of these variables, measured in any of the previous studies, were found to differ significantly between the two conditions created by those investigators.

Different trends for the different conditions are illustrated by results obtained for gazing elsewhere, self-fidgeting, head-shaking, and rocking movements: Increasing trends for evaders occurred on gazing elsewhere and self-fidgeting, the strongest differences appearing in the third period; decreasing trends for

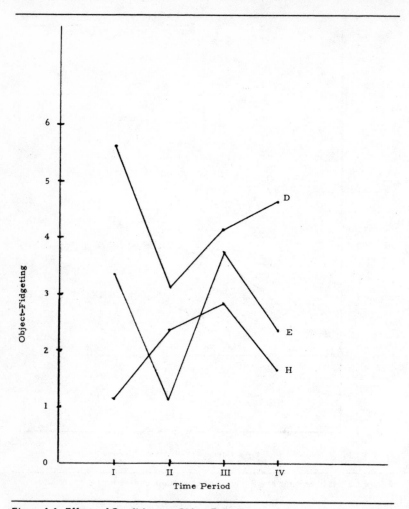

Figure 4.4 Effects of Conditions on Object-Fidgeting

evaders occurred on head-shaking and rocking movements, with the largest condition differences appearing in the first period. Condition differences for certain junctures appeared for object-fidgeting, gazing at the interviewer, and self-fidgeting: Deceivers and evaders fidgeted with objects more than honest subjects in the first time period ($F = 3.10$, $p < .06$; see Figure 4.4). Deceptive and evasive subjects gazed more often during the first and second periods (see Figure 4.5), while they self-fidgeted more

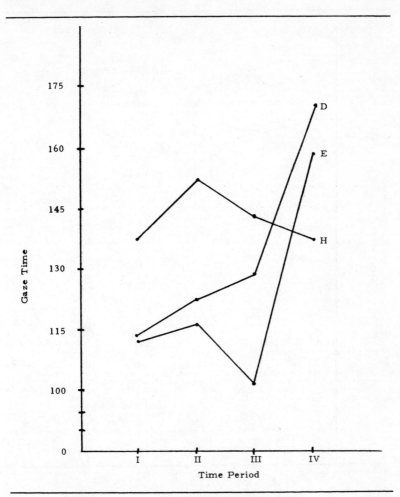

Figure 4.5 Effects of Conditions on Gaze Time at Interviewer

during the first and third time periods (F = 2.4, p < .06). These results indicate that some NVBs show effects only in the form of trends or during certain time periods. Implied by these findings is a broader conception of the ways by which NVBs discriminate among intentions.

INTERVIEW-POSTINTERVIEW DIFFERENCES

Certain variables showed condition effects only for deviations from baseline frequencies. Most notable in this regard are

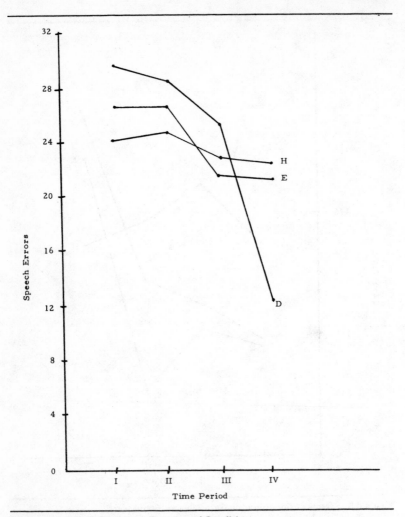

Figure 4.6 Speech Errors as a Function of Condition

speech errors: Deceivers made more speech errors relative to the postinterview period than did evaders and honest subjects ($F = 1.9$, $p < .09$; see Figure 4.6). This finding provides additional information that contradicts the conclusion based on Mehrabian's (1972) results. In that study only weak condition effects were obtained; baseline data were not collected. Combined with the results for speaking frequency, the data indicate that deceivers made more errors in fewer statements relative to the post-interview period than did their evasive and honest counterparts.

Other baseline effects are also interesting. The gaze aversion shown for both deceivers and evaders during the interview was reversed dramatically during the postinterview period (see Figure 4.5): These subjects often focused their gaze directly on the interviewer when no longer required to be deceptive, suggesting a "relaxation" effect ($F = 3.2$, $p < .01$). The suppression of leg movements for evaders contrasted with the accentuation of foot movements for these subjects in the postinterview period. Emphasized by all of these results is the importance of collecting baseline or "out-of-role" data. Certain variables show condition effects only for comparisons of deviation from baseline frequencies.

ROLE-PLAYING EFFECTS

Results obtained for five nonverbal behaviors illustrate another type of effect. Each of the conditions required that subjects enact a rather complex role not unlike assignments made to international diplomats. Such role obligations are subject to demeanor constraints that should be reflected in nonverbal behavior. The demeanor constraints, taking the form of suppressed behavior, are seen in significantly fewer facial displays, less head-nodding, fewer self-adaptors, less trunk swivel, and less frequent statements in the interview than in the postinterview period. (The effect is illustrated in Figure 4.7, where trends for trunk swivels are shown.) Taken together, these differences suggest that subjects maintained a more controlled posture during the interview than during the postinterview (baseline) period. Variants on this theme by condition are seen in the interactions summarized above and in the discriminant analysis results described below.

MULTIPLE NONVERBAL ASSESSMENTS

The results illustrate the value of measuring a large number of NVBs. Multiple assessments advance the state of the art by contributing findings not obtained in earlier work. They also

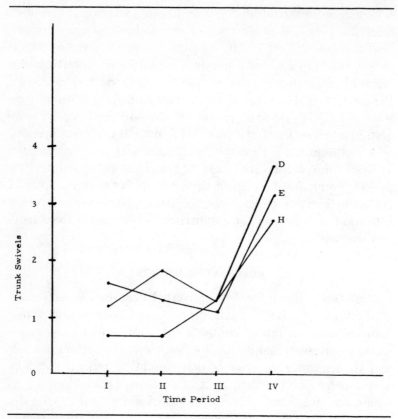

Figure 4.7 Trunk Swivels as a Function of Condition

serve to extend the range of observations likely to contribute to inferences about intentions. We were able to demonstrate effects for direct deception (speech errors, object-fidgeting, and speaking frequency), for indirect deception (leg and foot movements, gazing elsewhere, head-shaking, rocking, and self-fidgeting), and for both types of deception compared to honesty (gaze time at interviewer, facial displays, self-fidgeting, and gaze frequency at interviewer). Multiple measurements provide alternative indicators that may be useful when all channels are not available to the observer (such as leg and foot movements for a speaker who stands behind a podium, eye movements for an actor seen from a distance). Also, they provide *comple-*

mentary indicators, bolstering one's confidence in the inferences made. Moreover, they enable an investigator to address the question, Which *combination* of NVBs successfully discriminates among the conditions? This issue is addressed in the next section.

Discriminant Analysis

The aim of discriminant analysis is to determine whether it is possible to distinguish statistically between two or more groups in the sense of being able to tell them apart. We want to know whether deceivers, evaders, and honest subjects can be distinguished on the basis of observable nonverbal behaviors. By weighting and combining a set of measured NVBs in a linear fashion, we hope to find one or several dimensions on which the deceptive subjects are clustered at one end, honest subjects at the other, and evasive subjects, perhaps, in between. The technique contains the essential features of both analysis of variance and correlational analysis, namely, discrimination among independent variables (conditions) and interrelationships among dependent variables (NVBs). For this reason, among others, it is a particularly appropriate analytical approach to the problem.

Discriminant analysis offers a number of features that serve our purposes. These features can be divided into analysis and classification (Klecka, 1975). Analytic aspects provide several tools for the interpretation of data. Among these are statistical tests for measuring the success with which the nonverbal variables actually separate the groups when combined into the discriminant functions. The ordering of the variables is arranged along a function whose identification is provided in much the way that factors are labeled in factor analysis. The order is determined by weighting coefficients that can be interpreted much the same as in multiple regression. They serve to identify the variables that contribute most to differentiation of the groups or conditions. Listed in order of importance, these discriminating NVBs are shown below.

Discriminant analysis is also a powerful classification technique. The technique identifies the likely group membership of a subject when the only information known is his values on the discriminating NVBs. By classifying the subjects used to derive the functions, comparing predicted group membership with actual group membership, and observing the proportion of correct classifications, we can determine empirically the success in discrimination. These proportions are given in tables that summarize the number of known cases correctly predicted. The numbers shown in the tables are derived from computations that result in classification scores.

Classification equations take the form of

$$C_i = c_{i1} V_1 + c_{i2} V_2 + \ldots + c_{ip} V_p + c_{i0}$$

where C_i is the classification score for group i, the c_{ij}'s are the classification coefficients with c_{i0} being the constant, and the Vs are the raw scores on the discriminating variables. There is always a separate equation for each group; for this experiment, each subject will have three scores. The subject is classified into the group with the highest score. These scores can also be converted into probabilities of group membership. The rule of assigning a subject to the group with the highest score is equivalent to assigning him to the condition for which his NVBs indicate he has the greatest probability of membership. Particularly useful are the classification equations derived from the smallest subset of discriminating NVBs. These equations require the least information for computing classification scores.

Two sets of analyses were computed. The first sought to identify the discriminating NVBs across the time periods of the interview. The second examined the heart of the interview, defined as the middle eight minutes. Designed to capture the time-period aspect, the latter analysis was performed in lieu of including the three time periods as separate variables. Proceeding in stages, the analysis plan consisted of moving from the largest to the smallest discriminating subset. This was done by first entering all variables, then selecting the top ten steps for entry in the next phase, the top six for entry in a third phase, and, finally, the top three (or smallest discriminating subset) for

TABLE 4.2 DISCRIMINANT FUNCTION COEFFICIENTS AND
CLASSIFICATION RESULTS FOR TOTAL INTERVIEW

Function I: "Animation"		Function II: "Control"	
Head-shaking	−1.99	Head-shaking	−1.58
Gaze time at interviewer	−1.21	Head-nodding	+1.30
Head-nodding	+1.12	Foot movements	−.76
Leg movements	+1.08	Gaze time at interviewer	−.61
Arms crossed	+1.08	Speaking frequency	−.57
Object-fidgeting	+1.07	Gaze frequency elsewhere	−.50
Rocking movements	+.70	Leg movements	−.37
Gaze frequency elsewhere	+.39	Rocking movements	−.25
Speaking frequency	−.30	Object-fidgeting	−.07
Foot movements	+.22	Arms crossed	−.02

Classification Results

		Predicted Group Membership		
Actual Group	*No. of Cases*	*Honest*	*Evasive*	*Deceptive*
Honest	10	9	0	1
Evasive	10	1	8	1
Deceptive	10	1	1	8

Percentage of cases correctly classified: 83.33%

entry in a fourth phase. The ranking of NVBs on each function
and classification results are presented here.

TOTAL INTERVIEW

The two significant functions obtained from an analysis of
the top ten NVBs are shown in Table 4.2.[1] The standardized
discriminant function coefficients indicate the rank order of the
variables and the direction of their contribution. Although the
order of the variables differs somewhat between the functions,
the primary difference is the sign of the coefficients. The
positive contribution of most variables to the first function
suggests high activity or "animation"; the negative contribution
of these variables to the second function suggests inactivity or
"control." Classification results are also presented in Table 4.2.

Of 30 subjects, 25 were classified correctly: nine in honesty, eight in evasion, and eight in deception. Similar results were obtained for an analysis of the "top six" NVBs (24 of 30 subjects correctly classified).

The smallest subset of NVBs producing a significant function was identified. This consisted of three variables which, when listed in order of importance, are leg movements, object-fidgeting, and gaze time at the interviewer.[2] Coefficients and classification results are shown in Table 4.3. Good separation between the groups resulted in rather impressive classification of the cases, particularly with respect to honest and deceptive subjects: Overall, 77 percent of the subjects were correctly classified. The following equations were used for classifying subjects on the basis of the top three NVBs:

Honesty: $C_H = -.005$ (leg movements) $+ .022$ (gaze time at interviewer) $- .032$ (object-fidgeting) $- 5.99$ [1]

Evasion: $C_E = .020$ (leg movements) $+ .014$ (gaze time at interviewer) $+ .081$ (object-fidgeting) $- 4.79$ [2]

Deception: $C_D = -.002$ (leg movements) $+ .016$ (gaze time at interviewer) $+ .038$ (object-fidgeting) $- 4.24$ [3]

where C is the classification score for the condition. That score is computed by summing the product of the weights times the coded NVB values and adding (subtracting) the constant. The subject is placed in the condition with the highest classification score. When that score corresponds to the actual condition, the prediction is correct: These equations produced correct predictions for 23 of 30 subjects.

Several observations can be made on the basis of the discriminant analysis results. First, consistent with our technical approach, the results served to isolate a subset of NVBs that can be used in other applications. Illustrating the value of an empirical approach, the resulting subset of NVBs could not be identified on the basis of existing theory. Second, the analysis of variance results summarized above bolster our confidence in the variables isolated by the discriminant analysis. Main effects

TABLE 4.3   DISCRIMINANT FUNCTION COEFFICIENTS AND
CLASSIFICATION RESULTS FOR "TOP THREE"
FUNCTION

Function: "Animated Aversion"	
Leg Movements	+ .77
Object Fidgeting	+ .71
Gaze Time at Interviewer	− .69

Classification Results

		Predicted Group Membership		
Actual Group	*No. of Cases*	*Honest*	*Evasive*	*Deceptive*
Honest	10	8	0	2
Evasive	10	1	5	4
Deceptive	10	0	0	10

Percentage of cases correctly classified: 77%

or interactions were obtained for nine of the ten discriminating variables, and for each of the three variables isolated as the smallest subset. Third, most of the nonverbal channels are represented by the discriminating NVBs. The only category not in the list is gestures (illustrators, object adaptors, self-adaptors, and facial displays). These may be the NVBs that can be controlled more easily by the subject, a conclusion reached also by Ekman and Friesen (1974a).

HEART OF INTERVIEW

The significant function obtained from the analysis of the middle portion of the interview is shown in Table 4.4. This function, labeled "controlled directness," produced a high degree of separation between the groups: Mean discriminant scores of groups are 1.41 (H), .97 (E), and −2.38 (D). Such separation resulted in extremely accurate classification of subjects: Only one of the 30 subjects was misclassified (see Table 4.4).

The analysis process continued until the smallest subset of variables producing a significant function was identified. This

TABLE 4.4   DISCRIMINANT FUNCTION COEFFICIENTS AND
             CLASSIFICATION RESULTS FOR "HEART OF
             INTERVIEW"

Function: "Controlled Directness"	
Head-shaking	+ 2.28
Gaze time at interviewer	+ 2.03
Gaze frequency at notes	− 1.77
Head support	+ 1.26
Trunk swivel	− 1.32
Rocking movements	− 1.21
Speaking frequency	+ 1.18
Gaze frequency at interviewer	+ 1.12
Leg movements	− .80
Hands crossed	+ .72

Classification Results		Predicted Group Membership		
Actual Group	No. of Cases	Honest	Evasive	Deceptive
Honest	10	10	0	0
Evasive	10	0	10	0
Deceptive	10	0	1	9

Percentage of cases correctly classified: 96.6%.

set consisted of four NVBs which, when listed in order of steps, are leg movements, head support, gaze frequency at notes, and speaking frequency. When listed in order of relative contribution to the function, the NVBs are gaze frequency at notes, head support, speaking frequency, and leg movements (Table 4.5).

Of interest is the finding that leg movements emerged as the first step in both the total interview and the heart-of-interview analyses. The other variables found to discriminate in the smallest subset differ for the two analyses. The classification results shown in Table 4.5 indicate that 63 percent of the subjects were classified correctly. Most of the misclassifications occurred in the evasion condition; six of eleven misclassified

TABLE 4.5 DISCRIMINANT FUNCTION COEFFICIENTS AND
CLASSIFICATION RESULTS FOR "TOP FOUR"
FUNCTION

Function: "Top Four"	
Leg movements	.02
Head support	.76
Gaze frequency at notes	−.79
Speaking frequency	.69

Classification Results				
			Predicted Group Membership	
Actual Group	No. of Cases	Honest	Evasive	Deceptive
Honest	10	7	0	3
Evasive	10	1	4	5
Deceptive	10	2	0	8

Percentage of cases correctly classified: 63.33%.

subjects were evaders. Reflecting some confusion between evasion and deception, one-half of the evaders were classified as
deceivers. More impressive classification results would emerge if
we combined evasive and deceptive subjects. Such a combination produces 80 percent correct classification.

Similarities and differences in results obtained from the two
types of analyses can be noted. Like the functions obtained for
the analysis of the entire interview, most of the nonverbal
channels are represented, with the notable exception of gestures. Leg movements prove to be the best discriminator in both
analyses. However, contrasting postures are suggested by the
different functions: Positive contributions from gazing at the
interviewer and speaking frequency, combined with the negative
contribution of gazing at notes, suggest a directness not found
in the total interview analysis; more controlled movements, as
revealed in head support, low trunk swivel, low rocking, and so
on, are characteristic of the heart of the interview. Also, whereas the equations for the top three NVBs can be used for total
interview predictions, the top ten NVB results would seem more
useful for heart-of-interview predictions. However, the classifi-

cation results obtained from the top four NVBs are still consid-erably better than those obtained from experts, a topic to which we now turn.

The practical utility of prediction equations turns on the question, How much better are statistical predictions than those based on less formal procedures? Stated this way, the issue can only be resolved by comparing the outcomes of predictions based on alternative methods. A step in this direction was taken by asking coders to guess the condition of their subject(s). Recall that the coders were assigned specific nonverbal chan-nels. For this reason their guesses are quite likely to be based on those particular behaviors. While such a focus provides a limited test of the issue, it does address the question whether specific channels contain relevant information. That certain channels do indeed contain relevant information is suggested by recent find-ings obtained by Fugita et al. (1980). These investigators found that detectors did better in judging deception when their focus was limited to the categories of facial displays and eye contact. Further elucidation is provided by the following analysis.

Chi-square analyses of the guessing data were computed for each nonverbal behavior. Guesses of the subject's condition were compared to his actual assigned role. Significant or near-significant chi squares were obtained for four variables: speech errors (χ^2 = 16.20, p < .01), gaze time at interviewer (χ^2 = 19.46, p < .001), gaze time at camera (χ^2 = 21.17, p < .001), and gaze frequency at interviewer and camera (χ^2 = 8.47, p < .10). Clearly, the guessing data do not approach the accu-racy of classification derived from the prediction equations. They do, however, suggest another implication of considerable interest.

Closer inspection of the contingency tables indicates more precisely where the accurate predictions were made. Honest subjects were predicted rather accurately for the three gazing variables: 10 of 10 for gaze time at interviewer and for gaze time at camera; 9 of 14 for the combined gaze frequency at interviewer and at camera. Evasive subjects were classified accurately for the paralinguistic variables: 9 of 12 for speech errors; 7 of 10 for speaking time. Coders' guesses for deceptive subjects were largely inaccurate. Questions suggested by these data are whether there are more subtle visual cues for detecting honesty and more subtle paralinguistic cues that can be used to detect evasion: What is it about a subject's gaze that leads to correct inferences about his honest intentions? What aspects of voice quality or tone suggest evasion?

Another test of the issue was provided by asking experts, whose attention was not focused on specific channels, to judge each subject's condition. Three oil company executives from the Houston area were recruited for the task. Each was responsible for negotiating major projects in areas where "actual" intentions of an opposite number are critical. Each claimed to have developed skills for detecting deception. These skills would be tested by our task.

The experts were shown each of the 30 taped interviews over a three-day period. They were told that some subjects were required to deceive the interviewer, others were asked to mislead him, and still others were told to present honest answers to his questions. Each of these postures was defined in a manner similar to the scenarios given the subjects. Their task was to judge whether the subject was deceptive, evasive, or honest. In addition, they were asked to indicate the extent to which they were confident in each judgment and to elaborate, if possible, on the cues used to make the judgment.

Classification results are shown in Table 4.6. The percentages of correct classifications by the experts were 43 percent, 30 percent, and 27 percent, respectively. None of the experts approached the level of correct classification attained by the prediction equations: None was significantly above chance expectations. Equally interesting are the results of the confidence ratings. The experts were just as confident about their wrong judgments ($\overline{X} = 2.7$) as they were about their right judgments ($\overline{X} = 2.6$). Relatively few judgments were regarded as

TABLE 4.6   EXPERT JUDGMENTS

Expert I-Classification Results

Actual Group	No. of Cases	Predicted Group Membership		
		Honest	*Evasive*	*Deceptive*
Honest	10	3	3	4
Evasive	10	2	5	3
Deceptive	10	2	3	5

Percentage of cases correctly classified: 43%.

Expert II-Classification Results

Actual Group	No. of Cases	Predicted Group Membership		
		Honest	*Evasive*	*Deceptive*
Honest	10	3	5	2
Evasive	10	3	4	3
Deceptive	10	5	2	3

Percentage of cases correctly classified: 30%

Expert III-Classification Results

Actual Group	No. of Cases	Predicted Group Membership		
		Honest	*Evasive*	*Deceptive*
Honest	10	4	3	3
Evasive	10	2	2	6
Deceptive	10	3	5	2

Percentage of cases correctly classified: 27%

even slightly doubtful (Table 4.7). Their confidence seemed based on faith in their intuitions; few judgments were based on an explicit strategy for making inferences. Training would seem to be in order.

These results bolster the value of the statistical approach used in this study. The prediction equations were better "detectors" of deception than were experts skilled in the art of detection. However, further work is needed to assess the generality of the results. An attempt is being made to determine whether the prediction equations perform as well in other contexts, with

TABLE 4.7   EXPERT CONFIDENCE IN JUDGMENTS

	(1) Extremely Confident	(2) Quite Confident	(3) Slightly Confident	(4) Slightly Doubtful	(5) Quite Doubtful	(6) Extremely Doubtful
Judged Wrong	8	21	15	12	4	0
Judged Right	3	9	13	5	0	0

Mean judged wrong = 2.7.
Mean judged right = 2.6.

other subjects. Comparisons with other types of experts (such as foreign policy analysts) are also planned. The outcome of these experiments will enable us to evaluate the plausibility of using the discriminating nonverbal displays as material in training regimens. They would also enable us to address the question of whether trained detectors of deception are also good at being deceivers.

CLASSIFICATION OF NEW CASES

The evidence presented above shows that the equations classify subjects more accurately than do the experts. Generality would be attested to by correct classification of new cases, subjects whose coded NVBs were not used to develop the equations. Correct classification of new cases of known intentions would be compelling evidence for application.

The test of generality was made by analyzing data from three male subjects. Each subject was randomly assigned to one of the three conditions; condition assignment was not known to either the interviewer or the coders. The format was identical to that used in the original experiment. Two coders, working independently, coded the "top ten" NVBs (see Table 4.2) directly from the videotapes. Frequencies or time were inserted in each of the three classification equations derived from the top three analyses.[3] Computations were made for all three equations for each subject; each case was assigned to the group with the highest score. According to Klecka (1975), the highest score is equivalent to the greatest probability of group membership.

TABLE 4.8   CLASSIFICATION EQUATION PREDICTIONS FOR
             NEW SUBJECTS

Predicted Intention	Honest[a]		Actual Intention Evasive[a]		Deceptive[a]	
Honest	2.87[b]		.73		.84	
		3.61[c]		.51		.79
Evasive	2.78		1.44		1.65	
		2.92		1.28		1.26
Deceptive	1.97		.42		1.95	
		2.32		.25		1.60

a. Boxed scores are the highest classification scores in the column; in each case the highest score is the correct prediction.

b. Classification score for coder 1.

c. Classification score for coder 2.

Results are shown in Table 4.8. Each cell of the matrix contains classification scores for the two coders. The highest scores for each coder are those found in the diagonals; in each case, for both coders, the correct prediction was made. Of interest is the observation that correct predictions would not result from reliance on any *one* of the three NVBs: Most leg movements were not made by the evasive subject; the honest subject did not spend the most time looking at the interviewer. Rather, correct predictions resulted from a weighted-linear combination of the variables. It is that combination that is likely to prove useful for predictions of new samples.

These are impressive results, particularly since they were obtained from information on only three NVBs for three subjects. While arguing for relevance, however, this is a limited test of the generality issue. More extended tests would consist of larger samples of new subjects and situations. The procedure is particularly relevant to special samples but can also be used to assess generality to subjects that represent groups on which it is difficult to accumulate large numbers for a complete design (for example, other cultures, foreign policy analysts). Results comparable to those obtained above would attest to generality; divergent results would alert the investigator to sources of differences, such as culture or occupational experiences. Such tests are in progress. Their outcome will determine the extent to which confidence can be placed in predictions of subjects/actors whose intentions are not known a priori.

Correlation Patterns as a Function of Condition

Highlighted by the findings reported above are particular NVBs whose frequency distinguishes among the conditions. This is only one type of effect. Another function served by nonverbal behavior is covariation. Addressed here is the issue of whether there are combinations of behaviors whose covariation or co-occurrence distinguishes among the conditions. Included in these combinations are NVBs that may not distinguish between the conditions in terms of frequencies. Indeed, some may occur relatively infrequently. What is observed are *similar levels* across the total interview session or within time periods. An aim of this analysis is to develop empirical profiles of sets of covarying NVBs.

The analysis of variance results, reported above, indicate considerable within-group variation for a number of NVBs. One approach is to treat these as nondiscriminating variables, discounting their value as indicators. Another approach is to take advantage of the observed variation by examining *covariation* among different NVBs. Rejecting the former in favor of the latter, we contend that clusters of covarying NVBs provide useful information. For example, suppose we have two types of deceivers, the "fidgeters" and the "nonfidgeters." If we observe that the former show high levels of head activity (nodding and shaking) while the latter show little activity in this channel, we can conclude that these NVBs go together in terms of relative levels. This result is reflected in high correlations among fidgeting, nodding, and shaking for deceivers. This is what is meant by discrimination in terms of patterns. Such patterns highlight *combinations* of NVBs, providing information that can be used also to distringuish deceivers from evaders and honest subjects.

The patterns sought could be identified by performing cluster analyses of correlation matrices. This was done across the time periods and within the time periods of the interview. Focusing on covariation, the former consisted of examining three intercorrelation matrices, one for deception-condition subjects, another for evasive subjects, and a third for those in the honest condition. Focusing on co-occurrence, the latter analyses consisted of examining nine intercorrelation matrices, three time-period matrices for each condition. Of interest is the question, Which patterns are stable from one phase of the interview to another? The analysis sought to identify reoccurring patterns that included the top ten discriminating NVBs.

The same procedure was applied to each matrix: First, all statistically significant correlations between pairs of variables were isolated; second, clusters of three or more variables were formed on the basis of the sizes of the intercorrelations. Interestingly, each of the clusters obtained was unique to a condition. Particularly impressive is the size of many of the correlations, with some NVBs accounting for as much as 81 percent of the variation in others.

COVARIATION ACROSS TIME PERIODS

Each condition produced a pattern that was relatively easy to recognize. A highly cohesive set of relationships among head and body movements was found for deceivers: Similar amounts of swivel and rocking movements occurred with both nodding and shaking activity (Figure 4.8). Another significant pattern merits mention. Noted by Ekman and Friesen (1974b) as a source of "leakage," coordinated hand movements (illustrators, self-adaptors, hands crossed) were also found to form a pattern for deceivers. (Correlations among these NVBs were .87, .81, and .77.) An interesting pattern for evaders is shown in Figure 4.9: The more time the evader spent talking, the fewer were his

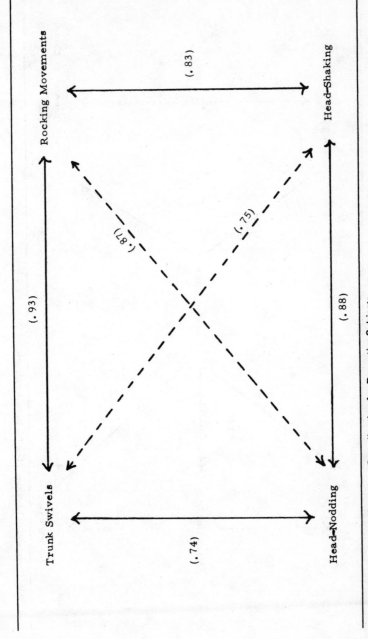

Figure 4.8 Body-Head Movement Coordination for Deceptive Subjects

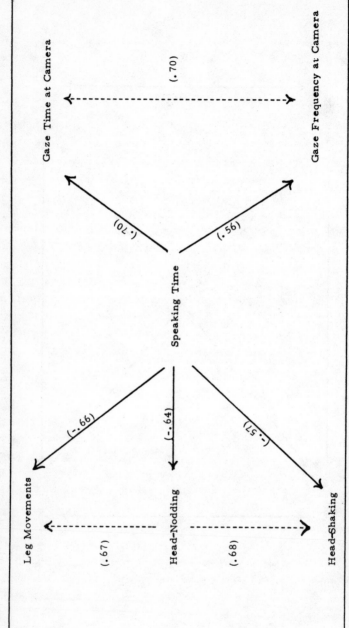

Figure 4.9 Correlates of Speaking Time for Evasive Subjects

leg movements, head nods, and head-shaking while focusing attention more often and for more sustained periods at the camera. This picture of the evasive speaker suggests averted gazes at the interviewer when talking and high leg movements when not talking (see results on frequencies above). Like evasion, the honest pattern shows correlates of speaking time. Unlike evaders, however, honest correlated movements consisted of facial displays, rocking motions, and crossed hands (Figure 4.10). Moreover, speaking time was not related to gazing at the camera. Such gazing was instead related to illustrators (r = .65) and to head support (r = .85). This picture of the honest speaker is similar to that suggested by the results on frequencies: controlled movements while talking.

Correlated NVBs are a particular type of deception clue. Discriminating among conditions, distinct patterns can serve as a source of evidence about intentions. Awareness of this evidence may prevent misclassification due to receiver and demeanor biases, that is, the tendency to interpret expressions (or appear) as honest/dishonest regardless of what they are (Zuckerman et al., 1979: 393). Even more useful are patterns of co-occurring or simultaneous behaviors. Taking the form of a display package, these patterns are easier to observe than those that merely covary. We turn next to the results of an analysis designed to discover NVB patterns that reoccur from one phase to another.

COVARIATION WITHIN TIME PERIODS

The results reported above leave open the question of where to look for the covarying patterns: Some patterns may reoccur from one time period to the next; others may be limited to certain phases of the interview. To explore this question, a set of intercorrelation matrices was computed for each of the three time periods. Emphasizing efficiency rather than breadth of observations, the analysis focused on only the top ten discriminating variables.

The discriminant analysis results discussed above provide an observational criterion: The conditions can be distinguished on

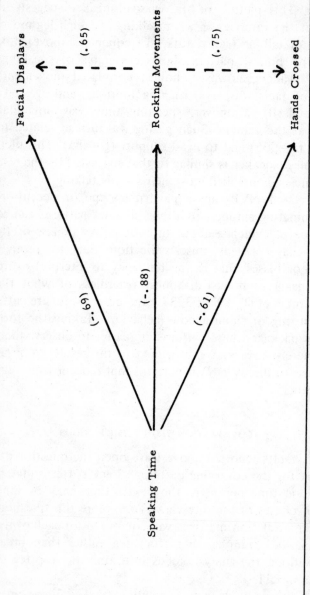

Figure 4.10 Correlates of Speaking Time for Honest Subjects

the basis of ten or fewer NVBs (see Table 4.2). The correlational analyses reported here address the question, Do the discriminating variables also cluster into observable patterns?[4] The results indicate a reoccurring pattern for deceivers; evaders and honest subjects display patterns that are limited to certain time periods. Additionally, some bivariate relationships reoccur in each time period.

High intercorrelations among rocking movements, head-nodding, and head-shaking occur for deceivers in each time period. Rocking and shaking correlated with frequency of gazes elsewhere in the first time period, while nodding and shaking correlated with speaking frequency in the second and third periods (see Figure 4.11). The rocking/nodding/shaking cluster is particularly significant. Included in the body-head movement cluster shown in Figure 4.8, these NVBs can be observed to covary during each phase of the interview. (Trunk swivel, the other NVB in the body-head cluster, was not among the top ten variables and thus was not included in the time-period analysis.) Since this pattern does not occur for either evasive- or honest-condition subjects, it serves as another indicator of deception.

Consistent patterns do not occur for evasive or honest subjects. Evaders show a pattern among leg movements, head-nodding, and head-shaking for the third time period. Honest-condition subjects show a strong pattern among gaze time at the interviewer, nodding, and shaking for the second time period: more time spent looking at the interviewer, less nodding, and less shaking. Consistent bivariate relationships do, however, appear for each of these conditions, including leg movements and nodding for evaders ($r_1 = .47$; $r_2 = .70$; $r_3 = .58$), and gaze time at interviewer and head-shaking for honest subjects ($r_1 = -.72$; $r_2 = -.76$; $r_3 = -.63$). Other pairs of variables covary during selected time periods, including legs and feet for honest subjects (second and third periods), nodding and shaking for honest subjects (first and second periods), and gaze frequency elsewhere and head-shaking for deceivers (first and second periods).

Several conclusions are worth noting. First, covarying head and body movements observed repeatedly from one phase to

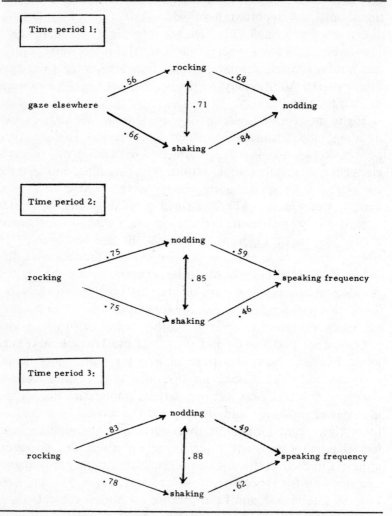

Figure 4.11 Co-Occurring Patterns for Deceptive Subjects in Each Time Period

another seem to indicate deception. Second, nodding and shaking appear as part of patterns for each condition; these NVBs are also among the best discriminators in the top ten analysis (Table 4.2). Third, leg movements distinguish evaders from deceivers and honest subjects in terms of both frequencies (Figure 4.1) and covariation. Finally, the controlled posture shown by honest subjects when speaking (Figure 4.10) is also apparent when gazing at the interviewer within each time period.

These results are limited in terms of comparability with the patterns obtained *across* time periods. Direct comparisons are possible from analyses of matrices that include all of the NVBs. Those analyses, currently in progress, will reveal other patterns that reoccur from one period to another. However, those results notwithstanding, the analyses reported above make an important contribution. They suggest that deception clues can be provided from observations (frequencies or covariation) of a small number of nonverbal behaviors.

Correlates of Psychological States as a Function of Condition

Another way NVBs can distinguish among conditions is through psychological states. Some behaviors derive their meaning *primarily* from a relationship to underlying feelings rather than in terms of frequencies or correlation patterns. Indeed, this is seen to be the case for gazing at notes, object adaptors, eye blinks, shoulder shrugs, and trunk swivels. Each of these behaviors reflected different states for different conditions. Other behaviors, whose frequencies and/or correlation patterns differ for different conditions, are understood better because of correlations with feelings. This is the case for such NVBs as gazing at the interviewer, gazing elsewhere, leg movements, head-shaking and -nodding, and object-fidgeting. Both of these types of results are discussed in this section.

Psychological states play an important role in the process of inferring intentions. This process is illustrated by the model shown in Figure 1.1. In that model, states mediate between intentions and observed behavior. Condition (intention) differences in correlations between states and NVBs indicate how the mediation process works. Discriminating between conditions are NVBs whose meaning is different for the different conditions. However, other findings provide useful interpretations. Some NVBs may be functionally equivalent in the sense of having similar meanings for different intentions. The same NVB may refer to different states for each of the intentions or have the same meaning for the different intentions. Each of these interpretations is suggested by the results.

Viewed here from the standpoint of the subject, psychological states refer to subjective feelings. These feelings were assessed by responses to a set of postinterview questions; the questions took the form of seven-point scales. Correlations between responses and NVBs were computed for each of the experimental conditions: For each condition a 26 (states) by 25 (NVBs) correlation matrix was analyzed.[5]

The results are organized first by condition and then by nonverbal behaviors. The former is intended to show how psychological states provide explanations for behavior observed in each condition. The latter shows that certain NVBs have different (similar) meanings for the different conditions. These two interpretations are highlighted by the findings.

HONEST SUBJECTS

The gazing pattern for honest subjects suggests a distinction between the meanings of looking *at* and looking *away* from the interviewer. Looking at the interviewer indicates involvement and dominance; looking away indicates uninvolvement, less interest, and detachment. The more time the subject spent looking at the interviewer, the more he felt involved and dominant. More frequent gazes elsewhere indicated less interest and involvement. Subjects who spent more time looking at the interviewer spent less time looking elsewhere ($r = -.66$). Taken together, these findings suggest two types of honest subjects: involved (looks at interviewer) and uninvolved (looks elsewhere). Also, frequent gazing at notes indicated less interest and a less serious approach, just as looking at the camera indicated detachment; subjects who looked at their notes frequently also looked often at the camera ($r = .60$). The similar meaning attached to gazing at notes, at camera, and elsewhere reinforces the distinction between looking at and looking away from the interviewer. Direction of gaze can take the form of an involvement index for honest subjects: The larger the difference between looking *at* and looking *away*, the more involved is the subject.

Also indicating involvement and interest are leg movements and speaking frequency. More leg movements and more frequent statements were made by more involved honest subjects. Other psychological states are reflected by other NVBs. Feelings of inadequacy and insecurity in performing the role are suggested by trunk swivels and head-shaking. More trunk swivels were shown by honest subjects who felt that they were less in control, more apprehensive, more stressful, more unpleasant, and suspicious; more head-shaking was displayed by subjects who felt less effective and less dominant. Also, calmer, less serious subjects displayed more shoulder shrugs.

EVADERS

The distinction between looking at and looking away is also significant for evaders. But rather than involvement and interest, looking reflects tension and stress. More time spent looking at the interviewer indicated tense feelings; frequent gazes away indicated less tension and stress. Subjects who spent more time looking at the interviewer gazed less frequently at the camera ($r = -.72$). These findings provide an explanation for both the averted gazes from the interviewer (Figure 4.5) and the frequent gazing elsewhere (Figure 4.2) shown by evasive subjects: Looking away from the interviewer served to reduce the tension felt by these subjects while performing their role. That this tension was relieved is indicated by the dramatic increase in time spent looking at the interviewer (and decrease in frequency of gazes elsewhere) by evasive subjects.

Involvement and interest are also indexed for evaders. Similar to the finding for honest subjects, gazing at the interviewer indicated involvement for evaders. In addition, frequent trunk swivels and object adaptors also indicated involvement. Gazing at the interviewer correlated with object adaptors ($r = .65$), both indicating involvement and similarity between own and assigned positions; perhaps involvement was a function of similarity between own and assigned positions. Reduced interest and involvement was indicated by frequent object-fidgeting and head-nodding.

Meaning can also be attributed to the high frequency of leg movements shown by evaders (Figure 4.1). More leg activity indicated less assertive feelings. In fact, each of the behaviors included in the intercorrelated cluster of leg movements, head-nodding, and head-shaking (Figure 4.9) has similar meaning: less in control, less assertive, more apprehensive, and less comfortable. The opposite meaning is suggested by eye blinks and by trunk swivels: more eye blinks correspond to more certain and easier defense of positions; more trunk swivels suggest greater confidence, dominance, and effectiveness. The high negative correlation between eye blinks and head-shaking ($r = -.75$) suggests two types of evaders. One is the confident subject who is identified by frequent blinking; the other is the apprehensive subject who is seen to shake his head often. This contradiction is explored further.

Postinterview self reports indicated that the evaders were significantly more assertive, confident, in control, dominant, and satisfied with the defense of their positions than were the deceivers and honest subjects. These findings suggest a self-assured and successful role player. A different picture emerges, however, when the nonverbal data are considered. Correlations computed within the evasion condition showed that more leg movements were associated with less assertiveness ($r = .77$),[6] with effort in the defense of positions ($r = -.56$), with anxiety ($r = -.54$), and with uncertainty ($r = .49$). Gazes elsewhere correlated with feelings of being relaxed ($r = .63$) and calm ($r = .66$). Suggested here is the unsure and nonassertive subject whose role assignment is difficult. How can these contradictory findings be reconciled?

One explanation relates to the concept of leakage (Ekman and Friesen, 1969a).[7] The NVBs qualified the meaning of the verbal data: The evaders were not as assertive, confident, or in control as claimed. Feelings of nonassertiveness seemed to occur during periods of silence, when frequent leg movements were seen (r $_{leg/speaking\ time}$ = -.66). Another interpretation turns on the distinction between process and outcome. The non-verbal data reflected feelings aroused during the performance; evasive subjects felt uncertain and tense while performing the role. The verbal data may have been appraisals of a completed task, reflecting feelings of success in accomplishing a difficult assignment. More in line may have been verbal reactions assessed *during* the interview: those articulations may have indicated the feelings that correlated also with the nonverbal behaviors.

These findings suggest a general hypothesis. It is apparent that such NVBs as leg movements and gazes elsewhere reflect feelings aroused by role. Evasion was probably the most difficult of the three assigned postures. If so, these NVBs ought to be observed in complex situations. Experimental variation of task complexity is feasible. Moreover, by separating complexity from evasion, it would be possible to evaluate effects of each on observed behaviors.

DECEIVERS

Unlike the honest subjects and evaders, the deceivers did not make evident nonverbal behaviors associated with involvement and interest. What was evident, however, were psychological states associated with the intercorrelated cluster of trunk swivels, rocking movements, and head-shaking (Figure 4.8). Each of these component behaviors reflected such feelings as relaxation, certainty, and easiness in defending positions; more body-head movements were displayed by subjects who were more relaxed, certain, confident in defense, and, for trunk swivels, more assertive and more confident. While not correlated with those NVBs, crossed hands also reflected relaxed and certain feelings. More relaxed and certain feelings characterized deceivers who crossed their hands often; these deceivers also viewed the exchange as competitive. Providing the opposite indication are object adaptors. Subjects who showed many object adaptors felt less assertive, more apprehensive, less interested, and viewed the exchange as more cooperative than did those who displayed fewer adaptors.

Tension and stress are indicated for deceivers by shoulder shrugs and illustrators. More shrugs were displayed by subjects who felt more stress while performing their role; more illustrators were related to less tension. It is of some interest to note that the frequent object-fidgeting shown by deceivers (Figure 4.4) was not a sign of irritability: It indicated control over performance. On the other hand, facial displays did reflect irritability. More facial displays were shown by more irritable deceivers.

NONVERBAL BEHAVIORS

The results discussed above are summarized in Table 4.9. These results can also be organized in terms of the NVBs. Some NVBs have a different meaning for the different conditions. In some cases, we can observe functionally equivalent behaviors, that is, different NVBs that have similar meanings for different conditions. In other cases, different NVBs reflect different feelings for the same intention, as well as for different intentions. Psychological states add a dimension of meaning to the results reported in the earlier sections. This observation is documented by the following findings.

Trunk Swivels. This NVB reflected similar feelings for deceptive and evasive subjects. For deceivers, the more the swivels, the more relaxed, assertive, confident, certain, and the easier they defended their positions; for evaders, the more the swivels, the more effective, involved, dominant, and confident they felt. For honest subjects, trunk swivels reflected opposite feelings: Subjects who displayed more swivels felt less in control, more stressful, more unpleasant, more suspicious, more apprehensive, and angrier. Particularly impressive is the consistency of the findings for each intention. Deceptive and evasive subjects who display swivels present the profile of the confident, assertive, and involved interviewee, while honest subjects who exhibit swivels convey the message of uncertainty and nervousness about their role.

Shoulder Shrugs. This NVB reflects opposite feelings for deceptive and honest subjects. Deceivers who shrugged often

TABLE 4.9   NONVERBAL BEHAVIORS AND PSYCHOLOGICAL STATES: SELECTED RELATIONSHIPS

Condition	Nonverbal Behavior	Psychological States	Relationships
Honesty	Gaze time at interviewer	Involved, dominant	More time spent looking at interviewer, more involved (−.71), more dominant (−.92)
	Gaze frequency elsewhere	Interest, involvement	More frequent gazes elsewhere, less interest (−.60), less involvement (.70)
	Gaze frequency at notes	Interest, seriousness	More frequent gazes at notes, less interest (−.66), less serious (.77)
	Leg movements	Interest, involvement	More leg movements, more interest (.80), more involvement (−.68)
	Speaking frequency	Involvement, similarity of own and assigned positions	More frequent statements, more involvement (−.81), more similar own and assigned positions (.64)
	Trunk swivels	In control, stress, pleasant, suspicious, apprehensive, anger	More swivels, less in control (−.71), more stressful (−.65), more unpleasant (.65), more suspicious (−.75), more apprehensive (.85), angrier (−.65)
	Head-shaking	Effective, assertive, dominant	More shaking (.65), less effective (−.66), less assertive (.66), less dominant (.67)
	Shoulder shrugs	Calm, serious	More shrugs, calmer (.83), less serious (.73)
Evasion	Gaze time at interviewer	Tension, involvement, similarity of own and assigned ¡ positions	More time spent looking at interviewer, more tense (−.67), more involved (−.63), more similar own and assigned positions (.62)
	Gaze frequency elsewhere	Tension, stress	More frequent gazes elsewhere (−.63), less tension (.71), less stress (.63)

(Continued on p. 162)

TABLE 4.9   NONVERBAL BEHAVIORS AND PSYCHOLOGICAL
STATES: SELECTED RELATIONSHIPS (continued)

Condition	Nonverbal Behavior	Psychological States	Relationships
Evasion (Cont.)	Gaze frequency at notes	Calm, pleasant, viewed as cooperative exchange	More frequent gazes at notes, calmer (.66), more pleasant (−.66), viewed exchange as more cooperative (.91)
	Leg movements	Assertiveness	More leg movements, fewer assertive feelings (.77)
	Head-nodding/ shaking	In control, involved, difficulty in defending position, comfort, apprehension	More nodding, less in control (−.67), less involved (.81), more difficult to defend positions (.60), less comfortable (.72); more shaking, less comfortable (.60), more apprehensive (.79)
	Trunk swivels	Effectiveness, involved, dominant, confident	More swivels, more effective (.78), more dominant (−.62), more confident (−.63)
	Eye blinks	Ease and effort in defending positions, certain	More adaptors, more similar own and assigned positions (.81), more involved (−.98)
	Object-fidgeting	Serious, interest	More fidgeting, less serious (.81), less interest (.65)
Deception	Gaze time at interviewer	Similar own and assigned positions, calm, pleasant, trusting	More time spent looking at interviewer, more similar own and assigned positions (.69), calmer (.70), more pleasant (−.72), more trusting (.65)
	Gaze time at camera	Pleasant, interest	More time spent looking at camera, less pleasant (.80), less interested (.74)
	Trunk swivels	Ease and satisfaction in defending positions, relaxed, assertive	More swivels, easier to defend positions (−.73), more relaxed (.76), more assertive (−.64),

TABLE 4.9 Continued

Condition	Nonverbal Behavior	Psychological States	Relationships
			more confident ($-.72$), more certain ($-.83$)
	Rocking movements	Ease of defense, relaxed, certain	More rocking, easier defense ($-.73$), more relaxed (.69), more certain ($-.83$)
	Head-shaking	Ease in defending positions	More shaking, easier defense of positions ($-.64$)
	Hands crossed	Relaxed, certain, view of exchange	More hand-crossings, more relaxed (.73), more certain ($-.65$), viewed as a competitive exchange ($-.68$)
	Object adaptors	Assertive, apprehensive, interest, view of exchange	More adaptors, less assertive (.64), more apprehensive (.69), less interested (.61), more viewed as a cooperative exchange (.85)
	Shoulder shrugs	Stress	More shrugs, more stressful ($-.65$)
	Illustrator gestures	Tension	More illustrators, less tension (.66)
	Object-fidgeting	In control	More fidgeting, more in control (.66)
	Facial displays	Irritability	More displays, more irritable (.71)

felt more stressful than those who displayed few shrugs. Honest subjects who displayed many shrugs indicated calm feelings; this relationship was particularly strong ($r = .83$).

Gazing Pattern. As noted above, the pattern of looking *at* and *away* from the interviewer had different meanings for evaders than for honest and deceptive subjects. Evaders felt tense when looking at the interviewer; their tension was relieved when they could direct their gaze elsewhere. This pattern seems to be the nonverbal expression of evasion, especially when we consider the feelings associated with gazing for honest and deceptive subjects. For honest subjects. looking at the interviewer indicated involvement and interest; looking away was a sign of being uninvolved or detached. The results for deceivers were more similar to those for honest subjects than to those for the evaders: Looking at the interviewer reflected calm, pleasant, and trusting feelings; looking at the camera was associated with less pleasant and less interested feelings.

Object-Fidgeting. This NVB had different meanings for deceptive and evasive subjects. As noted above, deceivers who often fidgeted with objects felt that they were more in control of their enactments. Evaders indicated less interest if they fidgeted often with objects. The meaning attributed to fidgeting by evaders was similar to that reflected by honest subjects' gazing away from the interviewer: Both were less interested or less serious about their enactments. The similar feelings associated with these NVBs render them functionally equivalent behaviors for evaders and honest subjects.

Head-Nodding. Like trunk swivels for honest subjects, frequent head-nodding indicated less control, less involvement, more difficulty in defending positions, and fewer comfortable feelings on the part of evaders. These similar meanings render swivels and nodding as functionally equivalent behaviors for honest and evasive subjects.

Illustrators. Less tension was felt by deceivers who displayed frequent illustrator gestures than by those who displayed few gestures. For evaders, less tension was felt by subjects who gazed elsewhere or at their notes. For honest subjects, frequent shoulder shrugs correlated with calmness: more shrugs indicated calmer feelings. Similar meaning assigned different NVBs renders these behaviors (illustrators, gazing elsewhere, shrugs) functionally equivalent; each is an indicator of reduced tension in the context of a particular intention.

Object Adaptors. Like trunk swivels for honest subjects, object adaptors indicated more apprehensive and fewer assertive and interested feelings for deceivers. Once again, the evidence suggests that different NVBs serve similar functions for different intentions.

Speaking Frequency. More frequent statements were made by those honest subjects who felt more involved and viewed their own positions to be similar to the assigned positions. Involvement and similarity of positions were indicated by more time spent looking at the interviewer and by frequent object adaptors for evaders. Involvement may be a function of perceived similarity between own and assigned positions ($r_{involvement/similarity}$ = −.40, p < .05 for N = 30; the more involved, the more similar own and assigned positions). They are indicated by different behaviors for honest (speaking frequency) and evasive (gaze at interviewer, object adaptors) subjects.

The relationships shown in Table 4.9 and discussed above can be summarized in terms of fewer psychological states and nonverbal behaviors. Most of the relationships turn on one of three types of states and involve a subset of the total number of assessed NVBs. One type of state is involvement or interest. Evasive and honest subjects displayed behaviors whose meaning indicated involvement. Another type of state is tension or stress. Evasive and deceptive subjects displayed behaviors that correlated with these feelings. A third state can be construed as confidence or effectiveness. Subjects in each of the three conditions demonstrated relationships between these types of feelings and selected NVBs. Correlations among the 26 questions indicated considerably stronger relationships between variables within a type (for example, assertive-confident, stress-anxious) than between types of states (such as assertive-tense, stress-involved). This evidence suggests factors that reflect primarily "honesty" (involvement), "direct and indirect deception" (stress), and "role-playing" (effectiveness). Interestingly, evasion shows relationships for two factors, one primarily involving honest subjects, the other involving deceivers; this is consistent with the notion that evaders were defined as neither completely honest nor completely deceptive. Verification of these observations awaits the results of a factor analysis.

A subset of NVBs can be identified as indicating either high or low involvement, stress, or effectiveness. Summarized in Table 4.10, these NVBs reflected one or more types of states for at least two of the conditions. Suggested here are possible

TABLE 4.10   OBSERVED BEHAVIORS AND TYPES OF PSYCHOLOGICAL STATES

	Type of State		
Observed Behavior	*Involvement*	*Stress*	*Confidence*
More time spent looking at interviewer	More involved (H)[a] More involved (E)[b]	More stress (E) Less stress (D)[c]	
Many trunk swivels		More stress (H) Less stress (D)	Less confident (H) More confident (E) More confident (D)
Frequent head-shaking			Less confident (H) Less confident (E) More confident (D)
Frequent gazing at notes or camera	Less involved (H) Less involved (D)	Less stress (E)	
Frequent gazes elsewhere	Less involved (H)	Less stress (E)	
Many leg movements	More involved (H)		Less confident (E)
Frequent shoulder shrugs	Less involved (H)	Less stress (H) More stress (D)	
Frequent fidgeting with objects	Less involved (E)		More confident (D)
Frequent object adaptors	More involved (E) Less involved (D)		Less confident (D)

a. honest condition
b. evasion condition
c. deception conditon

combinations of NVBs that can be used as signals of intentions: looking at versus looking away or leg movements versus shoulder shrugs for high and low involvement by honest subjects; looking at interviewer versus object-fidgeting for high and low involvement by evaders: looking at versus looking away for high and low stress felt by evaders; shrugs versus swivels or looking at the interviewer for high and low stress experienced by deceivers; swivels and shaking for low confidence by honest subjects; swivels versus shaking, leg movements, or nodding for high or low confidence by evaders; and head-shaking or object-fidgeting versus object adaptors for high or low confidence by deceivers. These should facilitate the process of going from observations (NVB frequencies) to inferences (intentions, states). They can also serve as a basis for a next step, which consists of assessing impressions made from various NVB displays (see Chapter 7).

Conclusion

The multimethod research strategy used in this project provided technical and theoretical products. The technical products consisted of identifying a subset of NVBs that discriminate among the conditions. Some variables were shown to distinguish the conditions in terms of level or frequency; others were part of a cluster of covarying behaviors whose pattern was unique to a condition. Theoretical products consisted of discovering nonverbal correlates of psychological states. Construed as intervening variables, the psychological states are seen to mediate the relationship between NVBs and intentions. The findings contribute to the process of inferring intentions from behavior. They also make evident the fact that the same NVBs may reflect different states for different intentions.

This experiment produced more information about concealing and revealing intentions than currently exists in the literature. The information is organized in terms of functions of NVBs. Functions refer to ways observations can be used to detect intentions. The only function addressed in previous experiments was discrimination by frequencies (Ekman et al., 1976; Harrison et al., 1978; McClintock and Hunt, 1975; Mehrabian, 1972; Streeter et al., 1977). Not explored in any of this work is discrimination by covariation or by correlates of psychological states. Moreover, none of the investigators attempted to develop a predictive model, limiting his focus to condition differences per se.

Particularly notable are findings that distinguish indirect from direct deception, those that show condition effects in

certain time periods, and those that indicate effects for differences from baseline data. Leg movements and gazing elsewhere
discriminated evaders from both deceivers and honest subjects:
More leg movements and more frequent gazes elsewhere were
made by evaders. Self-fidgeting, head-shaking, rocking movements, and object-fidgeting were among the NVBs that showed
time-period effects, such as a decreasing trend in frequency of
self-fidgeting contrasted with increasing trends of head-shaking
and rocking movements for evaders. Speech errors and gaze
time at the interviewer produced dramatic differences from
baseline-period observations: Deceivers made more speech
errors and deceivers and evaders spent more time looking away
from the interviewer during the three interview periods. Illustrating the value of our analytical and measurement approach,
these findings extend the range of observations that contribute
to inferences about intentions.

These results suggest the importance of distinguishing among
early, middle, and late displays shown for certain variables.
They also highlight the importance of baseline data. Our time-
period data indicate that condition differences may take the
form of different trends or be limited to certain junctures of the
interview: None of the variables involved in time period by
condition interactions was found to differ significantly between
the deception and honest conditions in the earlier studies (see
Mehrabian, 1972; McClintock and Hunt, 1975; Ekman et al.,
1976). Our baseline-difference data indicate that condition
differences may occur only for comparisons of deviations from
baseline frequencies: Baseline-difference effects occurred for
variables that showed no effect (number of statements), weak
condition effects (speech errors), or similar condition effects
(leg movements) in Mehrabian's study. Moreover, whereas
Mehrabian showed weak condition effects and McClintock and
Hunt found no difference for eye contact, our baseline-
difference data indicated accentuated gaze aversion during the
interview.

These comparisons make clear the value of an analytical
approach that probes relationships missed by conventional
assessment of condition main effects. Other results are, however, more directly comparable. These can be summarized.

(1) Facial Pleasantness. Opposite results obtained by Mehrabian (1972) and by McClintock and Hunt (1975) can be explained in terms of subjects' anxiety: more pleasantness (smiles/frowns) was found for Mehrabian's relatively low-anxiety subjects on deceptive than on honest communications; fewer smiles for McClintock and Hunt's deceptive answers may have been a result of tension, which, as the authors note, was aroused by the task. More facial displays, both positive and negative, for our direct and indirect deceivers may have reflected the low level of anxiety indicated by these subjects on a self-report measure; or we might be getting more smiles from relatively low-anxiety deceivers, more frowns from the high-anxiety subjects. Of interest will be the results of planned internal analyses that examine smiles versus frowns for low- and high-anxiety deceivers.

(2) Immediacy. Our gaze-aversion effect for deceivers versus honest subjects is similar to Mehrabian's finding of less immediate behaviors for deceptive responses. Eye contact was just one of several behaviors that combined to form his "immediacy" composite. Also included were the variables of touching, distance, and forward lean. Those behaviors were not assessed in our experiment.

(3) Leg and Foot Movements. Mehrabian's deception effect compares to the evasion effect obtained in our experiment: Mehrabian's deceptive responses showed fewer movements than his honest responses, while our deceivers showed fewer movements than our evaders. Moreover, the evaders showed *accentuated* leg movements, as noted above in the summary of the baseline-data effects.

(4) Speech Errors. A higher speech-error rate for Mehrabian's deceptive responses compares to our greater difference from baseline rates for deceptive subjects. Reflecting the complex argumentation demanded of subjects in our experiment, a high speech error rate was found in all conditions. This finding implies that a more sensitive index of deception in such situations may be differences from baseline levels.

(5) Speech Duration and Speaking Frequency. Opposite effects for speech duration obtained by Mehrabian (shorter speaking time when deceiving) and by Harrison et al., 1978 (longer answers when deceiving) compare to the nonsignificant

effect obtained in our experiment. The lack of differences obtained in our experiment may be explained by the interview format: similar structuring of questions in all conditions make differences in time spent talking unlikely to vary from one condition to another. Speaking frequency is less likely to be affected by such structuring. Indeed, differences from baseline data showed condition effects, with deceivers speaking less frequently than evaders or honest subjects.

(6) *Hand Movements.* Consistent with results obtained in other experiments, we found few significant condition main effects for hand movements. Nonsignificant condition effects were obtained by Ekman et al. (1976) for adaptors, by Mehrabian for gesticulations and self-/object manipulations, and by McClintock and Hunt for hand/arm gestures. Only illustrator gestures discriminated between deceptive and honest enactments in the Ekman et al. study. These results underestimate the importance of hand movements in deceptive interactions. Further analyses computed for our experiment show the following: Illustrators, self-adaptors, and crossed hands formed a strong cluster of covarying behaviors for deceivers; object- and self-fidgeting discriminated between deceivers and honest subjects for certain time periods, and, perhaps most compelling, object-fidgeting was the second most important variable to emerge from the stepwise discriminant analysis.

(7) *Voice Pitch and Response Latency.* Streeter et al. (1977) and Ekman et al. (1976) found that the average voice's fundamental frequency (pitch) was higher when subjects were lying than when telling the truth. Harrison et al. (1978) showed that deceptive answers were more hesitant as revealed in a measure of response latency. These results add two more variables to the set of discriminating paralinguistic responses found in our study. While neither was assessed here, each will receive attention in further stages of the project.

(8) *Other Nonverbal Behaviors.* Just as hand movements yielded few significant effects in more than one study, trunk swivels and head-nodding also failed to produce condition main effects. Like our results, Mehrabian and McClintock and Hunt found weak effects for swivels or posture shifts. Similarly head-

nodding was nonsignificant in both Mehrabian's and our experiment. It is instructive to note also that eye blinks, shoulder shrugs, head support, and crossed arms yielded nonsignificant condition effects in this study: None of these variables was measured in any of the previous experiments.

Approaching the problem from a different direction, discriminant analysis provided more concentrated results. Relatively accurate condition predictions were made from a combination of three NVBs—leg movements, gaze time at the interviewer, and object-fidgeting. Classification equations containing only these NVBs did much better than experts: 77 percent correct classification versus an average of about 35 percent for three experts. Implications for a more efficient observational strategy are suggested by these results. Efficiency is increased when an observer can base his or her inferences on a small subset of behaviors.

Another function served by NVBs is discrimination among conditions in terms of covariation. Highlighted by the correlational results are certain behaviors. Head movements (nodding and shaking) co-occur with other behaviors for each of the conditions; leg movements distinguish evaders from deceivers and honest subjects as a correlate of nodding, as well as a frequently occurring behavior; and rocking movements, nodding, and shaking form an intercorrelated cluster that occurs in each of the three time periods for deceivers. Moreover, implications for the concept of display packages are suggested by the correlations computed within time periods. The co-occurring patterns can be used to develop profiles of "typical" deceivers, evaders, and honest subjects.

Emphasizing meaning, the nonverbal correlates of psychological states illustrate a third function of nonverbal behaviors. This function is based on the view that NVBs reflect feelings more directly than they reflect intentions: The relationship between NVBs and intentions is mediated by psychological states. A predominant theme in the literature on nonverbal communication is the relationship between emotions and observed behavior (Harper et al., 1978). Such a relationship is implied by the concepts of leakage and deception clues (Ekman and Friesen,

1969a); it is the guiding assumption for research on the primary emotions (Ekman et al., 1972). Placed in the context of this project, the relationship is seen to turn on three types of states: involvement (primarily for honest and evasive subjects), stress (salient for the evaders and deceivers), and confidence (reflecting the challenge of role-playing). Involvement is indexed for honest subjects by the pattern of looking at versus looking away from the interviewer; for evaders, by looking at the interviewer versus object-fidgeting. Stress is indexed by looking at versus looking away from the interviewer for evaders, and by shrugs versus trunk swivels for deceivers. Confidence is indexed by such NVBs as trunk swivels (honest, evasive), head-shaking (honest, evasive, and deceptive), leg movements (evaders), and object-fidgeting (deceivers). These results are suggestive (see note 5). They contribute to a model of inferring intentions from behavior; they also make plausible the tasks of developing and refining indicators of emotions expressed in the context of political decision-making.

Identified by the results summarized here is a smaller set of NVBs that would seem to be candidates for measurement in further work. This short list is shown in Table 4.11. Each of these behaviors satisfies the criteria of reliability and/or relevance. Reliability was assessed by correlations computed between ratings made by independent coders (see note 1). Relevance was judged by significant results obtained for discrimination among conditions or high correlations with psychological states. Only trunk swivel fails to achieve high reliability, but qualifies because of correlational results. (An attempt is being made to bolster the reliability of this variable.) Only crossed arms fails to enter into significant relationships, but qualifies because of very high reliability. These are the NVBs assessed in the next-step studies mentioned below.

Based on the results of this study, what advice would we offer the observer/analyst and where would we focus our next steps in the research? Specific suggestions include the following:

(1) Concentrate on leg movements and looking elsewhere for clues to evasion: The leg movements are likely to occur during periods of silence when the subject feels less assertive; frequent gazes else-

TABLE 4.11 SHORT-LIST NVBs BASED ON CRITERIA OF
RELIABILITY AND IMPORTANCE

	Reliability	Relevance
1. Gaze time at interviewer	.95	ANOVA results; Top three in D.A.;[a] correlational relationships
2. Leg movements	.99	ANOVA results; Top three in D.A.; correlational relationships
3. Object-fidgeting	.86	ANOVA results; Top three in D.A.; correlate of feelings
4. Gaze frequency elsewhere	.64	ANOVA results; Top ten in D.A.; correlate of feelings
5. Foot movements	.91	ANOVA results; Top ten in D.A.; correlate of feelings
6. Speech errors	.81	Baseline difference for deceivers (not included in D.A. or correlational analyses)
7. Rocking movements	.82	Correlation pattern for each posture; correlate of feelings; Top ten in D.A.
8. Head-nodding	.86	Top ten in D.A.; correlation patterns; correlate of feelings
9. Speaking frequency	.70	Top ten in D.A.; correlate of feelings; borderline trends for mean differences
10. Trunk swivels	(<.6)	Correlate of numerous feelings for each posture; correlation pattern for deceivers
11. Illustrator gestures	.84	Correlate of feelings
12. Head support	.87	Correlational patterns and correlate of feelings
13. Arms crossed	.97	———

NOTE: The average reliability for the above (excluding trunk swivels) is .84; note that this is better
than the Ekman FACS average reliability reported as .76 (Ekman et al. 1980).
a. D.A.=discriminant analysis

where are likely to occur during periods of stress, serving to reduce
the tension.

(2) Note the time spent looking at the interviewer for clues to direct
and indirect deception; the deceivers/evaders should be seen to
spend less time looking than during a baseline period.

(3) Monitor the pattern of rocking movements, head-shaking, and
nodding. These NVBs should covary for deceivers; they seem to
reflect feelings of confidence and certainty.

(4) Use the observed frequencies of leg movements and object-fidgeting, as well as the time spent looking at the interviewer as entries in classification equations; the computational results should lead to a relatively accurate prediction of whether a subject is concealing, evading, or revealing information.

(5) Note the pattern of looking at versus looking away from the interviewer. More time spent looking at as compared to looking away suggests high involvement for honest subjects, high stress for evaders.

(6) Use trunk swivels as an indicator of confidence and stress. Many swivels seem to indicate increased confidence for deceivers and evaders, decreased confidence for honest subjects. They may also suggest less stress for deceivers than for honest subjects; this difference may be related to their respective levels of confidence.

Several experiments, suggested by the work completed to date, are in progress. First, an attempt is being made to assess the generalizability of these results. The entire experiment has been replicated with foreign service officers and military attaches serving as subjects. Both males and females are included in the sample. Data collection has been completed, and the tapes are being coded using the short list of NVBs shown in Table 4.11. Similar results attest to generality; different results would highlight effects due to subject-population differences. Particularly interesting will be the results of an attempt to use the classification equations developed above to predict the condition of subjects in the replication study.

Second, another experimental condition has been developed. Referred to as "evasive but honest," the condition is an attempt to separate effects of evasion from deception. Similar effects for evasion and deception, obtained in this experiment, may have been due to the fact that evasion was another form of deception, that is, an attempt to mislead by not dealing with issues directly. Subjects from the Houston population were instructed to be honest with regard to the present situation but ambiguous concerning implications for the future. Special attention will be paid to a comparison between this condition and the evasion condition of the experiment reported in this chapter: Are the nonverbal displays more like those obtained for honest subjects, or do they replicate the findings obtained from evasive subjects? The latter results would suggest that the earlier findings (reported above) were due to evasion per se.

Finally, a third experiment is in progress. This is an attempt to separate the effects of stress from deception. Certain aspects of the interview situation were varied. Subjects are given less time to prepare positions and to perform in the presence of another person whose task is to evaluate "truthfulness," and are told to deceive in the face of new evidence. Special attention will be paid to a comparison between this condition and the deception condition of the experiment reported above. Differences between the conditions in self-reported stress attest to an effective manipulation. If effective, the manipulated situational stress can be separated from the posture (deception). Differences between conditions in nonverbal displays can then be attributed to aroused stress. A more definitive test of the issue would require an orthogonal design: high and low situational stress would be combined with deceptive and honest intentions. This type of design is planned as a next step in the research program.

NOTES

1. Only head-shaking did not produce a significant reliability coefficient. Computed reliabilities for the other variables in the discriminant function are as follows: gaze time (.95), head-nodding (.86), leg movements (.99), arms crossed (.97), object-fidgeting (.86), rocking movements (.82), gaze frequency elsewhere (.64), speaking frequency (.70), and foot movements (.91). Reliability coefficients are correlations between ratings made by two coders working independently; a smaller sample of subjects from each of the experimental conditions was used for the reliability study.

2. Particularly impressive reliability coefficients were obtained for these variables: leg movements (.99), object-fidgeting (.86), and gaze time at interviewer (.95).

3. Predictions based on the short-form equations are preferred to those derived from longer equations. Three-variable equations are more efficient, requiring fewer codes and computations than those based on ten NVBs.

4. As noted above, these analyses take advantage of within-condition variation. While discriminating *between* the conditions, these NVBs also showed variation in level or frequency from one subject to another in the same condition.

5. Conclusions based on these analyses should be viewed as tentative. More definitive results would derive from procedural and analytical changes. Assessments

of states would benefit from a procedure for recording feelings during the interview process. Analytical precision would be enhanced by using a partialling procedure or by factor analyzing the correlation matrix. Both of these considerations will be entertained in next steps.

6. The apparent inconsistency between "more leg movements, less assertive feelings" and relatively high assertive ratings is explained by the difference between within-group variance and between-group differences. Evaders who made frequent leg movements rated themselves lower on the assertive scale than those who made relatively few movements. The mean assertive rating for this group was, however, higher than the mean rating of the deceptive and honest groups. Similarly, the mean number of leg movements for the evaders was higher than the mean obtained for the other groups.

7. Leakage refers to behaviors that indicate consciously disguised or unarticulated feelings. Being able to identify these feelings is important. They are intervening variables that link the observed behaviors to intentions. Having identified them helps to explain why particular NVBs are seen when someone attempts to conceal information and why other NVBs are seen when that person reveals the "correct" information.

5

DECODING NONVERBAL CLUES
TO DECEPTION

Focusing on the actor, the experiment reported in the previous chapter demonstrated that certain nonverbal behaviors distinguish among deceptive, evasive, and honest intentions. These behaviors can be regarded as veridical cues to deception (DePaulo and Rosenthal, 1979). This is one approach to the study of deception. Another approach concerns the ability to detect lies from nonverbal cues. Focusing on the observer, this approach is followed by investigators who desire to identify the factors that determine *judgments* of deception (see Kraut, 1978; Zuckerman et al., 1979). It is represented by the experiment reported in this chapter.

The shift of focus from actor to observer is a change of concentration from elicited behavior to interpretation. Relevant here is the distinction between the coder and the perceiver. Whereas the coder merely records counted frequencies or times, the perceiver engages in an interpretive activity that consists of making inferences about motives or feelings from observed behaviors. Providing information to be processed mechanically, coders contribute to the process of identifying veridical cues to deception. Reacting to various displays, perceivers provide information about dimensions of the interpretive process. Coders provided the data for analyses reported in the previous chapter. Perceivers provide the data for the analyses reported below.

While emphasizing the distinction between the coder and perceiver roles, it is also important to note relationships. Coding results can be used to improve judgments of intentions. In general, people are not accurate decoders: A number of experiments, reviewed by DePaulo and Rosenthal (1979: 1718), suggest that "people's lay theories about clues to deception are not particularly accurate." Indeed, our expert results, reported in the previous chapter, are a case in point. Knowing the discriminating cues, however, could improve accuracy. At issue is whether improved sensitivity results from awareness of the distinction between signals and noise.[1]

But simply knowing the signals may not assure accuracy. Even casual acquaintance with recent developments in cognitive theory make evident the problems associated with judgment. The problems are perceptual and inferential. Perceivers are active interpreters who go beyond the information given. Just as they may be subject to perceptual illusions, they are also subject to faulty inferences. Assessments can be traced to the influence of prior theories and expectations, and are "insufficiently influenced by actual data configurations" (Nisbett and Ross, 1980: 16). Interfering with the transition from visual perception to inference, such expectations can be treated as sources of error. Overcoming these problems is a prerequisite to improving judgmental accuracy.

The problem is further complicated by the realization that there are barriers to change. Nisbett and Ross (1980: 286-287) speculate about three major barriers: "(a) our inability to directly observe our cognitive processes, (b) our susceptibility to inferential errors when confronted with particular vivid and personally-relevant information, and (c) our general tendency to be overly confident about whatever judgments and inferences we have happened to reach." People are generally disinclined to examine their judgments for the possibility of error. They rely on subjective impressions, and often express greater certainty about their judgments than closely reasoned analysis could justify (see Fischhoff et al., 1977). While acknowledging that these are very serious barriers in the path toward change, Nisbett and Ross express optimism about the prospects for change.

Remedies can be found in educational programs. Several types of programs are outlined by Nisbett and Ross. One

consists of presenting anecdotal material that can be compre-
hended in terms of daily experiences. Concrete examples of
inferential errors may be essential for understanding the problem, a first step toward altering standard operating procedures.
Another remedy may be the use of maxims or slogans such as
"Consider the actor's situation before jumping to conclusions
about his dispositions," and "It's an empirical question." However, while highlighting the problem, neither remedy provides a
procedure for reaching "correct" decisions. A third strategy
consists of a formal procedure. Referred to as formal inference
training, this strategy includes rules of statistical inference and
relatively simple judgment heuristics. Which type of procedure
is chosen depends largely on the nature of the problem. None
has been evaluated systematically to date. An attempt is made
here to evaluate the effectiveness of one particular form of
inference training.

In its most general form, inference training consists of teach-
ing people to process information systematically. The analytical
structure provided by the training is an alternative to idiosyncratic habits of thought. It is less likely to be misleading,
although there are limiting conditions for application. Its useful-
ness depends on a problem whose outcomes are knowable and
are distinguishable in terms of costs and benefits. When these
conditions are met, inference training confers advantages that
are both practical (correct judgments) and psychological
(bolsters defense of decisions, feeling of accomplishment).

The problem addressed here, that is, decoding intentions
from nonverbal clues, meets the conditions for application of
inference training. Clues are provided by the experimental
results discussed in the previous chapter (outcomes are knowable). The wrong judgment can lead to serious miscalculations,
especially in foreign policy/negotiation settings (outcomes are
distinguishable in terms of costs and benefits). At issue, however,
is whether inference structures are in fact beneficial. It is
conceivable that knowing how to distinguish nonverbal signals
from nonverbal noise is sufficient. The issue can be arbitrated
by the results of an experiment in which the effects of different
training procedures on judgment accuracy are compared.

A training workshop on nonverbal communication provided an opportunity to conduct the experiment. Decoders were foreign training officers whose responsibilities included sensitizing others to the importance of nonverbal behavior. These participants were shown alternative videotapes, each scripted for nonverbal behaviors and intentions. They were to distinguish among the presentations in terms of the actor's intentions to reveal or conceal information. Procedural details are discussed before the results are presented. The chapter concludes with a discussion of implications and next steps.

Procedures

Three scripted enactments of the role of Soviet ambassador to the United States were prepared. Each was a depiction of a deceiver, an evader, or an honest diplomat. Each posture was portrayed in a six-minute interview dealing with two issues, the invasion of Afghanistan and troops in Europe. The same actor portrayed each of the three postures. He was interviewed by one of the authors (DD), who served as moderator.

The verbal scripts were prepared by the actor, who was told to follow the instructions given subjects in the experiment reported in Chapter 4. These scripts were responses to standard questions on the two issues, written on cue cards for ease of presentation. The nonverbal scripts were those behaviors found to distinguish among the three conditions in the experiment reported above: For the deceiver role, the actor fidgeted with his glasses, gazed away from the moderator occasionally, made several speech hesitations, and showed occasional rocking movements. The evasive enactment consisted of frequent leg and foot movements, looking around the room, occasional fidgeting with glasses, and head-shaking during the early part of the interview. For the honest enactment, the actor looked at the interviewer frequently, showed occasional illustrators and head shakes, and made few facial displays (smiles or frowns). Timing was also scripted; the actor was told, through the use of cue cards, when to display each NVB.

Rehearsals and repeated "takes" were necessary before a final version was produced. Often this involved juxtaposing new segments with completed portions of the interview. Also juxtaposed were an introductory statement and moderator questions: This procedure was designed to ensure that the observed variation from one enactment to another would be limited to the actor's behavior. These tasks were handled by a professional videotape editing service, whose technicians also managed the color-mixing procedures.[2]

The tapes were shown to members of three workshop sessions held at Hurlburt Air Force Base (Hurlburt Field, Florida) during the 1980-1981 year. The workshops were part of a course on cross-cultural communication designed for foreign training officers from various government agencies. The sessions had 23, 18, and 19 members respectively. The tapes were presented in three different orders (H, E, D or D, E, H or E, D, H). Members of the class were divided into three groups, each assigned a room for viewing the films. This procedure was used to prevent an order effect, that is, results attributable to the sequence of portrayals or position of a particular portrayal. Class members were told not to use a process of elimination, that each decision should be independent of the others. They were not to assume that each of the three portrayals was depicted on alternative tapes.

Reactions were recorded on three six-page questionnaires, each filled out immediately after viewing one of the tapes. Respondents (decoders) were told that the actor was assigned to one of three sets of instructions: honest, evasive, or deceptive representation. The respondents were provided and read the instructions prior to answering the questions. The actor was rated on kind of intention (deceptive, evasive, honest), degree of each intention (extent to which he was being deceptive), confidence in these judgments, attributed feelings (15 seven-step scales), impressions (30 seven-step scales), and nonverbal and verbal cues used in making judgments (chosen from 21 cues). Before viewing the tapes, workshop members were given a particular training procedure; each session was subject to a different procedure: global lecture, technical briefing, or inference training. We turn now to a description of these procedures.

The four conditions are referred to as a global lecture, a technical briefing, inference training, and audio-only. With the exception of audio-only, each condition is an attempt to sensitize decoders to nonverbal cues. Audio-only was instituted as a control condition in order to evaluate effects of exposure to nonverbal cues per se. The conditions consisted of training exercises, each taking about half an hour to complete. Each condition is described in order of execution.

Global Lecture. Prior to viewing the three tapes, members of Workshop I were given an orientation lecture on nonverbal communication. Topics covered included the meaning of nonverbal behavior, the relation between NVBs and psychological states, ways in which NVB can be used to diagnose intentions, multiple-channel displays, leakage, types of deception, the distinction between encoding and decoding, and the advantages of a technical approach to the study of nonverbal behavior. This lecture was introduced as an attempt to sensitize workshop members to the importance of NVB and to communicate the view that certain NVBs may convey information about feelings and intentions. The discussion drew, to a large extent, on the material presented in Chapters 1, 2, and 3 of this volume.

Technical Briefing. Prior to viewing the tapes, members of Workshop II were given a technical briefing on experimental results. The briefing consisted of a graphic presentation of findings obtained in the experiment reported in Chapter 4. Differences in condition frequencies of leg movements, object-fidgeting, gaze direction, looking around the room, and speech hesitations were illustrated. Discriminant analysis results were also presented. These NVBs were highlighted as signals which, unlike other behavior, can be used to distinguish among intentions. Handouts of definitions (see Table 4.1, Chapter 4) and a signals chart were distributed. The signals chart took the following form:

Nonverbal Behavior	Distinguishes Between
Looks away from camera	H < D and E
Fidgets with glasses	H < D and E
Speech hesitations	D > H and E
Leg movements	E > D and H
Looking around room	E > D and H

No attempt was made to train members on how to use the findings to make inferences about intentions.

Inference Training. Members of Workshop III were given inference training prior to viewing the tapes. The procedure consisted of three parts. The first part entailed a briefing, with viewcharts, on key experimental results, including the comparison of discriminant and expert predictions. Findings were then translated into signals and noise, the distinction turning on whether an NVB discriminated among the experimental conditions. Third, the procedure for inferring intentions from nonverbal displays was demonstrated in the form of a flowchart (Figure 5.1). The chart was explained in terms of four tracks: honest versus evasive *or* deceptive, and evasive versus deceptive tracks. Seldom looking away from the camera and seldom fidgeting with glasses lead to a decision of honest; often looking away and frequent fidgeting lead to a decision of *not* honest. The latter decision leads to a search for more evidence: Much leg activity suggests a tentative diagnosis of evasion; frequent looking around the room, when combined with leg activity, leads to a decision of evasion. On the other hand, infrequent leg activity when observed in conjunction with speech hesitations signals deception.

The strategy is an organized method for processing information about five nonverbal cues. This is the essential distinction between a technical briefing (where critical cues are identified)

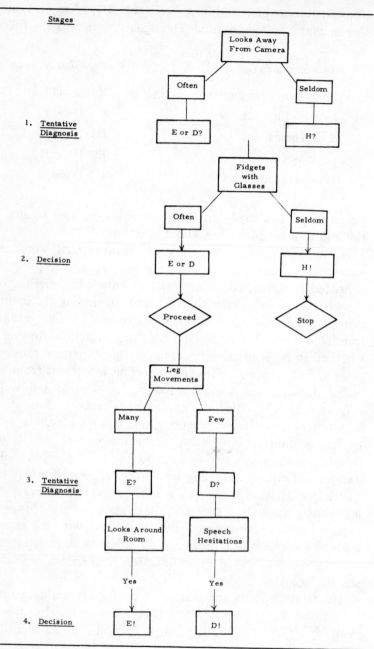

Figure 5.1 Strategy Used for Inference Training

and inference training. By no means should such an aid be construed as an algorithm; it requires perceptual rather than calculational decisions (see note 1). When asked, following the judgment task, if this aid was helpful, *all* decoders agreed; no one indicated that he was confused by the flowchart.

Audio-Only. Members of Workshop III were also asked to make judgments based only on the audio version of the three enactments. This task preceded inference training and viewing of the tapes. It followed a lecture, given in an earlier session, on nonverbal communication, comparable to the global-orientation lecture. Decoders were told "to listen carefully to *what the actor says* and judge whether you think he is being deceptive, evasive, or honest according to the instructions that he received." As in the other conditions, they were told not to use a process of elimination, that each decision should be independent of the others. At the conclusion of this task the class was reassembled for inference training. To prevent a systematic bias due to the earlier listening task, each inference-training group received the order used for another group in the audio-only presentations.

At the conclusion of the judgment task, in each condition, the class was assembled for a discussion of results. The results obtained from their judgments were compared to the percentage correct achieved in earlier conditions. (Only the Workshop I members, given a global lecture, could not benefit from condition comparisons.)

Experimental comparisons were made on responses to three types of questions: judgments of kind (honest, evasive, deceptive), degree (extent to which H, E, or D), and confidence in these judgments. Of particular interest is an evaluation of the impact of inference training on number of correct judgments. We turn now to the results.

Results

Results are summarized in terms of percentage correct judgments in Table 5.1. Large gains are shown for the technical-

TABLE 5.1   PERCENTAGE CORRECT JUDGMENTS BY
CONDITION AND PORTRAYAL

	Deception	Percentage Gain	Evasion	Percentage Gain	Honesty	Percentage Gain
Global lecture	13		43		52	
Technical briefing	39		67		50	
Technical vs. global		+26		+24		(−2)
Inference training	74		84		74	
Inference vs. technical		+35		+17		+24
Audio-only	39		53		58	
Inference vs. audio		+35		+31		+16

briefing over the global-lecture condition for judgments of
deception and evasion (+26, +24), for inference training over
technical briefing on all three portrayals (+35, +17, +24), and
for inference training over audio-only for all portrayals (+35,
+31, +16). Statistical evaluation of the results is organized in
terms of three sets of planned comparisons: global lecture
versus technical briefing, technical briefing versus inference
training, and audio-only versus inference training.[3] Results
obtained for each comparison are presented in turn.

GLOBAL LECTURE VERSUS TECHNICAL BRIEFING

The global-lecture condition (Workshop I) is compared to the
technical-training condition (Workshop II) for the deceptive,
evasive, and honest portrayals. Number of correct versus incorrect judgments and perceptions of extent to which each portrayal was seen as honest, evasive, or deceptive are evaluated.
Also presented are the results of an analysis of confidence
ratings.

Number Correct Versus
Incorrect Judgments

The Deceiver. Three of the 23 global-lecture condition decoders judged the deceiver as deceptive; 7 of 18 technical-
briefing decoders made the correct judgment. These results are
depicted in Table 5.2.

TABLE 5.2   NUMBER OF CORRECT AND INCORRECT
JUDGMENTS BY CONDITION

	Correct	Incorrect	Total Decoders
The Deceiver			
Global	3	20	23
Technical	7	11	18
The Evader			
Global	10	13	23
Technical	12	6	18

The difference, as evaluated by chi square, is statistically significant (χ^2 = 5.19, with 1 df, p < .025, one-tailed). The technical briefing improved judgment accuracy: More decoders who received a technical briefing were correct than those whose orientation consisted of a general lecture. The incorrect judgments were divided equally between evasive and honest for the global-lecture decoders; the 11 incorrect technical judgments were divided into 5 for evasion and 6 for honest.

The Evader. Of 23 global-lecture decoders, 10 judged the evader as evasive; 12 of 18 technical-briefing decoders made the correct judgment. These results are also depicted in Table 5.2.

The difference, as evaluated by chi square, is statistically significant (χ^2 = 3.22 with 1 df, p < .05, one-tailed). Once again, the technical briefing improved judgmental accuracy: More technical decoders were correct than global decoders. Interestingly, all of the incorrect judges in both conditions misclassified the evader as a deceiver.

The Honest Portrayal. About the same proportion of correct judgments of the honest portrayal were made in both conditions: 12 of 23 in the global-lecture condition and 9 of 18 in the technical-briefing condition. The technical briefing did not improve accuracy over that obtained for the global condition. Misclassifications were divided about evenly between the deceiver and the evader for global-condition decoders, while twice as many incorrect technical-condition decoders perceived deception as opposed to evasion.

TABLE 5.3   SUMMARY OF RESULTS FOR PERCEIVED
             INTENTIONS: GLOBAL LECTURE

Actual	Honest	Perceived Evasive	Deceptive	χ_r^2 (Friedman statistic)
Honest		>	=	7.95 (p<.02)
Evasive	>		=	30.06 (p<.001)
Deceptive	=	=		4.79 (p<.10)

NOTE: The symbols in the charts are to be interpreted as follows: greater than (>) means that the portrayal is judged as more like the actual than the alternative; the equals sign means that the portrayal is *not* judged as more like the actual than the alternative.

In summary, significant gains due to a technical briefing occurred for decoding the deceptive and evasive portrayals. The percentage gains are depicted in Table 5.1.

**Perceptions of Degree
of Each Portrayal**

Decoders were also asked to "indicate the degree to which each of the representation styles was present in [each] film." This question provided a measure of the extent to which the correct portrayal was perceived. Differences between ratings for each perceived style by actual portrayal were evaluated by the Friedman Analysis of Variance by Ranks (Siegel, 1956). Results are depicted in the form of matrices for each condition.

Global Lecture. The honest portrayal was perceived as more honest than evasive but not distinguished significantly from deception; the evasive portrayal was seen as more evasive than honest but not distinguished significantly from deception; and the deceiver was not seen as more deceptive than evasive or honest. These findings are summarized in Table 5.3.

Decoders correctly distinguished honesty from evasion. While actual honesty was perceived to be somewhat more honest than deceptive, the difference was not large enough to be statistically significant. The evasive portrayal was seen as somewhat more deceptive than evasive, while the deceptive portrayal was viewed as somewhat more honest *and* somewhat more evasive than deceptive. These differences were not, however, significant.

TABLE 5.4   SUMMARY OF RESULTS FOR PERCEIVED
             INTENTIONS: TECHNICAL BRIEFING

Actual	Honest	Perceived Evasive	Deceptive	χ_r^2 (Friedman statistic)
Honest		=	=	2.43 (p>.10)
Evasive	>		>[a]	28.6 (p<.001)
Deceptive	>	>		7.31 (p<.05)

NOTE: See note to Table 5.3.

a. predicted direction

Technical Briefing. The honest portrayal was not perceived as more honest than either evasive or deceptive; the evasive portrayal was seen as more evasive than honest or deceptive; and the deceiver was seen as more deceptive than honest or evasive. These findings are depicted in Table 5.4.

These results support the evidence shown above: Decoders were able to distinguish evasion and deception from the alternatives; they had more difficulty discriminating honesty from deception or evasion, although the trend was in the predicted direction. Moreover, this analysis provides evidence that is relatively precise, that is, of the form "more deceptive than evasive" as opposed to "deceptive rather than evasive."

The decoders were particularly good at perceiving the extent to which a portrayal was deceptive. Additional probes suggest an explanation. Correct judges of degree used the salient cues of object-fidgeting and speech hesitations more than did the incorrect judges: None of 10 correct judges used object-fidgeting, while only 4 of 8 incorrect judges indicated use of this cue (χ^2 = 1.83 with 1 df, p < .10, one-tailed); 7 of 10 correct judges used speech hesitations, while only 1 of 8 incorrect judges relied on this cue (χ^2 = 3.85 with 1 df, p < .025, one-tailed).[4] Apparently correct judgments of degree of deception depended largely on ability to perceive the salient cues. And significantly more correct judgments of degree were made following a technical briefing than after the global lecture (χ^2 =

6.58 with 1 df, p < .01, one-tailed).[5] Further evidence of gains in judging deception is provided by an analysis of the confidence ratings.

Confidence Ratings

Analyses of confidence ratings were completed for the technical-briefing decoders. Correct judges of deception were significantly more confident in their judgments than were incorrect judges ($\overline{X}_c$ = 1.86, $\overline{X}_i$ = 3.27; t = 3.53, p < .001). Correct judges of evasion and of honesty were not more confident of their judgments than were the incorrect judges (for evasion, $\overline{X}_c$ = 2.08, $\overline{X}_i$ = 2.17; for honesty, $\overline{X}_c$ = 2.11, $\overline{X}_i$ = 2.78). The more that judges of deception perceived that style in the film, the more confident they were in their judgments; conversely, the less they perceived deceptive intentions in the deception portrayal, the less confident they were in their judgments (r_s [Spearman rank correlation coefficient] = .53, p < .001). The relationship between extent to which honesty was seen in the honest portrayal and confidence in that judgment was weak (r_s = .35, p < .10); there was no relationship between perceptions of evasion and confidence in judgements (r_s = .10, n.s.).

It seems that when a decoder was correct in his judgment of deception, he knew it: Decoders of deception were quite confident that they had correctly judged deception when in fact they were correct. While less than half of our technical-briefing sample judged deception correctly, those who did were rather convinced that their judgments were accurate. Not so for perceptions of honesty: Correct judges were only somewhat more confident in their judgments than were incorrect judges, and they were only somewhat more confident in judgments that honesty was the predominant style represented in the honest film.

Judgments of evasion present a different picture. Recall that evasion was successfully distinguished from both honesty and deception, and 67 percent of the sample made correct judgments. Why were they not more confident in their judgments?

TABLE 5.5   NUMBER OF CORRECT AND INCORRECT
              JUDGMENTS BY CONDITION

	Correct	Incorrect	Total Decoders
The Deceiver			
Technical	7	11	18
Inference	14	5	19
The Evader			
Technical	12	6	18
Inference	16	3	19
The Honest Portrayal			
Technical	9	9	18
Inference	14	5	19

A plausible explanation is in terms of a "ceiling effect" for judgments of evasion: All decoders rated evasion as either "high" (N = 12) or "moderate" (N = 6); confidence ratings were largely divided between "quite a bit" (N = 12) and "some" (N = 5). In order to produce a significant correlation between judgments and confidence ratings, most decoders would have had to indicate "complete confidence" in their judgments; only one observer of evasion was willing to admit to such confidence.

TECHNICAL BRIEFING VERSUS INFERENCE TRAINING

The technical-briefing sample (Workshop II) was compared to the inference-training sample (Workshop III) on number of correct versus incorrect judgments for the deceptive, evasive, and honest presentations.

Number of Correct Versus Incorrect Judgments

The Deceiver. Of 18 technical-briefing-condition decoders, 7 judged the deceiver as deceptive; 14 of 19 inference-training-condition decoders made the correct judgment. These results are depicted in Table 5.5.

The difference, as evaluated by chi square, is statistically significant ($\chi^2 = 6.09$, with 1 df, $p < .01$, one-tailed). Inference training improved judgment accuracy; more decoders who received inference training were correct than those who were given a technical briefing. Of the 5 incorrect decoders, 4 made faulty inferences, monitoring the signals correctly but drawing the wrong conclusions (honest or evasive). Only one of the incorrect judgments was due to faulty monitoring: The decoder indicated that he saw frequent leg activity and heard infrequent hesitations, leading him to a judgment of evasion.

The Evader. Of 18 technical-condition decoders, 12 judged the evader as evasive; 16 of 19 inference-condition decoders made the correct judgment. These results are shown in Table 5.5.

The difference, as evaluated by chi square, approaches significance (χ^2 = 2.65, with 1 df, p < .06, one-tailed). Once again, the inference training improved judgmental accuracy: More inference decoders were correct than were technical decoders. This result is particularly impressive considering that there was little room for improvement from the technical condition (67 percent correct technical to 84 percent correct inference). All three incorrect judgments resulted from faulty inferences, each accounting for the signals but resulting in the wrong decision, that is, deception.

The Honest Portrayal. Of 18 technical-condition decoders, 9 judged the honest portrayal to be honest; 14 of 19 inference-condition decoders made the correct judgment. These results are depicted in Table 5.5.

The difference, as evaluated by chi-square, is significant (χ^2 = 3.33, with 1 df, p < .05, one-tailed). Here, too, inference training improved accuracy: More inference decoders than technical decoders were correct. Of the 5 incorrect judgments, 4 were due to faulty monitoring. These decoders simply failed to record the correct signals, leading them to make the wrong decision: deception. It is interesting to note that while most of the incorrect honest decoders made monitoring errors, the incorrect evasive and deceptive decoders made inferential errors. However, these are the exceptions. An overwhelming number of

TABLE 5.6   NUMBER OF CORRECT AND INCORRECT
JUDGMENTS BY CONDITION

	Correct	Incorrect	Total Decoders
The Deceiver			
Audio	7	11	18
Inference	14	4	18
The Evader			
Audio	10	9	19
Inference	16	3	19
The Honest Portrayal			
Audio	11	8	19
Inference	14	5	19

inference decoders made the correct judgment in response to each of the portrayals.

AUDIO-ONLY VERSUS INFERENCE TRAINING

The audio-only sample (Workshop III) was compared to the inference-training treatment (Workshop III) on number of correct versus incorrect judgments and on perceptions of the extent to which each portrayal was seen as honest, evasive, or deceptive. Confidence ratings were also compared.

**Number of Correct Versus
Incorrect Judgments**

Three statistical comparisons were made. The audio-only condition was compared to the inference-training condition for each of the three portrayals. These are matched samples; each member of Workshop III was exposed to both conditions. Since the two samples are not independent, the differences are evaluated by the McNemar Test for the Significance of Changes, a nonparametric statistic for related samples. Moreover, since the expected frequencies are less than five, probabilities are also determined according to the binomial test (Siegel, 1956: 66-67).

The Deceiver. Of 18 audio-only decoders, 7 were correct.[6] The comparison between audio and inference conditions is depicted in Table 5.6.

The difference, as evaluated by the McNemar Test, corrected for continuity (Siegel, 1956: 64), is significant (χ^2 = 4, with 1 df, p < .025, one-tailed). The exact probability computed by the binomial test is .02. Clearly, the inference training made a difference: More correct and fewer incorrect judgments of honesty were made following inference training than for audio-only judgments.

The Evader. Of 19 audio-only decoders, 10 were correct. The comparison with the number correct and incorrect in the inference-training condition is shown in Table 5.6.

The difference, as evaluated by the McNemar Test, corrected for continuity, is significant (χ^2 = 4.17, with 1 df, p < .025, one-tailed). The exact probability, computed by the binomial statistic, is .016. Once again, inference training made a difference: More correct and fewer incorrect judgments were made following inference training than for the audio-only judgments.

The Honest Portrayal. Of 19 audio-only decoders, 11 were correct. The comparison between audio-only and inference training is depicted in Table 5.6.

The difference, as evaluated by the McNemar Test, is not significant (χ^2 = 1.28, with 1 df, p > .10, one-tailed). The probability level is not decreased by the binomial test (p = .227). While the difference is in the predicted direction, it does not approach significance. It is nevertheless interesting to note that a comparison of judgments of "degree of honesty" does approach significance. The exact probability, computed by the sign test for related samples, is .09. Inference-training decoders judged the honest enactment as *relatively honest* more than did the audio-only decoders. Thus, inference training did improve judgments of "degree" but not of "kind." The issue of discrimination among portrayals by degree is now pursued further.

Perceptions of Degree
of Each Portrayal

Workshop III decoders were also asked to "indicate the degree to which each of the representation styles was present in

TABLE 5.7   SUMMARY OF RESULTS ON PERCEIVED
             INTENTIONS: AUDIO-ONLY

Actual	Honest	Perceived Evasive	Deceptive	χ_r^2 (Friedman statistic)
Honest		=	=	3.53 (NS)
Evasive	>		=	20.44 (p<.001)
Deceptive	=	=		1.44 (ns)

NOTE: See note to Table 5.3. for interpretation of symbols.

[each] film." As noted above, this question provided a measure of the extent to which the correct and alternative portrayals were perceived in each enactment. It makes feasible an analysis of the extent to which the actual portrayal is distinguished from each of the other possibilities. Differences between ratings for each actual portrayal by perceived style were evaluated by the Friedman Analysis of Variance by Ranks (Siegel, 1956). Results are depicted in the form of matrices for each condition, audio-only and inference training.

Audio-Only. The evasive portrayal was perceived as more evasive than honest but not distinguished significantly from deception; the honest portrayal was not seen as more honest than either evasive or deceptive; and the deceiver was not seen as more deceptive than evasive or honest. These findings are summarized in Table 5.7.

Decoders were able only to distinguish evasion from honesty when they had access to the verbal channel. None of the other paired comparisons (honest versus evasive, deceptive versus honest, and so on) approached significance by the Wilcoxon matched-pairs signed ranks test. Better discrimination was obtained for the global-lecture condition (two paired comparisons were significant) and for the technical-briefing condition (four comparisons were either significant or approached significance). The comparisons suggest that access to nonverbal channels per se aids the decoder. More than this, access with inference training improves discrimination considerably, as will be shown next.

TABLE 5.8   SUMMARY OF RESULTS ON PERCEIVED
INTENTIONS: INFERENCE TRAINING

Actual		Perceived		
	Honest	Evasive	Deceptive	χ_r^2 (Friedman statistic)
Honest		>	>	9.89 (p<.01)
Evasive	>		>	30.56 (p<.001)
Deceptive	>	>		16.40 (p<.001)

NOTE: See note to Table 5.3.

Inference Training. All comparisons were significant: The honest portrayal was perceived as more honest than either evasive or deceptive; the evasive portrayal was seen as more evasive than honest or deceptive; and the deceptive portrayal was perceived as more deceptive than either honest or evasive. These findings are depicted in Table 5.8.

Decoders were able to distinguish the actual from both alternatives in each case. For each enactment, one paired comparison was stronger than the other, although both were significant: For the honest portrayal, the larger difference was between degree of judged honesty and evasion, the difference between honest and deceptive also being significant by the Wilcoxon matched-pairs test ($z = 1.65$, $p = .0495$)[7] ; for the evasive portrayal, the larger difference was between evasive and honest, the difference between evasive and deceptive also being significant by the Wilcoxon test ($z = 1.76$, $p = .0392$); and for the deceptive portrayal, deception was distinguished from honesty and evasion, the latter approaching significance ($z = 1.63$, $p = .0516$). These are impressive findings. Inference training improved discrimination over all previous conditions, enabling decoders to distinguish successfully between the scripted intention and the alternatives for each presentation.

Confidence Ratings

The difference between correct and incorrect judgments is not reflected in the confidence ratings. There were no differences between the mean confidences assigned a correct or incorrect judgment for either the inference-training condition or the audio-only condition. As much confidence was shown by audio ratings as by inference-condition ratings. Moreover, degree of confidence was not related to extent to which decoders judged the actual style in the film. Spearman rank correlations were computed for each portrayal within the two conditions. The inference-condition coefficients were .29 (honest), -.32 (evasive), and .20 (deceptive). The audio-only-condition coefficients were .38 (honest), -.33 (evasive), and -.04 (deceptive). Only three of these coefficients approached significance, two of them being in the opposite direction. These results indicate only weak relationships between accuracy and confidence, suggesting either overconfidence in incorrect judgments or underconfidence in correct decisions.

Interestingly, however, inference-training decoders were more confident in their judgments, whether right or wrong, than were the technical-briefing decoders of Workshop II. For judgments of kind (H, E, or D), decoders of the honest portrayal showed more confidence following inference training ($\overline{X}$ = 2.00) than after the technical briefing ($\overline{X}$ = 2.44, t = 1.43, p < .10, one-tailed); decoders of the evasive portrayal were more confident following inference training ($\overline{X}$ = 1.68) than after the technical briefing ($\overline{X}$ = 2.11, t = 2.34, p < .025, one-tailed), and for the deceptive portrayal, inference-training decoders showed more confidence ($\overline{X}$ = 1.84) than those whose judgments followed a technical briefing ($\overline{X}$ = 2.72, t = 1.48, p < .10, one-tailed). Confidence ratings of judgments of degree (amount of honesty, evasion, deception) showed the same pattern: For honesty, inference $\overline{X}$ = 2.11, technical $\overline{X}$ = 2.67, t = 2.54, p < .01, one-tailed; for evasion, inference $\overline{X}$ = 1.89, technical $\overline{X}$ = 2.28, t = 1.47, p < .10, one-tailed; and for deception, inference $\overline{X}$ = 1.89, technical $\overline{X}$ = 2.56, t = 3.19, p < .001, one-tailed. Thus, inference-trained decoders were both more accurate *and* more confident in their judgments than were the decoders exposed to a technical briefing.

Discussion

The analyses computed above suggest the following conclusions:

(1) Reliance on verbal cues results in inaccurate judgments: Judgments based on audio-only were no more accurate than those based on audiovisual presentations without prior training or briefing.

(2) A technical briefing results in some improvement in judgmental accuracy: Separating signals from noise per se improves judgments over a condition where such separation is not made explicit.

(3) Inference training improves judgmental accuracy: Augmenting the ability to distinguish between signals (relevant cues) and noise (irrelevant cues) with a strategy for processing the signals clearly improves judgments.

(4) More confidence in judgments, whether right or wrong, was expressed following inference training than after a technical briefing.

Each of these findings is discussed briefly.

Access to the verbal channel only resulted in, at best, about 50 percent correct judgments. Actually, the categorical judgments (H, E, or D) suggest better accuracy than was in fact the case. A less optimistic picture is presented by the analysis of "degree of style": Decoders were able only to discriminate evasion from honesty. Apparently, barely detectable differences of degree, that is, one step on the four-step scales, led to correct categorizations. Even though the discrimination was not significant, it was just enough, in some cases, to lead to a correct classification. These results should dispel suspicions that the verbal message provided useful clues for detecting deception. Judgments were not better than nonverbal access per se (the global-lecture condition). Nonverbal signals improved discrimination, however, when decoders were made aware of the signals (the technical-briefing condition).

A technical briefing improved accuracy over that obtained following a global lecture. Better discrimination among the alternatives for the evasive and deception portrayals was also obtained for technical as compared to audio. The improvement seems due to the essential dimension of difference among the conditions, namely, awareness of the distinction between signals and noise. However, even here the best result achieved was 67 percent correct judgments (evasive portrayal). Further improvement was hypothesized to result from adding an inference strategy. Correct monitoring was not enough; a processing strategy would be necessary. Indeed, this was the case.

The evidence presented above clearly supports the hypothesis that inference training makes a difference. Even where there was limited room for improvement, as in judgments of evasion, significant improvement occurred (67 to 84 percent correct). Strong effects on judgments of kind and degree underscore the contention, made in the social judgment literature, that processing aids are essential. Emphasized in this literature are shortcomings of social judgment. Less clear are the detailed procedures needed to aid decoders. Application of strategies is determined by "appropriateness" (Nisbett and Ross, 1980: 42). The strategy adopted here was tailored to a problem in which five (nonverbal) cues appeared in different combinations for each of three portrayals. It consisted of a series of sequential decisions along tracks that proceeded from tentative to final decisions (see Figure 5.1). Such a process of elimination worked: Only 14 percent of all judgments made seemed to be characterized by faulty inferences; other incorrect judgments were due to faulty monitoring. While the benefits of inference training must be balanced against cost considerations, it is worth noting that its use "can pay enormous dividends when recurrent, conceptually identical problems are modelled formally" (Nisbett and Ross, 1980: 278; see also Slovic, 1976).

Whether the same strategy is appropriate for tasks with *different* features remains to be determined. A next step will entail applying the strategy to other presentations. One possibility is enactments that use more combinations of scripted cues (for example, seven nonverbal cues) and more role portrayals (such as an additional "evasive but honest" condition, as described in Chapter 4). This problem will consist of more tracks and tentative decisions than shown in Figure 5.1. It can be compared to a technical briefing. Of interest is whether the differences in judgment accuracy between these conditions (inference versus technical) are comparable to the differences reported above. Another possibility is to use real-time interview material. The problem might consist of an attempt to distinguish between high- and low-stress periods. Having isolated the discriminating NVBs, the investigator can prepare an inference-training regimen for processing those cues. Once again, to assure comparability with the scripted-portrayal experiments, this procedure should be compared to a technical briefing. Moreover, a control condition should be designed: Another group can make judgments of stress on the basis of a visual-only presentation.

Finally, a comment on the confidence results is in order. These results suggest that confidence ratings were related more to training condition than to accuracy: Inference-training decoders were more confident in their judgments than were technical-briefing decoders, and few correlations between confidence and judgments approached significance. Only the technical-briefing decoders of the deception portrayal showed significant covariation between judgments of deception and confidence (r_s = .53). Condition or prior experience is a more important determinant of accuracy than subjective confidence. Supporting the literature on overconfidence (see Fischhoff et al., 1977), this finding indicates that stated confidence is not a good predictor of judgmental accuracy.[8]

NOTES

1. We are dealing here with issues of perception and inference. The goal is to improve judgments in situations where decisions must be made without the benefit of mechanical calculation aids. The availability of such devices would enable an analyst to use the classification equations derived from analyses reported in the previous chapter. Whether observers can compute an algorithm without such devices is an unresolved issue. It seems appropriate to assume that in many situations such calculation is simply not feasible.

2. Inquiries with respect to use of the videotapes for research purposes should be addressed to the senior author (DD).

3. This strategy was determined by design considerations. The global versus technical and technical versus inference comparisons are based on independent

samples and proceed from the most general (global) to the most detailed (inference) treatments. The audio-only versus inference evaluation is a comparison of treatments administered on the same sample, necessitating the use of matched-sample statistics described below.

4. Differences in salient cue usage were not found for correct versus incorrect judgments of the evasive and honesty portrayals.

5. Note also that differences between the conditions on judgments of *degree* of deceptive representation are stronger (10 of 18 judges rated deception "high") than judgments of *kind* (7 of 18 were correct; see analysis above).

6. One decoder was not included in this comparison; he arrived late for the first audiotape which, in his room, was the deceiver.

7. For large samples, significance is evaluated in terms of the exact probability associated with the value of a computed z statistic. Siegel (1956) showed that z is an excellent approximation to the p value obtained by computation of the sum of the ranked differences for the Wilcoxon test.

8. Prediction can be construed in terms of multiple regression where training condition and subjective confidence are the predictors and perceived intention is the criterion. Most of the variance would be expected to be accounted for by training condition. Nonsignificant coefficients and partial correlations would be expected to be obtained for confidence.

6

MODELS OF PERCEIVED HONESTY,
EVASION, AND DECEPTION

Improving detection accuracy is one part of the problem of decoding. Another part consists of accounting for *variation* in perceptions. The former was addressed in experiments on the conditions for effective decoding: Significant gains were shown for inference training as compared to a technical briefing and to a global lecture on nonverbal communication (Chapter 5). The latter is addressed by a modeling exercise designed to identify the factors that covary with decoder judgments.

A goal of decoder training is to reduce variation in judgments. This is done by providing decoders with an information-processing model. That such a procedure is successful is attested to by the results of inference training: 84 percent correct classifications for evasion; 74 percent for deception and honesty. However, it must be noted that the adequacy of a model depends, in part, on the nature of the stimulus materials. For scripted displays the critical parameters or sources of variation are known. For displays shown *in situ,* the critical variables are less evident, making difficult the task of devising a model. Without a processing model it is likely that judgments will vary considerably, as was shown to be the case in the global and technical conditions. Such variation provides an opportunity to learn about how observers select and process information presented during deceit, evasion, or honesty.

How observers discount some factors and weight others preferentially is an empirical issue of some importance. By noting what is being attended to, the analyst can determine the relative importance of global impressions and specific behaviors.

By noting the perceptions elicited by different displays, the impression manager can orchestrate his or her presentations for planned effects. Both purposes are aided by a robust model that can predict judgments in a variety of situations. The aim of this exercise is to construct such a model: It is to be a model that both accounts for substantial portions of the variation in judgments and yields rather precise estimates of relative importance of the isolated factors or components.

Our approach to model construction consists of correlating decoders' ratings of degree of deceptiveness, honesty, or evasion with a number of cues, disregarding the actual truthfulness or deceptiveness of the message. Types of cues include attributed feelings, observed NVBs, and global impressions. Each variable was measured on a scale ranging from, for example, "very stressful" to "very relaxed," or, in the case of the NVBs, "seldom occurring" to "often occurring." While observers were not told to form impressions before judging intentions, they were asked to record impressions in the context of "what accounted for the judgment." Judgments of intentions are regarded as one factor in a cluster of perceptions; the model serves to define the specific perceptions that covary. An example of this type of analysis is the correlational exercise performed for the experiment reported in Chapter 4.

Only a few previous studies have taken this approach. Most notable are the studies by Krauss and his associates (1976) and by Kraut (1978). These investigators found that impressions of nervousness and discrepancy varied directly with attributed deceit, while perceptions of the speaker as serious and empathic varied inversely with suspicions of deception. Other variables include especially long or short response latencies, and such observed NVBs as self-adaptors, postural shifts, hand gestures, smiling, and responses that appear vague, implausible, and lacking in detail. Some of these cues did, in fact, distinguish deceptive from nondeceptive responses, but most other cues that were correlated with observer judgments of deception bore little or no relationship to the actual deceptiveness of the messages (see also DePaulo et al., 1980).

These results provide clues about relevant variables. Most were included in this study. Although, as Kraut (1978) observed, it is unlikely that any behavior is invariably perceived as a signal to deception, some are likely to emerge in the context of our investigation. This study provides an opportunity to evaluate previous results. It also enables us to contribute new results relevant to the diplomatic context: Considerably more variables were assessed than in the earlier studies. Moreover, by treating the variables as components of a model, a first attempt is made to ascertain the best linear combination and to evaluate relative importance of different types of clues.

Here, as elsewhere in the research program, the importance of context as a determinant of inferred motives or intentions is emphasized. Specific attributed feelings and impressions are likely to vary with changes in setting and type of lies (such as stealing objects versus policy dissimulation; see DePaulo and Rosenthal, 1979). This argument does not however diminish the importance of impressions. Indeed, decoder impressions are construed as variables that intervene between observed displays and inferred intentions (Figure 1.1, Chapter 1). Reacting to observed verbal and nonverbal behavior, decoders attribute psychological states to the actor. These attributions are posited as a basis for observer's judgments of the actor's intentions. But they may be misleading. Impressions may not derive from critical clues or lead to the correct inference about intentions. Such implications are addressed in the analyses reported below. An assessment is made of the relative contribution of critical nonverbal clues (signals) and global impressions to the inference process.

The analyses are diagnostic. They are intended to provide answers to questions such as whether decoders rely more on their impressions or on specific behaviors as bases for judgments. This question is not a hypothesis: The literature is merely suggestive, providing some leads but no theory. Rather, *the results* can be treated as hypotheses to be tested by experiments where specific impressions are made orthogonal to specific NVBs. In this way causal relations among impressions, behaviors, and inferences can be established.

Procedures

Recall that decoders rated each of three portrayals (honest, evasive, deceptive) on a number of scales. They were asked first to record their judgments of kind (honest, evasive, or deceptive), degree (extent of honesty and so on), and confidence in these ratings. Second, they rated the actor in terms of how they thought "he actually felt while performing the role" (attributed feelings). Third, they were to indicate how often each of 21 nonverbal behaviors occurred. Finally, they rated the actor on a set of scales that represented a variety of impressions that he seemed to convey. The data were obtained from participants in the Workshop I and Workshop II sessions of cross-cultural communications classes held at Hurlburt Field. Forty-one decoders reacted to each of the three scripted portrayals.[1]

The analysis was designed to account for *variation* in perceptions of intentions. Such a focus entails examining those judgment ratings where a certain amount of variation is observed. For example, a scripted portrayal that yields many correct judgments presents little variation to be accounted for, as was the case for inference-training decoders (Workshop III) or, to a lesser extent, for reactions to the evasive portrayal following a technical briefing (Workshop II). Reactions of global and technical decoders to the honest and deceptive portrayals showed considerable variation for each of the "degree of intention" scales. Particularly scattered were judgments of honesty and deception in response to the honest portrayal, and judgments of evasion in response to the deception portrayal. For this reason, these particular scales were used as criterion variables in the analysis.

It is important to note the distinction between responses elicited by *different* portrayals and different responses elicited by the *same* portrayal. The former, which has implications for impression management, is an attempt to relate aspects of a presentation to perceptions. This issue is addressed in Chapter 7. The latter, which pertains to determinants of variation in judgments, seeks to ascertain the factors that seem to lead to a response of "honest" rather than "deceptive." This issue is addressed here.

The predictors are those impressions, attributions, and observed NVBs that account for variation in judgments. Conceptual and empirical criteria were used to winnow the "chaff" from the "grain." First, the scales were divided into types of attributions (stress or confidence), impressions (liking, respect, trust, or potency), and nonverbal behaviors (scripted versus nonscripted). Second, correlations were computed among the predictor and the criterion scales. Highly intercorrelated variables within a category were either combined to form a composite scale or only one was used to represent the common underlying dimension (see Kim and Kohout, 1975: 341). Third, the reduced set of variables were correlated. The reduced matrix was examined for high correlations between predictor scales (such as relaxed-tense) and the criterion scale (degree of honesty); also examined were correlations among the predictors. Surviving variables were those that correlated with the criterion, were representative of a dimension, and were not highly correlated with predictors that represented other dimensions. This procedure was repeated for each of the three criterion variables.

The predictors were used in multiple regression analyses. Three analyses were computed, one for judged honesty, another for judged evasion, and a third for judged deception. While not causal in a narrow sense, the models do highlight the set of relevant perceptions that covary with judgments of intentions. Information provided includes overall predictability of the linear combination (multiple R^2) and the relative importance of different predictors (coefficients, partial correlations, and order of steps). Direct and stepwise regressions were computed. The direct procedure was developed by Wiens (1979) as part of the Mathtech ECON package. Particularly relevant and unique is a procedure that tests for multicollinearity among the explanatory variables; results of this test have implications for the reliability of the partial regression coefficients. The stepwise procedure was computed by the SPSS multiple regression subprogram (Kim and Kohout, 1975). We turn now to the results obtained by these procedures.

Results

The results are presented for each scale (perceived honesty, evasion, deception) separately. First, the isolated predictors are listed by the order in which they emerged from the stepwise program. Second, the regression statistics are presented; these include the coefficients, t statistics, partial correlations with the dependent variables, and the multiple R^2. Third, the pattern of interdependence among the predictors is depicted in terms of a matrix of partial Rs, multiple R^2s, and partial t statistics. Finally, the resulting prediction equation is shown as a model of perceived honesty, evasion, or deception.[2]

PERCEIVED HONESTY

The correlational analysis identified four predictor variables. These were entered into a stepwise regression program. The first variable to emerge is referred to as a global qualities index. It consists of the sum of the ratings on certain versus apprehensive and reliable (dependable) versus unreliable (undependable). This variable accounted for 58 percent of the variance in perceived honesty. A significant increment in variance explained was produced by the second variable, ratings of sense of humor. Adding this variable to the global qualities index resulted in 65 percent of the variance accounted for. The third variable, ratings of aggressiveness, produced a nonsignificant increment in variance explained, increasing the amount of explained variance by 2 percent. The fourth variable, an NVB index consisting of the sum of ratings of looking away from the camera and object-fidgeting, incremented variance explained by less than 1 percent.

The regression statistics are presented in Table 6.1. Significant coefficients and partial Rs were obtained for the global qualities index and for perceived sense of humor. Perceived aggressiveness produced a borderline-significant coefficient and a relatively low partial R with the dependent variable. A test of the hypothesis that all coefficients are zero produced a highly significant F ratio (F = 18.53, 4 and 36 df, p < .001), indicat-

TABLE 6.1 REGRESSION STATISTICS FOR PERCEIVED HONESTY

Variable	Coefficient	Standard Deviation	t Statistic	Partial R
Global qualities index	.19	.04	4.94*	.64
Perceived sense of humor	− .22	.08	2.77*	.42
Perceived aggressiveness	− .11	.08	1.33	.22
NVB index	.03	.06	.48	.08
Intercept	1.89	.56	3.41*	

* significant below .05 level

TABLE 6.2 PATTERN OF INTERDEPENDENCE AMONG PREDICTORS: PERCEIVED HONESTY

	Global Qualities	Sense of Humor	Aggressiveness	NVB Index
Global qualities index	.31[a]	− .27[b]	− .26	.30
Perceived sense of humor	− 1.72[c]	.15	.10	− .23
Perceived aggressiveness	− 1.64	.61	.22	− .23
NVB index	1.91	− .33	− 1.64	.23

a. Amount of variance accounted for by predictor on all others (numbers on diagonal).
b. Partial correlation between respective variables (numbers above diagonal).
c. t statistics associated with the partial correlation between these variables (numbers below diagonal).

ing that this hypothesis should be rejected. Together, the predictor variables explained 67 percent of the variance in perceptions of honesty.

The pattern of interdependence among the predictors is shown in Table 6.2. The R^2 of the regression of each predictor variable on all the others is shown on the diagonal; the partial correlations between the variables in the regression are shown above the diagonal, and the t tests of the partial correlations are shown below the diagonal. It will be noted that all of the coefficients are small, the largest being the multiple R^2 for the global qualities index (.31). A chi-square test of the hypothesis that the correlation matrix lacks any collinearity was performed and rejected ($\chi^2 = 7.42$, 6 df, n.s.). We conclude, on the basis of this evidence, that the coefficients are reliable estimates of relative importance.

The model of perceived honesty takes the form of the following prediction equation:

$$P_h = 1.89 + .19 \text{ (global qualities index)} + (-.22) \text{ (perceived}$$
$$\text{sense of humor)} + (-.11) \text{ (perceived aggressiveness)}$$
$$+ .03 \text{ (NVB index)}$$

where P_h is the extent to which an actor is perceived as honest, and the components are ratings made on the respective scales. The last component, NVB index, can be dropped from the equation, adding very little to the explained variance in perceived honesty. An implication of these results is that actors who are perceived as more certain and reliable, who have a good sense of humor, and who appear nonaggressive are likely to be regarded as honest. Moreover, this judgment does not seem to depend on specific perceived NVBs.

PERCEIVED DECEPTION

Three predictor variables were identified by the correlational analysis. The first variable to emerge from the stepwise regression was the global qualities index. Defined as the combination of the certain versus apprehensive and reliable versus unreliable scales, this variable accounted for 43 percent of the explained variance in perceived deception. A significant increment in variance explained was produced by the second variable, the NVB index (looking away from camera + object-fidgeting). Of the explained variance, 49 percent was accounted for by the two variables. A third variable, sense-of-humor ratings, increased the explained variance to 53 percent. (The multiple R for this set of variables is .73.)

The regression statistics are shown in Table 6.3. Significant coefficients and partial Rs were obtained for the global qualities index and for the NVB index. Perceived sense of humor pro-

TABLE 6.3   REGRESSION STATISTICS FOR PERCEIVED
DECEPTION

Variable	Coefficient	Standard Deviation	t Statistic	Partial R
Global qualities index	−.16	.04	3.40*	.49
NVB index	−.18	.08	2.14*	.33
Perceived sense of humor	.17	.11	1.62	.26
Intercept	3.38	.56	6.06*	

* significant below .05 level

TABLE 6.4   PATTERN OF INTERDEPENDENCE AMONG
PREDICTORS: PERCEIVED DECEPTION

	Global Qualities	NVB Index	Sense of Humor
Global qualities index	.26[a]	.38[b]	−.31
NVB index	2.54[c]	.19	−.08
Perceived sense of humor	−2.01	−.50	.14

a. Amount of variance accounted for by predictor on all others (numbers on diagonal).
b. Partial correlation between respective variables (numbers above diagonal).
c. t statistics associated with the partial correlation between these variables (numbers below diagonal).

duced a borderline-significant coefficient and partial correlation. A test of the hypothesis that all coefficients are zero resulted in a highly significant F ratio (F = 13.14, 3 and 37 df, p < .001), indicating that this hypothesis should be rejected.

The pattern of interdependence among the predictors is shown in Table 6.4. Although two of the three t ratios are significant (below the diagonal), none of the partial Rs (.38, −.31, and −.08) are strong enough to cause any concern. Moreover, the highest percentage of variance accounted for by any predictor on all the others (on the diagonal) is only 26 percent. The amount of collinearity contained in the matrix is negligible. Once again, we conclude that the coefficients can be regarded as reliable estimates of relative importance.

The model of perceived deception takes the form of the following prediction equation:

$$P_d = 3.38 + (-.16) \text{ (global qualities index)} + (-.18) \text{ (NVB index)}$$
$$+ .17 \text{ (perceived sense of humor)}$$

where P_d is the extent to which an actor is perceived as dishonest, and the components are ratings on the respective scales. It is interesting to note similarities and dissimilarities to the equation for honesty. The same components are scored in an opposite direction: Actors who appear more apprehensive and undependable, often look away from the camera and fidget with objects, and have a relatively poor sense of humor are likely to be perceived as deceitful. This outcome is not surprising, since the perceived honesty and perceived deception scales are correlated ($r = -.65$). More interesting is the difference in importance of the NVB index. A significant coefficient and partial correlation for deception contrasts with nonsignificant results obtained for honesty. This difference is discussed below.

PERCEIVED EVASION

Three predictors were identified by the correlational analysis. An NVB index was the first variable out of the stepwise regression. This index consisted of three behaviors: looking away from the camera, fidgeting with objects, and speech hesitations. Of the explained variance in perceived evasion, 34 percent was accounted for by this variable. A very strong increment in variance explained was shown for the second variable, a global qualities index. This index consisted of two scales, certain versus apprehensive and relaxed versus tense. Together with the NVB index, this variable accounted for 51 percent of the explained variance. The third variable to emerge in the regression was perceived aggressiveness. A significant increment in explained variance resulted from adding this variable. The additional 5 percent brought the total amount of explained variance to 56 percent. (The multiple R for this set of variables is .75.)

The regression statistics are shown in Table 6.5. Significant coefficients and partial Rs were obtained for each of the variables. As was the case for the analyses of honesty and deception, the hypothesis that all coefficients are zero was rejected (F

TABLE 6.5   REGRESSION STATISTICS FOR PERCEIVED
            EVASION

Variable	Coefficient	Standard Deviation	t Statistic	Partial R
NVB index	− .13	.04	3.64*	.51
Global qualities index	− .12	.03	4.07*	.56
Perceived aggressiveness	.15	.07	2.06*	.32
Intercept	3.38	.43	7.90*	

* significant below .05 level

TABLE 6.6   PATTERN OF INTERDEPENDENCE AMONG
            PREDICTORS: PERCEIVED EVASION

	NVB Index	Global Qualities	Perceived Aggressiveness
NVB index	.13[a]	.21[b]	− .32
Global qualities index	1.29[c]	.05	.12
Perceived aggressiveness	− 2.08	.73	.11

a. Amount of variance accounted for by predictor on all others (numbers on diagonal).
b. Partial correlation between respective variables (numbers above diagonal).
c. t statistics associated with the partial correlation between these variables (numbers below diagonal).

= 15.75, 3 and 37 df, p < .001). The pattern of inter-dependence among the predictors is shown in Table 6.6. Only one of the three partial correlations differs significantly from zero, and that is merely a correlation of .21. None of the multiple R^2s (on the diagonal) even approaches significance. This pattern does not depart from orthogonality as shown by a chi-square test (χ^2 = 3.22, 3 df, n.s.). We conclude that there is no multicollinearity and that the coefficients are reliable estimates of relative importance.

The model of perceived evasion resulting from the above analyses is as follows:

$$P_e = 3.38 + (-.13) \text{ (NVB index)} + (-.12) \text{ (global qualities index)} + .15 \text{ (perceived aggressiveness)}$$

where P_e is the extent to which the actor was seen as evasive, and the components are ratings on the respective scales. Similarities and dissimilarities to the other models are instructive. Like the deception model, the NVB index is a strong predictor and the direction of effects is the same: More looking away, object-fidgeting, and speech hesitations, more apprehension and tension, and more aggressive perceptions covaried with judgments of evasion. Like the honest model, perceived aggressiveness emerged as a predictor variable. However, some findings are unique to this model: The NVB index includes speech hesitations as well as looking away and object-fidgeting, and the global qualities index substitutes the relaxed-tense scale for reliable (dependable)-unreliable (undependable). Implications of these findings are now discussed.

Discussion

The results reported above suggest the following conclusions:

(1) Impressions are an important aspect of the judgment process. Certain impressions were found to account for a large amount of the variance in each of the three judgments of intentions.

(2) Specific nonverbal behaviors account for a large portion of the variation in judgments of deception and evasion but not honesty. Observations of certain NVBs are used in the process of determining the extent to which an actor is deceptive, as well as the extent to which he or she is evasive.

(3) Judgments of evasion are based on some variables not used in judgments of honesty and deception. Impressions of relaxed versus tense and observations of speech hesitations are used in the process of inferring the extent to which an actor is evasive.

(4) Some of the findings confirm results obtained in earlier studies; other findings are new, not reported previously. More firmly established findings are provided by the confirmatory results; findings that may be relevant to the context of this study are provided by the new results.

Each of these conclusions is discussed briefly.

When confronted with the same enactment, different decoders reported different impressions. They also recorded different judgments of the actor's intentions, and the two types of variables were highly correlated. Although not proven by the results, the relationship between the variables is likely to proceed *from* impressions *to* judgments of intentions. That such a sequence may be dysfunctional is shown in this situation. Rather than depending on known cues, many decoders followed their impressions; for example, if the actor appeared apprehensive, the decoder expected him to be dishonest.[3] This strategy was misleading (see the results on percentage correct judgments reported in Chapter 5). To overcome these "habits of thought," a training procedure was devised. Referred to as inference training, the procedure produced very little variation in judgments, with as many as 84 percent correct classifications of the evasive portrayal (Table 5.1, Chapter 5).

Global impressions were the predominant source of variation in judgments of perceived honesty (58 percent of the variance), and less so for judgments of deception (43 percent of the variance) and evasion (27 percent of the variance). The NVB index explained a significant amount of the variance for judgments of evasion (34 percent) and deception (26 percent), but was a negligible source of variation for judgments of honesty. The partial correlation between the NVB index and perceived honesty (.08) indicated that the simple correlation (.41) was spurious, accounted for by correlations between NVBs and the impression variables. This was not the case for deception and evasion, where partial correlations of .33 and .51 were statistically significant. These differences may have been the result of processes used to infer honesty that were different from those used to infer deception and evasion.

One reconstruction of decoder information-processing is based on response to *perceived* animation. Decoders' judgments of perceived honesty followed from impressions formed from responses to the general lack of animation in the honest portrayal. For some, the lack of animation conveyed the impressions of certainty and reliability; for others, the actor was viewed as apprehensive and unreliable. It was these global

impressions, rather than specific NVBs, that determined judgments. A different process led to judgments of deception and
evasion. Decoders used the information on specific NVBs along
with the general impressions evoked by the portrayals. They
responded to two signals, noticing the difference between frequent looking away (fidgeting) and infrequent looking away
(fidgeting); added to these NVBs was speech hesitation, a scripted cue in the portrayal used to develop the model of perceived
evasion. While using these cues correctly, decoders were also
guided by their impressions. Incorrect judgments were a result
of relying on impressions and cues that did not distinguish
deception from evasion but merely discriminated these intentions from honesty. This reconstruction is conjectural; a more
definitive interpretation awaits evidence from experiments
wherein the process is traced through time.

The coefficients for perceived evasion were more similar in
direction (apprehensive, frequent looking away) and size (relative weights for impressions and for NVBs) to those obtained
for deception than for honesty. This is not a surprise: Evasion
was defined essentially as indirect deception. Conceivably,
opposite results would be obtained for perceptions of a fourth
posture, evasive but honest, developed as another condition in
the nonverbal coding project (see Chapter 4). More interesting,
however, are the differences between evasion and deception.
Unlike the judgments of deception (and honesty), perceived
evasion covaried with impressions of relaxed versus tense and
with observations of speech hesitations. If, as we suspect, evasion is viewed as the most difficult of the three postures, it
follows that decoders are likely to attribute high levels of
tension and apprehension to the role. Impressions of reliability
(or dependability) may form a dimension that distinguishes
only between deceptive and honest actors. Response to speech
hesitations, seen to be characteristic of evaders, might also be
due to the perceived uncertainties of the assignment.

Some of the results are similar to those obtained in the earlier
studies by Krauss et al. (1976) and Kraut (1978). Those investigators found that perceived deception was associated with

responses that appear uncertain or vague, with an apparent lack of seriousness, with nervous fidgeting, and with impressions of "nervousness." Similarly, we have found that perceived deception covaries with impressions of apprehension, unreliability, object-fidgeting, and impressions of tension (for evaders).[4] These variables may be the attributes associated with deception in general, as it occurs in a variety of settings. Such repeated confirmation makes plausible the contention that this set of variables approaches the status of theory. Other variables found to be associated with deception are new findings: Deceivers were seen to look away from the camera often and appeared to have a poor sense of humor; evaders were seen as aggressive and exhibited frequent speech hesitations. These variables may be the attributes associated with the diplomatic context of this study or with the type of orchestration designed for the experiments. These variables should be regarded as hypotheses. With each isolated as a key predictor in the context of this study, further experimentation is in order.

Finally, a word on limitations and next steps. The results reported above are not to be taken as the last word on the issue of perceptions. We regard the exercise as largely heuristic. We are sensitive to possible limitations. For example, by using a paring procedure for isolating predictors, we may have, to an extent, capitalized on chance, arguments about "remarkability" notwithstanding (Saunders, 1970). Furthermore, if the decoders did not consider their ratings of impressions as "accounting for" judgments of perceived intentions, the prediction equations may simply be metaphors. Both these limitations are empirical issues: We can estimate the extent of shrinkage in predictability based on the equations (see Campbell, 1975), and we can assess the effects of a procedure in which ratings are made sequentially. The former evaluation entails applying the equations to new data sets.[5] The latter evaluation entails an experiment where impression data are collected before, and without knowledge of eventual, ratings of perceived intentions.[6] These tasks are proposed next steps. Meanwhile, a number of interesting results have been obtained from the analyses reported here. In the spirit of caution, we offer these results as hypotheses to be tested in other settings.

Implications from this analysis for the concept of impression management are only indirect. The analysis does not explore the relationship between actual displays and impressions. It was an attempt to explain variation of responses to the *same* portrayal: Different decoders responded differently to the same stimulus. Needed is an analysis that compares responses to the *different* portrayals. The results of such an analysis, which have more direct implications for impression management, are reported next.

NOTES

1. Each portrayal was a six-minute presentation of "Soviet positions" on two issues, troops in Europe and invasion of Afghanistan. The actor was scripted to perform a set of nonverbal behaviors that varied for the different portrayals (see Chapter 5 for descriptions).

2. Special thanks go to Robert Procelli for aid in data preparation, programming, and computations.

3. It should be noted, however, that impressions may be functional in other situations. Where reliable cues cannot be isolated, decoders are forced to rely on their general impressions. Not all impressions are necessarily misleading: Certain impressions can be linked to postures or display packages, leading to correct judgments of intentions. The research objective here is to separate valid from invalid impressions.

4. A step not taken in the previous studies was the development of predictive models. This study is a first attempt to provide estimated weights for each variable.

5. An opportunity to collect validation data was provided by Workshop III. However, the inference-training procedure largely precluded variation in judgments of intentions, and the audio-only condition precluded obtaining ratings of observed NVBs. Both are necessary aspects of the modeling exercise.

6. In addition, a nonscripted actor and untrained decoders would be desirable. These features would assure variation in judgments, making opportunistic selection of dependent variables unnecessary.

7

IMPACT OF PORTRAYALS
ON PERCEPTIONS

The work reported in Chapter 6 is a correlational analysis. Focusing on variation *within* the scripted displays, the analysis isolated covarying indicators of perceived intentions. The work reported in this chapter is an experimental analysis. Focusing on variation *between* the displays, the analysis isolates variables that discriminate among the actual portrayals. Systematic manipulation of the displays enables us to relate the discriminating variables (perceptions) to differences in the nonverbal behaviors. The results address the issue of impression management: Knowing the relationship between displays and perceptions renders an actor more effective in his attempts to manage impressions.

A number of studies have shown that impressions are conveyed through multiple nonverbal channels. The display package concept is emphasized in these studies: For example, forward trunk lean, frequent head nods, and more time spent looking contribute to judgments of empathy; sustained gazing at close distances combined with relaxed vocalizations convey credibility (see the section in Chapter 2 on multiple channels). Similarly, the recent study by Kraut (1978), reviewed in Chapter 6, showed that judgments of deceptiveness were inferred from such clues as "nervous" fidgeting and gesturing, implausible replies, and replies that were too long or too short, too quick or too slow. These are perceived cues. Like the findings obtained above, the cues bore little or no relationship to the actual degree of deceptiveness in the message, that is, the veridical cues. These findings suggest that impressions are misleading. Even so, they are important elements in the inference process. For this reason, among others, it is necessary to probe relationships between the impressions and *known frequencies* of NVBs. Such probes will make evident the sources of misleading inferences about intentions.

Procedures

The analysis is a comparison of the three actual portrayals in terms of elicited impressions. Each portrayal is a scripted display of selected NVBs. Differences between the displays were on seven behaviors: leg movements (evader), foot movements (evader), looking around the room (evader), speech hesitations (deceiver), fidgeting with objects (deceiver and evader), looking away from camera (deceiver and evader), and head-shaking (evader and honest). Attributed feelings, impressions, and observed behaviors were the same scales used for the modeling exercise of Chapter 6. Data were obtained from the 41 members of Workshops II and III. The difference, as noted above, is a between-portrayal analysis versus an analysis of perceptual variation within portrayals. Means were computed for each scale, and differences were analyzed by analysis of variance.

Discriminant analyses were also performed. These analyses were designed to isolate the best set of discriminating variables. Addressed here is the question whether a smaller set of impressions separate the experimental groups (three actual portrayals). First, however, the subset of scripted behaviors was entered into a discriminant analysis. The results of this procedure serve as a check on the manipulation. The scripted behaviors should discriminate among the portrayals as well as show differences between the means in a direction that coincides with the programmed NVB frequencies.

Results

Means, F ratios, and discriminant analysis results are shown for the scripted NVBs and for the impression variables. The analysis of the NVBs was designed as a check on the manipulated behaviors. The analysis of the impressions was designed to determine whether different perceptions were elicited by the different displays. Implications of the results follow.

SCRIPTED NONVERBAL BEHAVIORS

The means and F ratios for each scripted NVB are shown in Table 7.1. All of the F ratios are highly significant. The actor was seen to move his legs more often, look around the room more frequently, shake his head, and move his feet more often when he was being evasive than when he played a deceptive or an honest role. Fidgeting with glasses and speech hesitations distinguished the deceptive and evasive portrayals from the honest, while looking away from the camera somewhat more prevalent in the evasive than in the deceptive portrayal. It is also interesting to note that the top two variables to emerge from the discriminant analysis, leg movements and object-fidgeting, were also the top two in the analysis of the nonverbal coding experiment (Chapter 4). Not only were these the best discriminators of the different intentions; they were also responded to

TABLE 7.1 MEANS AND F RATIOS FOR THE SCRIPTED NONVERBAL BEHAVIORS

Behaviors[a]		Portrayal		Univariate F Ratio[b]
	Honest	Deceptive	Evasive	
Leg movements	.93	1.17	2.63	28.71
Fidgeting with glasses	1.22	2.54	2.51	21.25
Looking around at room	.85	1.42	2.39	14.96
Head-shaking	1.10	1.05	1.78	3.67
Speech hesitations	.81	1.71	1.83	7.75
Foot movements	1.00	1.27	2.71	26.16
Looking away from camera	1.27	2.07	2.78	15.66

NOTE: Listed in order of stepwise discrimination.

a. All behaviors were assessed on a scale ranging from "never" (0) to "often" (3).

b. All significant below .001 level, except head-shaking ($p < .03$).

as salient behaviors whose frequency of occurrence differed for the three enactments.

The group centroids and classification results obtained from a discriminant analysis of the scripted NVBs are shown in Table 7.2. The first function, accounting for 63 percent of the variance, separates the evasive portrayal from deceptive and honest. This reflects the pattern of seeing more leg and foot movements, more looking around the room and head-shaking for the evasive portrayal. Indeed, this is as it should be: The evader was scripted for this display. The second function, accounting for 37 percent of the variance, separates the three portrayals from one another. It reflects primarily the fact that the deceptive portrayal is clearly distinguished from the honest portrayal for most behaviors, especially looking away, fidgeting, leg movements, hesitations, and looking around. This too is essentially correct: Only leg movements were the same for the deceptive and honest portrayals. Seventy-six percent of the cases were classified correctly on the basis of the coefficients derived from the functions (see Table 7.2, part b). We conclude, on the basis

TABLE 7.2   GROUP CENTROIDS AND CLASSIFICATION RESULTS FOR BEHAVIORS

a. Centroids of Groups

Portrayal	Function I	Function II
Honesty	− .65	− .77
Deception	− .54	.82
Evasion	1.19	− .05

b. Classification Results

		Predicted Portrayal		
Actual Portrayal	No. of Cases	Honest	Evasive	Deceptive
Honest	41	33	5	3
Evasive	41	3	32	6
Deceptive	41	5	8	28

Percentage of known cases correctly classified: 76%

of these results, that the manipulation was effective; decoders noted the programmed differences in NVB frequencies.

IMPRESSIONS ELICITED BY PORTRAYALS

The means and F ratios are shown for the various impression scales, and for each of the perceived intention scales, in Table 7.3. Particularly compelling is the consistency of the mean differences: When the actor was evasive, he was seen as more anxious, uncertain, suspicious, confused, apprehensive, uncomfortable, unreliable, tactless, hostile, argumentative, uncooperative, and so on. He was also perceived as less honest, more deceptive, and more evasive in the evasive as compared to the deceptive and honest roles. Each of the F ratios is highly significant. Impressions of the deceptive portrayal are sometimes located between honest and evasive (especially, stressful, suspicious, confused, apprehensive) and at other times are more similar to the impressions elicited by the honest portrayal (note friendly, nonaggressive, compliant, considerate, and cooperative). While the actor-as-deceiver is seen as less honest, he is not perceived as much more deceptive or evasive than when he portrays honesty. These results indicate that the evasive portrayal conveyed impressions that distinguished it from the other enactments; the deceptive portrayal was not distinguished from the other enactments consistently across most scales.

A discriminant analysis was computed to determine the best subset of discriminating scales. All 22 scales were entered as variables.[1] Nine of these variables emerged from the stepwise procedures. Shown in Table 7.4, the order of variables in terms of discriminating power is as follows: argumentative, perceived honesty, uncooperative, perceived evasion, uncertain, hostile, tactless, suspicious, and anxious. These variables combine to convey the "image" of an actor who is not to be trusted and is generally disliked. Two functions were obtained. The first, accounting for 76 percent of the variance, separated impressions of the deceptive portrayal from the others, due probably to the variation in deceptive perceptions from one scale to another. Making the strongest contribution to this function, in

TABLE 7.3   MEANS AND F RATIOS FOR IMPRESSIONS AND
             PERCEIVED INTENTIONS

Scale	Portrayal			Univariate F Ratio[a]
	Honest	Deceptive	Evasive	
Stressful-relaxed[b]	4.83	3.90	3.07	12.17
Anxious-calm[b]	4.68	4.03	2.81	14.98
Pleasant-unpleasant[b]	3.22	3.67	4.37	6.97
Confident-uncertain[b]	2.52	3.20	3.78	8.00
Suspicious-trusting[b]	4.39	3.80	2.73	16.19
In Control-confused[b]	2.20	2.93	3.46	10.31
Certain-apprehensive[b]	2.85	3.63	4.46	11.56
Comfortable-uncomfortable[b]	3.07	3.66	4.56	9.60
Calm-irritable[b]	2.63	3.20	3.95	10.57
Angry-pleased[b]	4.83	4.39	3.83	8.87
Easy-difficult[c]	2.42	2.93	3.39	6.48
Reliable-unreliable[b]	3.33	3.74	5.29	17.75
Tactful-tactless[b]	2.54	2.92	3.90	10.71
Hostile-friendly[b]	4.48	4.21	3.44	6.37
Aggressive-nonaggressive[b]	3.53	3.68	2.98	3.19
Argumentative-compliant[b]	3.90	3.70	3.00	80.51
Considerate-conceited[b]	3.80	3.85	4.46	3.03
Uncooperative-cooperative[b]	4.28	4.28	3.05	11.32
Relaxed-tense[b]	3.08	3.77	4.88	13.63
Perceived Honesty[d]	1.98	2.45	3.35	26.40
Perceived Deception[d]	2.51	2.28	1.65	9.47
Perceived Evasion[d]	2.66	2.20	1.53	22.95

a. All significant below .01 level, except confident ($p<.045$) and considerate ($p<.052$).
b. Ranges from 1 (e.g., stressful) to 7 (e.g., relaxed).
c. Ranges from 1 (very easy) to 5 (very difficult).
d. Ranges from 1 (high) to 4 (not present at all).

terms of size of coefficient, is the impression of argumenta-
tiveness. The second function, accounting for 24 percent of the
variance, clearly separated evasion (group centroid = 1.00) from

TABLE 7.4 STANDARDIZED DISCRIMINANT FUNCTION
COEFFICIENTS FOR VARIABLES ON FUNCTIONS I
AND II

Variable	Function I	Function II
Argumentative	1.15	−.08
Perceived honesty	.05	.39
Uncooperative	−.43	.10
Perceived evasion	−.17	−.51
Uncertain	−.33	.06
Hostile	−.34	−.11
Tactless	.05	.31
Suspicious	.28	−.02
Anxious	−.22	−.11

NOTE: Variables listed in stepwise order.

TABLE 7.5 CLASSIFICATION RESULTS

		Predicted Portrayal		
Actual Portrayal	No. of Cases	Honest	Evasive	Deceptive
Honest	41	31	10	0
Evasive	40	3	35	2
Deceptive	40	2	2	36

Percentage of known cases correctly classified: 84%

deception (centroid = −.03) and honesty (centroid = −.94). The strongest contributing variables are the perceived intentions, honesty and evasion. Of the cases, 84 percent were classified correctly by the equations derived from these functions (Table 7.5). We conclude, on the basis of these results, that the portrayals had different impacts on decoder perceptions and that the impressions elicited by them were reflected also in judgments of intentions (perceived honesty, evasion).

Implications

The results reported here have implications for two processes. They help to explain the frequent misclassifications of intentions, thereby providing insight into the inference process. They suggest factors that elicit particular impressions, information that is relevant to the process of impression management. Each of these implications adds to the conclusions reached in Chapter 6. Each is discussed in turn.

The modeling results indicated that impressions are an important aspect of the judgment process (Chapter 6). These results indicate that different impressions were elicited by the actual portrayals, and these impressions often suggested *another* intention. The evader was perceived to be more like a deceiver. He was also viewed as unreliable, anxious, suspicious, hostile, argumentative, uncooperative, and so on. All of the incorrect judges (N = 19) misclassified the evader as a deceiver (see Chapter 5). The deceiver was rarely classified as deceptive (13 percent and 39 percent correct judgments for the global and technical conditions respectively; see Table 5.1, Chapter 5). More often, he was seen as either evasive (N = 15) or honest (N = 16). The near-equal number of misclassifications in the other two categories is reflected in the impressions data: The actual deceiver was sometimes perceived to be more similar to the actual evader, and at other times seen as more similar to the actual honest portrayal. Reinforcing the conclusion that impressions are important, these findings elucidate *the way in which* those impressions misled the decoders.

Both the scripted behaviors and the impressions successfully discriminated among the three portrayals. This means that decoders were responsive to the programmed differences[2] and that those displays elicited different impressions. It does not mean that we have established linkages between specific NVBs and specific impressions. The issue of whether the impressions were responses to the total display or to particular elements of that display remains to be resolved. Differences between particular NVBs (leg movements, looking around) and total amount of activity were confounded: We cannot tell whether the impressions elicited by the evasive portrayal were due to the particular combination of behaviors or due to animation per se. Moreover, it is possible that one or a few behaviors was particularly salient, accounting for the differences in impressions. These alternative interpretations are hypotheses to be explored in another experiment.

The alternative hypotheses can be arbitrated by results obtained from an experiment where selected combinations of cues are made orthogonal while controlling for total amount of animation. Three displays are to be compared: leg movements and looking around, leg movements and object-fidgeting, and looking around and object-fidgeting. A fourth display is created as a control: The actor would exhibit a high amount of activity while *not* moving his legs, looking around, or fidgeting with objects.[3] Further analytical specificity would be obtained by examining reactions to displays in which each cue would be manipulated separately. The results would benefit the impression manager. He would be alerted to the cues that convey deceptive intent. By controlling those cues (looking around, legs and fidgeting, total activity), he might avoid "looking deceitful."

This chapter concludes our report of analyses of data obtained from the workshops. In Chapter 5 we have demonstrated the effects of various training regimens on judgments of intentions. In Chapter 6 and here we have presented models to account for variation in perceptions of intentions and have determined the impact of the portrayals on a variety of impressions. Together, these efforts provide a basis for next steps. Included among these steps are assessing the effects of inference training on nonscripted (or differently scripted) displays, determining the generality of the perceptual models, and separating the effects on impressions of aspects of the scripted displays.

NOTES

1. The results from this analysis are regarded as more suggestive than definitive. The unfavorable ratio of cases (41) to variables (22) increases the chances of obtaining a significant discriminant function. However, our primary interest is the

order of the variables, not the amount of variance accounted for by the functions. Implications of the ratio between cases and variables for the stepwise order of the variables are not clear.

2. Analysis of selected NVBs not programmed to vary from one portrayal to another showed no differences in observed frequency of occurrence.

3. Another portrayal would consist of a display of all three behaviors. Here, however, care must be taken to separate the display of these salient NVBs from total amount of activity.

CONCLUSION

8

TOWARD AN ORGANIZING FRAMEWORK

The research reported in this volume, and elsewhere, has been influenced by the idea that behavior derives its meaning from the broader context in which it is displayed. This idea is the basis for the contention, made earlier, that "display rules" for nonverbal behaviors are likely to be different from one setting to another (see the opening to Chapter 4). The issue is not evaluated in this volume or elsewhere. An evaluation would entail systematic variation of context. Such variation has not been attempted here; the findings are relevant to one particular setting, namely, diplomatic interactions. Limited tests of the issue have, however, been made in other, related, environments (see Druckman et al., 1974). They can also be made with regard to nonverbal behavior.

Proper evaluation of context effects would consist of developing a series of experiments wherein context is varied and a large number of NVBs are assessed. The variables would derive from conceptual systems that enumerate types of NVBs and categorize types of contexts or situations. Relevant systems for classifying NVBs were reviewed in Chapter 1. These systems were developed to provide vocabularies for types of NVBs (Birdwhistell, 1970; Ekman and Friesen, 1969b), to describe characteristics of nonverbal channels (Dittmann, 1972), and to distinguish among functions served by different behaviors (Table 1.4, Chapter 1). Fewer taxonomies of situations exist. The basis for a taxonomy is provided by Goffman's analysis of expression games (see Chapters 1 and 4). He attempts to capture subtle aspects of situations with relevance to nonverbal displays. Emphasized by this analysis are structural dimensions of relationships. A more elaborate rendering of this theme is reviewed in this final chapter.

The need for a system that distinguishes among types of situations is recognized by each of the authors of this volume. Interest in developing such a system has been a primary concern of this volume's senior author (see Mahoney and Druckman, 1975). Aware of this concern, the other authors (RR and JB) suggested the potential relevance of a framework proposed by Jones and Thibaut (1958). This system is an attempt to depict alternative interaction structures, including the contingencies represented by diplomatic exchanges. For this reason, in particular, it seemed useful to introduce, or reintroduce, the reader to the concepts of this framework. Linkages between situation dimensions and nonverbal categories were not made by Jones and Thibaut. Nor have linkages been sought by other investigators, despite the fact that the Jones-Thibaut work preceded most of the nonverbal frameworks. Allusions to such linkages are made in this chapter, and the importance of developing hypotheses is promoted as a next step.

The Jones-Thibaut classification system is reviewed here by Rozelle and Baxter. It addresses complex interdependencies found in situations where nonverbal displays may be strategic (see Goffman, 1969). Regarded as a taxonomy of relationships, the system is divided into formal and substantive aspects. In discussing these aspects, the authors draw on examples from the diplomatic (Chapters 4, 5, and 6) and police-citizen (Chapter 3) settings referred to in earlier chapters.

The Formal System

The formal system involves three types of interaction: (1) noncontingent, (2) asymmetrically contingent, and (3) reciprocally contingent. The noncontingent form is actually a kind of nondirect interaction in that the actors only appear to be communicating with one another as a result of prescribed role behaviors. The behaviors involved are largely self-contained and independent. Examples of such interactions usually occur within formalized settings in which the actors play their assigned roles regardless of the content of the other participants' idiosyncratic speech or behaviors. Formal ceremonies at the signing of an international trade agreement or at academic graduation proceedings would be examples of this type of interaction. Many peace-keeping and crowd-control functions also fit this category.

The asymmetrically contingent form of interaction occurs when the behavior of one actor (the variable responder) is significantly (or fully) determined by the other actor (the standard responder), with the latter's behavior being determined by independent factors. The standard responder's behavior is largely controlled by a plan or script of interaction that not only specifies his course of action but also orients him to response possibilities on the part of the variable responder. The standard responder is usually in control of the *process*, whereas the variable responder most frequently determines the *outcome* of the interaction. An example familiar to police work would be the routine interview of a witness to an accident by the police officer. In this instance, the officer (standard responder) follows a predetermined set of instructions, controlling the process of the interview, with the witness responding appropriately to the question (in this case, the standard responder's "behavior"). Thus, the witness is the variable responder, his or her answers determining the outcome of the interaction. Of course, the outcome may be defined in several ways. Perhaps most relevant here would be the police officer's evaluation of the inter-viewee's credibility and accuracy.

This type of interaction is also characteristic of the *Meet the Press* format used in our series of experiments (Part II). The interviewer occupies the role of the standard responder with a predetermined outline of topics and questions that allows for control of the interview process. The interviewee is the variable responder, his or her answers determining the outcome of the interaction. Outcome may be defined in several ways and may be evaluated differently by the interview participants and observers. Outcome definitions are particularly complex in situations where the variable responder is in the role of a representative, since evaluations of such groups as constituencies, general audiences, and adversaries may be based on different and/or conflicting perspectives. These concerns are presented in elaborated form in the "boundary role conflict" literature (Adams, 1976; Druckman, 1977a), where attempts are made to describe the constraints, expectancies, and pressures linking representatives to groups. In *Meet the Press,* the interviewer is also under performance evaluation pressures to obtain salient and credible information. Such roles are highly competitive, and interviewer performance may be evaluated in terms of style and effectiveness as well as in terms of the performance of the variable responder.

A third type of interaction is described as reciprocally contingent. In this instance, neither actor (or subgroup of actors) is in complete control of process. Both are dependent on one another for information, interaction flow, and desired outcomes. This type of interaction is the most demanding on participants, since the assessment of behaviors (both self and other's) occurs simultaneously with continued appropriate execution of one's own behavior and its anticipated interpretation (on the part of the other) from one moment to the next. An example of this form in police work may be the questioning of a suspect who admits involvement, but where the desired outcome of the interaction is a clearer statement of guilt. In this situation, the behavior of the police officer is, in part, determined by successive responses of the suspect and vice versa.

The typical example in intergroup relations occurs in the area of bargaining and negotiations. In this situation, participants are dependent on each other for mutually desired outcomes. This type of interaction is sequential in form, offers and counteroffers are contingent on each other, and strategies of interaction change depending on their perceived effectiveness. Both parties are voluntarily engaged in an interaction in which commonalities and divergencies of interests and values are balanced in such a way that all involved judge that more is to be gained than lost by engaging in the relationship (Rubin and Brown, 1975; Druckman et al., 1977). This may be the most complex form of interaction from the perspective of nonverbal behavior, as it relates to impression formation and management. Each particpant must be skilled in decoding (interpretation) and encoding (presentation) procedures and be aware of the situational factors influencing both the other's and his or her own behavior. To date, research in nonverbal behavior has not addressed this type of interaction. Further complicating the situation are factors such as performance evaluation and boundary role conflict considerations. In international relations, cultural differences in nonverbal encoding and decoding practices are crucial determinants of effective communication (Watson and Graves, 1966; Collette, 1971; Garratt et al., 1981).

The three types of situations rarely occur in "pure" form. Most police-citizen interactions contain varying degrees of role-playing, controlling behavior, and mutually dependent behaviors. Perhaps the most prevalent combination occurring in the police officer's activities is that of the asymmetrically and reciprocally contingent interactions. Thus, while routinely questioning a witness to a crime, the variable responder's suspicious behavior during the process of the interview may cause the police officer (standard responder) to change the desired outcome from that of information-gathering to admission of guilt from the witness. When this outcome change occurs, the asymmetry of the interaction is reduced, since both participants begin monitoring each other's behavior to a greater extent, acting and reacting accordingly. It should be noted here that the complexity of the reciprocally contingent situation is amplified with the realization that the witness's desired outcome (information-giving) is different from the police officer's (admission of guilt), and the participant's perception of who is "in control" of the interaction (perception of asymmetry) may change depending on the content presented during the process.

In diplomatic transactions, roles of the interactants are perhaps not as clearly distinguished as in police-citizen interactions. For example, the interviewer in a *Meet the Press* format does not possess the power that an interviewer-police officer has, yet interviewer and interviewee often "debate" in the sense that an unexpected question or unanticipated answer can change the course of the interview and shift relative control over topics covered or arguments offered from one participant to the next.

As Jones and Thibaut indicate, the asymmetrically contingent interaction may also be transformed into a noncontingent interaction. This often occurs in political and diplomatic interviewing when the spokesperson for a particular point of view simply gives the "party line" in answering questions posed to him or her. In the police-citizen situation, the citizen may simply deny knowledge of any information requested by the officer or repeat the same limited information in response to a variety of questions. In such cases, no effective communication occurs.

The Substantive System

The substantive classification system proposed by Jones and Thibaut involves three types of outcomes which they label as "goals" of interaction: (1) facilitation of personal goal attainment, (2) the deterministic analysis of personality, and (3) the application of social sanctions. For each of these types of goals or desired outcomes, a process "set" is specified to promote better understanding of inferences made by the actors. According to Jones and Thibaut, the personal goal-attainment outcome is achieved by implementing a "value-maintenance" set, the deterministic analysis of personality outcome is best achieved by a "causal-genetic" set, and the application of social sanctions is most appropriately carried out by a "situation-matching" set.

When the value-maintenance set is used for personal goal attainment, four types of outcomes may be sought by the actor. One is a desire for clarifying information from others concerning important aspects of the environment. Although physical aspects of the environment are included, this orientation emphasizes social factors that tend to be more dependent on a perceived consensus from others, or on one's evaluation of information on the basis of the perceived credibility of the source. Examples of social aspects of the shared environment would be the perception of cues that aid in assessing personal characteristics such as how others attribute to the actor qualities of reliability, honesty, and expertise. This process may be thought of as "mediating external reality" about oneself and the shared environment.

A second outcome effected by the value-maintenance set involves attempts to seek "motivational and value support." This deals with a search for consensual validation of the actor's beliefs, attitudes, and values as they pertain to his or her behavior. Third, an outcome often pursued in this area is that of obtaining a favorable evaluation from others, regardless of any other information received or the maintenance of validation of the actor's values or beliefs. This situation is typified by the actor engaging in behavior he or she predicts will evoke supporting behaviors on the part of other people. In a sense, the actor is "manipulating" the others' actions.

A final outcome of the value-maintenance set is that of accomplishing some purposes that are "external to the interaction itself." Jones and Thibaut distinguish between two cases of this goal, both of which involve the actor's dependence on others for the attainment of the outcome. The first case specifies that others have control over the desired outcome to such an extent that they determine whether or not the actor achieves the goal. An example of this would be the officer's dependence on informers to make appropriate arrests. It should be noted that in this example, control shifts between officer and informant, depending on who is the actor, that is, the more dependent participant. This mutual exchange of control is an example of a shifting, asymmetrically contingent interaction.

In an interview such as *Meet the Press,* the interviewer depends on the foreign diplomat to respond in such a way that the interview is favorably evaluated by the audience. In addition, the diplomat-as-representative is somewhat dependent on the interviewer's questioning strategy; that strategy may not allow for a credible presentation, resulting in a desired evaluation by his constituency. Another possible outcome involves a goal that can only be obtained through the active cooperation of the participants in the interview. In this case, each participant is sensitive to the other's attributes (credibility, motivation, skill), which are seen as being instrumental to achieving a desired outcome.

In the present context, personal goal attainment through the use of a value-maintenance set would seem to focus primarily on the participant who is most dependent on the outcome of the interaction as this is facilitated by his or her self-presentation tactics. Thus, whether or not an ambassador is successful in being deceptive, evasive, or honest may depend on the proper execution of nonverbal and verbal behaviors during an interview. The same concern would be true for a citizen-suspect being interviewed by a police officer. Different cues may be associated with the various outcome goals and could aid in the attainment of successful impression *management* or in increased accuracy of impression *formation*.

The use of a causal-genetic set involves the determination of perceived behavioral causation in others. This type of set and its goal of accuracy is perhaps most relevant to the observer's, audience's, or interviewer's accurate detection of the evasive, deceptive, or honest self-presentations of the foreign ambassador in *Meet the Press* (Chapter 4). Likewise, the police officer is concerned with this set in attempting to decide the probable guilt of a suspect during an interview, based on the suspect's verbal and nonverbal behaviors. The actor attempts an evaluation on the basis of "accurate" information received from the other participant and/or others not directly involved in the interaction. Unlike the value-maintenance set, the actor's causal-genetic evaluation of the other does not necessarily involve consequences of the other's behavior that directly affect the actor himself. A general goal of the causal-genetic perceptual set is to identify behavioral acts that are intentionally determined and to distinguish between "true" and misleading intentions on the part of others. The extent to which an act (expression) is automatic or purposeful may be an important factor influencing an actor's judgment regarding its intentionality, while its outcomes in relation to the actor and to others may determine the attributions ascribed to it (Jones and Davis, 1965).

The situation-matching set is an attempt to form an evaluation of others on the basis of social norms and rules relevant to the interaction. In this perceptual set, the outcomes of others' behaviors are the primary concern for the actor. An example of a well-defined situation-matching set is a jurist deciding on the proper response to the outcome(s) of a specified behavior committed by the defendant. The "appropriateness" of certain behaviors is also a consideration here. An example would be the police officer's use of relevant cues and knowledge of expectancies in particular social settings, such as various sections of a city, in which similar behavioral acts may or may not be categorized as suspicious. In diplomatic relations, cross-cultural differences among interactants and proxemic factors would be relevant, particularly in the misinterpretation of behavior. Incorrect attributions of intent may result from inappropriate use of eye contact, self-adaptors, and interpersonal spacing among or between those representing different cultural traditions, such as might be experienced between an Arab and an Englishman (Collette, 1971).

Jones and Thibaut (1958: 177) do not elaborate, or make explicit, relationships between the formal and substantive classification systems for types of interactions except to note that "it would seem difficult to maintain either a causal-genetic or a situational-matching set under circumstances where there is a high degree of mutual or double contingency."

Application of the Systems

In relating these classification systems to the studies presented in this volume, the formal system is perhaps the most clearly applicable in categorizing the types of interaction involved. An important distinction must be made between the majority of studies in which the interactants were observed by a nonparticipating observer, and the studies in which data were based on judgments made by one of the actual participants in the interactions (see Garratt et al., 1981; Havis et al., 1981). Distinctions should also be made between explicit use of nonverbal behaviors and use of more global indicators ("impressions") to arrive at perceived intentions of the actor, as in the diplomacy studies. The research discussed in Chapter 5, illustrating the advantage of technically guided and conceptually modeled judgments of intentions over unguided global interpretations, is an example of the value of this distinction.

The diplomacy studies reported in Part II would most readily be categorized as asymmetrically contingent interactions in that the variable responder is the interviewee (the Soviet ambassador) and the standard responder is the press interviewer. In terms of substantive criteria, the interviewee would most likely be involved in the facilitation of personal goal attainment by invoking a value-maintenance set, whereas the press interviewer would attempt to identify processes influencing the actor's behavior and invoke a causal-genetic set. However, because of performance pressures, the interviewer would also be involved in personal goal attainment and, as a result of his boundary role conflict, the interviewee would probably utilize a causal-genetic set to attempt to interpret questions more adequately.

More knowledge of motivational sets, expectancies, and patterns of interaction could result from research that concentrates specifically on attributional processes and biases. For example, interviewer expectancies regarding the interviewee's qualities would be expected to generate dispositional attributions on the part of the interviewer. The interviewee, in turn, would have a tendency to attribute, as influences on his or her own behavior, such situational factors as the interviewer's questioning strategy and performance-evaluation pressures, disregarding the causal effects of his or her own attitudes on self-presentation. Comparable biasing factors could also apply to the interviewer. These, in turn, may affect, or be affected by, the type of nonverbal encoding and decoding engaged in by both players.

Reciprocally contingent interactions, such as negotiations, would represent a more complex example of attribution bias. In the present case, however, the observer who rates the films is instructed to employ dispositional expectancies and to invoke a causal-genetic set to determine the "true" intentions of the target on the basis of impression and/or behavioral cues.

Within this definitional framework, specification of behavioral and situational cues actually used in decoding self-presentation patterns and for making attributions of cause, as well as those presented in encoding processes, may more accurately identify goals of interaction outcome, information-processing set, and structure of the interaction. The studies reported in Chapters 5 and 6 are examples of attempts to delineate specific cues used in decoding an asymmetrically contingent interaction on the part of an observer using a causal-genetic set to determine "true" intentions of the target person. The discriminant function analyses performed on the data of the experiments reported in Chapter 4 are attempts to identify encoding cues that distinguish among different intentions within the same type of interaction. Whether the classification systems proposed by Jones and Thibaut will have operational utility is a question that awaits further examination, perhaps by systematically varying types of interactions across defined situation contingencies. Many of the subtleties of ongoing face-to-face interactions may be explicated by such procedures.

Nonverbal Behavior

The analysis described above may also be evaluated at a conceptual level. An important question becomes that of identifying whether such a reconceptualization moves the understanding of nonverbal behavior ahead appreciably. Historically, the understanding of nonverbal behavior is one of psychology's oldest problems. Indeed the analysis of facial expression of emotion represents one of the areas first approached systematically in psychological terms (Darwin, 1872; Woodworth, 1938; Wolff, 1948). Interest in other aspects of nonverbal behavior has a long history, an even longer background (Allport and Vernon, 1933), and a wide contemporary appeal (see Chapters 1 and 2).

Perhaps one reason for the early and continuing interest in the area is its focal position in what may be regarded as the fundamental dilemma of psychology, namely, how to understand purposeful action. To be sure, many nonverbal behaviors

are automatic and mechanical enough to be usefully conceptu-
alized by models drawn from the natural sciences. Pupillary
dilations, skin colorations, vocal patterns, perhaps even gestures,
gait, and many other nonverbal behaviors, may be well understood with the aid of structural and causal models of analysis
(Pepper, 1942; Harré and Secord, 1972; Giorgi, 1976). The
analytic approach delineating constituents of nonverbal acts and
tracing lawful or causal connections to underlying structures or
processes is a widely employed strategy of this orientation
(Birdwhistell, 1952, 1970; Kasl and Mahl, 1965). Similarly, the
search for individual consistency in external expressive forms as
an indication of the presence of relatively unique qualities is a
related approach of this orientation (Allport and Vernon, 1933;
Rosenthal, 1979).

At the same time, it seems equally clear that many behaviors
have an important volitional and purposive quality about them.
Eye winks, hand gestures, facial displays, bodily postures, and
other such behaviors have intentional and programmatic features that may be best understood by employing conceptual
models focusing on interactional and contextual analyses
(Pepper, 1942; Scriven, 1965). While such models may exchange the possibilities of control and precise prediction for the
goal of understanding, they may be better suited for appreciat-
ing many social-psychological phenomena, including nonverbal
behavior.

In some ways the root problem of the appreciation of nonverbal behavior is that of identifying those behaviors or behav-
ior-situation combinations that bespeak automatic and nonvoli-
tional expressions. Were there a glossary of behaviors or a
taxonomy of behavior occasions that could be consulted, research strategies aimed at control and prediction, perhaps even
causal modeling, could prove extremely productive. However,
since people are often quite self-conscious and since they are
themselves the consumer-users of such knowledge, the utility of
such an understanding may be quite limited. Michael Scriven
(1965) has posed the problem quite clearly. He argues that if
one aspires to a positivistic and predictive understanding of some

aspects of human conduct, such as a volitional nonverbal act, if one assumes that the explanatory system pertaining to that act is public (and therefore accessible to the subject) and precise (and therefore leads to one and only one predicted outcome among alternatives), and if one further assumes that the person concerned is counterpredictive, he or she may defeat or control the prediction at will. This same concern is expressed by Goffman (1969) in his analysis of "expression games" as described in Chapter 1. Nonverbal behavior is clearly an area of human conduct sufficiently volitional to qualify as problematic to predict. George Kelly (1969) observed that one of a person's main problems in social interaction is that of distinguishing winks from blinks—the tactical from the benign.

The systems of analysis proposed by Jones and Thibaut would seem to offer a useful way of conceptualizing some of the contextual features of social interaction that may facilitate further understanding of nonverbal behavior.

REFERENCES

ACKOFF, R. L. and F. E. EMERY (1972) *On Purposeful Systems.* Chicago: Aldine.

ADAMS, J. S. (1976) The structure and dynamics of behavior in organizational boundary roles, in M. D. Dunnette (ed.) *Handbook of Industrial and Organizational Psychology.* Chicago: Rand McNally.

ADDINGTON, D. W. (1971) The effect of vocal variation on ratings of source credibility. *Speech Monographs,* 38: 242-247.

––– (1968) The relationship of selected vocal characteristics to personality perception. *Speech Monographs,* 35: 492-503.

AIELLO, J. R. (1972) A test of equilibrium theory: Visual interaction in relation to orientation, distance, and sex of interactants. *Psychonomic Science,* 27: 335-336.

AIELLO, J. R. and S. E. JONES (1971) Field study of the proxemic behavior of young school children in three subcultural groups. *Journal of Personality and Social Psychology,* 19: 351-356.

ALLEN, B. V., A. N. WIENS, M. WEITMAN, and G. SASLOW (1965) Effects of warm-cold set on interviewee speech. *Journal of Consulting Psychology,* 29: 480-482.

ALLPORT, G. and P. VERNON (1933) *Studies in Expressive Movement.* New York: Macmillan.

ALTMAN, I. and E. E. LETT (1969) The ecology of interpersonal relationships: A classification and conceptual model, in J. E. McGrath, *Social and Psychological Factors in Stress.* New York: Holt, Rinehart & Winston.

ARGYLE, M. and J. DEAN (1965) Eye-contact, distance, and affiliation. *Sociometry,* 28: 289-304.

ARGYLE, M. and R. INGHAM (1972) Gaze, mutual gaze, and proximity. *Semiotica,* 6: 32-49.

ARGYLE, M., R. INGHAM, F. ALKEMA, and M. McCALLIN (1973) The different functions of gaze. *Semiotica,* 7: 19-32.

ARGYLE, M., M. LALLJEE, and M. COOK (1968) The effects of visibility on interaction in a dyad. *Human Relations,* 21: 3-17.

ASHLEY MONTAGU, M. F. (1971) *Touching.* New York: Columbia University Press.

ASHLEY MONTAGU, M. F. and F. MATSON (1979) *The Human Connection.* New York: McGraw-Hill.

AXELROD, R. and W. ZIMMERMAN (1979) The Soviet central press, lying, and Soviet foreign policy. Presented at the annual meeting of the American Political Science Association, Washington, D.C.

BADLER, N. I. and S. W. SMOLIAR (1979) Digital representations of human movement. *Computing Surveys*, 11: 19-38.

BANTON, M. (1964) *The Policeman in the Community*. London: Tavistock.

BATES, J. E. (1975) Effects of children's nonverbal behavior upon adults. Presented at the meeting of the American Psychological Association, Chicago.

BAXTER, J. C. (1970) Interpersonal spacing in natural settings. *Sociometry*, 33: 444-456.

BAXTER, J. C. and R. M. ROZELLE (1975) Nonverbal expression as a function of crowding during a simulated police-citizen encounter. *Journal of Personality and Social Psychology*, 32: 40-54.

BEATTY, J. and D. KAHNEMAN (1966) Pupillary changes in two memory tasks. *Psychonomic Science*, 6: 371-372.

BEEBE, S. A. (1974) Eye contact: A nonverbal determinant of speaker credibility. *The Speech Teacher*, 23: 21-25.

BERNE, E. (1964) *Games People Play*. New York: Grove Press.

BIRDWHISTELL, R. L. (1970) *Kinesics and Context*. Philadelphia: University of Pennsylvania Press.

——— (1952) *Introduction to Kinesics: An Annotation System for Analysis of Body Motion and Gesture*. Louisville, KY: University of Louisville.

BOOMER, D. S. (1965) Hesitation and grammatical encoding. *Language and Speech*, 8: 148-158.

——— (1963) Speech dysfluencies and body movement in interviews. *Journal of Nervous and Mental Disease*, 136: 263-266.

BOUCHER, J. D. and P. EKMAN (1975) Facial areas of emotional information. *Journal of Communication*, 25: 21-29.

BREED, G. R. and M. PORTER (1972) Eye contact, attitudes, and attitude change among males. *Journal of Genetic Psychology*, 120: 211-217.

BRUNEAU, T. J. (1973) Communicative silences: Forms and functions. *Journal of Communication*, 23: 17-46.

BURROUGHS, W., W. SCHULTZ, and S. AUTREY (1973) Quality of argument, leadership votes, and eye contact in three-person leaderless groups. *Journal of Social Psychology*, 90: 89-93.

CAMPBELL, D. T. (1975) Degrees of freedom and the case study. *Comparative Political Studies*, 8: 178-193.

CHANCE, M.R.A. (1962) An interpretation of some agonistic postures. *Symposia of the Zoölogical Society of London*, 8: 71-89.

CHAPPLE, E. D. and C. M. ARENSBERG (1940) Measuring human relations: An introduction to the study of the interaction of individuals. *Genetic Psychology Monographs*, 22: 3-147.

CLARK, W. R. (1975) A comparison of pupillary response, heart rate, and GSR during deception. Presented at the meeting of the Midwestern Psychological Association, Chicago.

CODDINGTON, A. (1968) *Theories of the Bargaining Process*. Chicago: Aldine.

COHEN, A. A. and R. P. HARRISON (1973) Intentionality in the use of hand illustrators in face to face communication situations. *Journal of Personality and Social Psychology*, 28: 276-279.

COLLETT, P. (1971) Training Englishmen in the nonverbal behavior of Arabs. *International Journal of Psychology*, 6: 209-215.

CONDON, W. S. and W. D. OGSTON (1966) Sound film analysis of normal and pathological behavior patterns. *Journal of Nervous and Mental Diseases*, 143: 338-347.

CONDON, W. S. and L. W. SANDER (1974) Neonate movement is synchronized with adult speech: Interactional participation and language acquisition. *Science*, 183: 99-101.

COSTANZO, F. S., N. N. MARKEL, and P. R. COSTANZO (1969) Voice quality profile and perceived emotion. *Journal of Counseling Psychology*, 16: 267-270.

DABBS, J. M., Jr. (1969) Similarity of gestures and interpersonal influence. Summary in *Proceedings of the 77th Annual Convention of the American Psychological Association*, 4: 337-338.

DANIELIAN, J. (1967) Live simulation of affect-laden cultural cognitions. *Journal of Conflict Resolution*, 11: 312-324.

DARWIN, C. (1872) *The Expression of the Emotions in Man and Animals*. London: Murray.

D'AUGELLI, A. R. (1974) Nonverbal behavior of helpers in initial helping interactions. *Journal of Counseling Psychology*, 21: 360-363.

DAVITZ, J. R. and L. J. DAVITZ (1959) The communication of feelings by content-free speech. *Journal of Communication*, 9: 6-13.

DePAULO, B. M. and R. ROSENTHAL (1979) Telling lies. *Journal of Personality and Social Psychology*, 37: 1713-1722.

DePAULO, B. M., M. ZUCKERMAN, and R. ROSENTHAL (1980) Detecting deception: Modality effects, in L. Wheeler (ed.) *Review of Personality and Social Psychology*, Vol. 1. Beverly Hills, CA: Sage Publications.

DEUTSCH, F. and W. F. MURPHY (1955) *The Clinical Interview*, Vols. 1 and 2. New York: International Universities Press.

DITTMANN, A. T. (1978) The role of body movement in communication, in A. W. Siegman and S. Feldstein (eds.) *Nonverbal Behavior and Communication*. Hilldale, N.J: Lawrence Erlbaum Associates.

––– (1972) *Interpersonal Messages of Emotion*. New York: Springer.

––– (1971) Review of *Kinesics and Context*, by R. L. Birdwhistell. *Psychiatry*, 34: 334-342.

DITTMANN, A. T. and L. G. LLEWELLYN (1969) Body movements and speech rhythm in social conversation. *Journal of Personality and Social Psychology*, 11: 98-106.

DONCHIN, E. (1979) Event-related brain potentials: A tool in the study of human information processing, in H. Begleiter (ed.) *Evoked Potentials in Psychiatry*. New York: Plenum Press.

DONCHIN, E. and J. B. ISREAL (1978) Event-related potentials–Approaches to cognitive psychology. Unpublished manuscript, Cognitive Psychophysiology Laboratory, University of Illinois.

DRUCKMAN, D. (1980) Social-psychological factors in regional politics, in W. Feld and G. Boyd (eds.) *Comparative Regional Systems*. New York: Pergamon.

––– (1977a) Boundary role conflict: Negotiation as dual responsiveness. *Journal of Conflict Resolution*, 21: 639-662.

––– (1977b) The person, role, and situation in international negotiations, in M. G. Hermann (ed.) *A Psychological Examination of Political Leaders*. New York: Free Press.

——— (1973) *Human Factors in International Negotiations: Social-Psychological Aspects of International Conflict.* Sage Professional Papers in International Studies 02-020. Beverly Hills, CA: Sage Publications.

——— (1971) Understanding the operation of complex social systems: Some uses of simulation design. *Simulation and Games,* 2: 173-195.

——— (1968a) Prenegotiation experience and dyadic conflict resolution in a bargaining situation. *Journal of Experimental Social Psychology,* 4: 367-383.

——— (1968b) Ethnocentrism in the Inter-Nation Simulation. *Journal of Conflict Resolution,* 12: 45-68.

——— (1967) Dogmatism, prenegotiation experience, and simulated group representation as determinants of dyadic behavior in a bargaining situation. *Journal of Personality and Social Psychology,* 6: 279-290.

DRUCKMAN, D. and T. V. BONOMA (1976) Determinants of bargaining behavior in a bilateral monopoly situation II: Opponent's concession rate and similarity. *Behavioral Science,* 21: 252-262.

DRUCKMAN, D., R. ROZELLE, R. M. KRAUSE, and R. MAHONEY (1974) Power and utilities in a simulated interreligious council: A situational approach to interparty decision making, in J. Tedeschi (ed.) *Perspectives on Social Power.* Chicago: Aldine.

DRUCKMAN, D., and K. ZECHMEISTER (1973) Conflict of interest and value dissensus: Propositions in the sociology of conflict. *Human Relations,* 26: 449-466.

DRUCKMAN, D., R. ROZELLE, and K. ZECHMEISTER (1977) Conflict of interest and value dissensus: Two perspectives, in D. Druckman (ed.) *Negotiations: Social-Psychological Perspectives.* Beverly Hills, CA: Sage Publications.

DUKE, M. P. and S. NOWICKI, Jr. (1972) A new measure and social-learning model for interpersonal distance. *Journal of Experimental Research in Personality,* 6: 119-132.

DUNCAN, S. D., Jr. (1974) On the structure of speaker-auditor interaction during speaking turns. *Language in Society,* 2: 161-180.

——— (1972) Some signals and rules for taking speaking turns in conversations. *Journal of Personality and Social Psychology,* 23: 283-292.

DUNCAN, S. D., Jr. and D. W. FISKE (1979) Dynamic patterning in conversation. *American Scientist,* 67: 90-98.

EKMAN, P. (1978) Facial expression, in A. W. Siegman and S. Feldstein (eds.) *Nonverbal Behavior and Communication.* Hillsdale, NJ: Lawrence Erlbaum Associates.

——— (1972) Universal and cultural differences in facial expressions of emotions, in J. K. Cole (ed.) *Nebraska Symposium on Motivation.* Lincoln: University of Nebraska Press, 207-283.

——— (1965) Communication through nonverbal behavior: A source of information about an interpersonal relationship, pp. 390-442 in S. S. Tomkins and C. E. Izard (eds.) *Affect, Cognition, and Personality.* New York: Springer.

EKMAN, P. and W. V. FRIESEN (1975) *Unmasking the Face: A Guide to Recognizing Emotions from Facial Clues.* Englewood Cliffs, NJ: Prentice-Hall.

——— (1974) Detecting deception from the body or face. *Journal of Personality and Social Psychology,* 29: 288-298.

——— (1974a) Detecting deception from the body or face. *Journal of Personality and Social Psychology,* 29: 288-298.

——— (1974b) Hand movements. *Journal of Communication,* 22: 353-371.

——— (1971) Constants across cultures in the face and emotion. *Journal of Personality and Social Psychology*, 17: 124-129.

——— (1969a) Nonverbal leakage and clues to deception. *Psychiatry*, 32: 88-106.

——— (1969b) The repertoire of nonverbal behavior: Categories, origins, usage, and coding. *Semiotica*, 1: 49-98.

——— (1968) Nonverbal behavior in psychotherapy research, in J. M. Shlien, H. F. Hunt, J. D. Matarazzo, and C. Savage (eds.) *Research in Psychotherapy*, Vol. 3. Washington, DC: American Psychological Association.

EKMAN, P., W. V. FRIESEN, and S. ANCOLI (1980) Facial signs of emotional experience. *Journal of Personality and Social Psychology*, 39: 1125-1134.

EKMAN, P., W. V. FRIESEN, and P. ELLSWORTH (1972) *Emotion in the Human Face: Guidelines for Research and an Integration of the Findings*. New York: Pergamon.

EKMAN, P., W. V. FRIESEN, and K. R. SCHERER (1976) Hand movement and voice pitch in deceptive interaction. *Semiotica*, 16: 23-27.

EKMAN, P., E. R. SORENSON, and W. V. FRIESEN (1969) Pan-cultural elements in facial displays of emotion. *Science*, 164: 86-88.

ELLSWORTH, P. C. (1975) Direct gaze as a social stimulus: The example of aggression, pp. 53-76 in P. Pliner, L. Krames, and T. Alloway (eds.) *Nonverbal Communication of Aggression*. New York: Plenum.

ELLSWORTH, P. C. and J. M. CARLSMITH (1968) Effects of eye contact and verbal content on affective response to a dyadic interaction. *Journal of Personality and Social Psychology*, 10: 15-20.

ELLSWORTH, P. C. and L. M. LUDWIG (1972) Visual behavior in social interaction. *Journal of Communication*, 22: 375-403.

ELLSWORTH, P. C. and L. D. ROSS (1976) Intimacy in response to direct gaze. *Journal of Experimental Social Psychology*, 11: 592-613.

EXLINE, R. V. (1963) Explorations in the process of person perception: Visual interaction in relation to competition, sex, and the need for affiliation. *Journal of Personality*, 31: 1-20.

EXLINE, R. V. and C. ELDRIDGE (1967) Effects of two patterns of a speaker's visual behavior upon the perception of the authenticity of his verbal message. Presented at the meeting of the Eastern Psychological Association, Boston.

EXLINE, R. V. and B. J. FEHR (1978) Applications of semiosis to the study of visual interaction, in A. W. Siegman and S. Feldstein (eds.) *Nonverbal Behavior and Communication*. Hillsdale, NJ: Lawrence Erlbaum Associates.

EXLINE, R. V., D. GRAY, and D. SCHUETTE (1965) Visual behavior in a dyad as affected by interview content and sex of respondent. *Journal of Personality and Social Psychology*, 1: 201-209.

FAST, J. (1971) *Body Language*. New York: Pocket Books.

FISCHER, M. J. and R. A. APOSTAL (1975) Selected vocal cues and counselors' perceptions of genuineness, self-disclosure, and anxiety. *Journal of Counseling Psychology*, 22: 92-96.

FISCHHOFF, B., P. SLOVIC, and S. LICHTENSTEIN (1977) Knowing with certainty: The appropriateness of extreme confidence. *Journal of Personality and Social Psychology*, 3: 552-569.

FODDY, M. (1978) Patterns of gaze in cooperative and competitive negotiation. *Human Relations*, 31: 925-938.

FRANK, R. S. (1977) Nonverbal and paralinguistic analysis of political behavior: The first McGovern-Humphrey California primary debate, in M. G. Hermann (ed.) *A*

Psychological Examination of Political Leaders. New York: Free Press.

FRANKEL, A. A. and J. BARRETT (1971) Variations in personal space as a function of authoritarianism, self-esteem, and racial characteristics of a stimulus situation. *Journal of Consulting and Clinical Psychology,* 37: 95-98.

FREEDMAN, N., T. BLASS, A. RIFKIN, and F. QUITKIN (1973) Body movements and verbal encoding of aggressive affect. *Journal of Personality and Social Psychology,* 26: 72-85.

FREUD, S. (1938) Psychopathology of everyday life, in A. A. Brill (ed.) *The Basic Writings of Sigmund Freud.* New York: Modern Library.

FRIEDMAN, H. S. (1979) Nonverbal communication between patients and medical practitioners. *Journal of Social Issues,* 35: 82-99.

FRIJDA, N. H. (1969) Recognition of emotion, pp. 167-223 in L. Berkowitz (ed.) *Advances in Experimental Social Psychology,* Vol. 4. New York: Academic.

FROMM-REICHMANN, F. (1950) *Principles of Intensive Psychotherapy.* Chicago: University of Chicago Press.

FUGITA, S. S., M. C. HOGREBE, and K. N. WEXLEY (1980) Perceptions of deception: Perceived expertise in detecting deception, successfulness of deception and nonverbal cues. *Personality and Social Psychology Bulletin,* 6: 637-643.

GALE, A., B. LUCAS, R. NISSIM, and B. HARPHAM (1972) Some EEG correlates of face-to-face contact. *British Journal of Social and Clinical Psychology,* 11: 326-332.

GARRATT, G. A., J. C. BAXTER, and R. M. ROZELLE (1981) Training university police in Black-American nonverbal behaviors: An application to police-community relations. *Journal of Social Psychology,* 113: 217-229.

GATTON, M. J. (1970) Behavioral aspects of interpersonal attraction. *Journal of Personality and Social Psychology,* 29: 586-592.

GIORGI, A. (1976) Phenomenology and the foundations of psychology, in J. K. Cole and W. J. Arnold (eds.) *Nebraska Symposium on Motivation.* Lincoln, Nebraska: University of Nebraska Press.

GITIN, S. R. (1970) A dimensional analysis of manual expression. *Journal of Personality and Social Psychology,* 15: 271-277.

GITTER, A. G., H. BLACK, and D. MOSTOFSKY (1972) Race and sex in the communication of emotion. *Journal of Social Psychology,* 88: 273-276.

GOFFMAN, E. (1969) *Strategic Interaction.* Philadelphia: University of Pennsylvania Press.

——— (1959) *The Presentation of Self in Everyday Life.* Garden City, NY: Doubleday.

GOLDBERG, G. N., C. A. KIESLER, and B. E. COLLINS (1969) Visual behavior and face-to-face distance during interaction. *Sociometry,* 32: 43-53.

GOLDMAN-EISLER, F. (1967) Sequential temporal patterns and cognitive processes in speech. *Language and Speech,* 10: 122-132.

GOULD, R. and H. SIGALL (1977) The effects of empathy and outcome on attribution: An examination of the divergent perspectives hypothesis. *Journal of Experimental Social Psychology,* 13: 480-491.

GRIFFITT, W. and R. VEITCH (1971) Hot and crowded: Influences of population density and temperature on interpersonal affective behavior. *Journal of Personality and Social Psychology,* 17: 92-98.

HAASE, R. F. and D. T. TEPPER, Jr. (1972) Nonverbal components of empathic communication. *Journal of Counseling Psychology,* 19: 417-424.

HAGGARD, E. A. and K. S. ISAACS (1966) Micromomentary facial expressions as indicators of ego mechanisms in psychotherapy, pp. 154-165 in L. A. Gottschalk and A. H. Auerbach (eds.) *Methods of Research in Psychotherapy.* New York: Appleton-Century-Crofts.

HALL, E. T. (1966) *The Hidden Dimension.* Garden City, NY: Doubleday.

——— (1964) Adumbration as a feature of intercultural communication. *American Anthropologist,* 6: 154-163.

——— (1963a) Proxemics—The study of man's spatial relations and boundaries, pp. 422-435 in I. Galdston (ed.) *Man's Image in Medicine and Anthropology.* Monograph Series 4. New York: International University Press.

——— (1963b) A system for the notation of proxemic behavior. *American Anthropologist,* 65: 1003-1026.

HARE, A. P. and R. F. BALES (1963) Seating position and small group interaction. *Sociometry,* 26: 480-486.

HARPER, R. G., A. N. WIENS, and J. D. MATARAZZO (1978) *Nonverbal Communication: The State of the Art.* New York: John Wiley.

HARRE, R. and P. SECORD (1972) *The Explanation of Social Behavior.* Oxford: Blackwell, 1972.

HARRISON, A. A., M. HWALEK, D. F. RANEY, and J. G. FRITZ (1978) Cues to deception in an interview situation. *Social Psychology,* 41: 156-161.

HAVIS, J. G., R. M. ROZELLE, J. C. BAXTER, and J. P. KIMBLE (1981) A comparison of the effects of positive and standard nonverbal and verbal behaviors on impression formation during a police-citizen encounter. Unpublished manuscript, Department of Psychology, University of Houston.

HEMSLEY, G. D. and A. N. DOOB (1975) Efect of looking behavior on perceptions of a communicator's credibility. Presented at the meeting of the American Psychological Association, Chicago.

HENLEY, N. M. (1973) Status and sex: Some touching observations. *Bulletin of the Psychonomic Society,* 2(2): 91-93.

HERMANN, M. G. (1977) Verbal behavior of negotiators in periods of high and low stress: The 1965-66 New York City Transit Negotiations, in M. G. Hermann ed.) *A Psychological Examination of Political Leaders.* New York: Free Press.

HERON, J. (1970) The phenomenology of social encounter: The gaze. *Philosophy and Phenomenological Research,* 31: 243-264.

HESS, E. (1975) The role of pupil size in communication. *Scientific American,* 233: 110-119.

——— (1965) Attitude and pupil size. *Scientific American,* 212: 46-54.

HESS, E. H. and S. B. PETROVICH (1978) Pupillary behavior in communication, in A. W. Siegman and S. Feldstein (eds.) *Nonverbal Behavior and Communication.* Hillsdale, NJ: Lawrence Erlbaum Associates.

HEWES, G. W. (1955) World distribution of certain postural habits. *American Anthropologist,* 57: 231-234.

HOFFMAN, S. P. (1969) An empirical study of representational hand movements. Doctoral dissertation, New York University. (Dissertation Abstracts 29 (1969), 4379B. University Microfilms 69-7960.)

HOLSTEIN, C. M., J. M. GOLDSTEIN, and D. J. BEM (1971) The importance of expressive behaviors, involvement, sex, and need-approval in induced liking. *Journal of Experimental Social Psychology,* 7: 534-544.

HOWELL, R. J. and E. C. JORGENSEN (1970) Accuracy of judging unposed emotional behavior in a natural setting: A replication study. *Journal of Social Psychology,* 81: 269-270.

IZARD, C. E. (1971) *The Face of Emotion.* New York: Appleton-Century-Crofts.

JANIS, I. L. and H. LEVENTHAL (1968) Human reactions to stress, in E. F. Borgatta and W. W. Lambert (eds.) *Handbook of Personality Theory and Research.* Chicago: Rand McNally.

JANISSE, M. P. (1976) The relationship between pupil size and anxiety: A review, pp. 27-48 in I. Sarason and C. Spielberger (eds.) *Stress and Anxiety,* Vol. 3. Washington, DC: Hemisphere (Wiley).

——— (1973) Pupil size and affect: A critical review of the literature since 1960. *Canadian Psychologist,* 14: 311-329.

JONES, E. E. and K. E. DAVIS (1965) From acts to dispositions: The attribution process in person perception, in L. Berkowitz (ed.) *Advances in Experimental Social Psychology,* Vol. 2. New York: Academic.

JONES, E. E. and R. E. NISBETT (1972) The actor and the observer: Divergent perceptions of the causes of behavior, in E. E. Jones, D. E. Kanouse, H. H. Kelley, R. E. Nisbett, S. Valins, and B. Weiner (eds.) *Attribution: Perceiving the Causes of Behavior.* Morristown, NJ: General Learning Press.

JONES, E. E. and J. THIBAUT (1958) Interaction goals as bases of inference in interpersonal perception, in R. Tagiuri and L. Petrullo (eds.) *Person Perception and Interpersonal Behavior.* Stanford, CA: Stanford University Press.

KASL, S. V. and G. F. MAHL (1965) The relationships of disturbances and hesitations in spontaneous speech to anxiety. *Journal of Personality and Social Psychology,* 1: 425-433.

KELLY, G. (1969) Humanistic methodology in psychological research, in B. Maher (ed.) *Clinical Psychology and Personality.* New York: John Wiley.

KELLEY, H. H. (1972) Attribution in social interaction, in E. E. Jones et al. (eds.) *Attribution: Perceiving the Causes of Behavior.* Morristown, NJ: General Learning Press.

KENDON, A. (1970) Movement coordination in social interaction: Some examples described. *Acta Psychologica,* 32: 100-125.

——— (1967) Some functions of gaze-direction in social interaction. *Acta Psychologica,* 26: 22-63.

KIM, J. and F. J. KOHOUT (1975) Multiple regression analysis: Subprogram regression, in N. H. Nie, C. H. Hull, J. G. Jenkins, K. Steinbrenner, and D. H. Bent (eds.) *Statistical Package for the Social Sciences.* New York: McGraw-Hill.

KLECK, R. E. and W. NEUSSLE (1968) Congruence between the indicative and communicative functions of eye contact in interpersonal relations. *British Journal of Social and Clinical Psychology,* 7: 241-246.

KLECKA, W. R. (1975) Discriminant analysis, in N. H. Nie, C. H. Hull, J. G. Jenkins, K. Steinbrenner, and D. H. Bent (eds.) *Statistical Package for the Social Sciences.* New York: McGraw-Hill.

KLEINKE, C. L., M. R. LENGA, T. B. TULLY, F. B. MEEKER, and R. A. STANESKI (1976) Effect of talking rate on first impressions of opposite-sex and same-sex interactions. Presented at the meeting of the Western Psychological Association, Los Angeles.

KLEINKE, C. L. and P. D. POHLEN (1971) Affective and emotional responses as a function of other person's gaze and cooperativeness in a two-person game. *Journal of Personality and Social Psychology,* 17: 308-313.

KNAPP, M. L. (1972) The field of nonverbal communication: An overview, pp. 57-72 in C. J. Steward and B. Kendall (eds.) *On Speech Communication: An Anthology of Contemporary Writings and Messages.* New York: Holt, Rinehart & Winston.

KNAPP, M. L., R. P. HART, G. W. FREDRICH, and G. M. SHULMAN (1973) The rhetoric of good-bye: Verbal and nonverbal correlates of human leave taking. *Speech Monographs,* 40: 182-198.

KRAUSS, R. M., V. GELLER, and C. OLSON (1976) Modalities and cues in the detection of deception. Presented at the meeting of the American Psychological Association, Washington, D.C.

KRAUSE, M. S. and M. PILISUK (1961) Anxiety in verbal behavior: A validation study. *Journal of Consulting Psychology,* 25: 414-429.

KRAUT, R. E. (1978) Verbal and nonverbal cues in the perception of lying. *Journal of Personality and Social Psychology,* 36: 380-391.

LaCROSS, M. B. (1975) Nonverbal behavior and perceived counselor attractiveness and persuasiveness. *Journal of Counseling Psychology,* 22: 563-566.

LAZARUS, R. S. (1966) *Psychological Stress and the Coping Process.* New York: McGraw-Hill.

LeCOMPTE, W. F. and H. M. ROSENFELD (1971) Effects of minimal eye contact in the instruction period on impressions of the experimenter. *Journal of Experimental Social Psychology,* 7: 211-220.

LEVITT, E. A. (1964) The relationship between abilities to express emotional meanings vocally and facially, pp. 87-100 in J. R. Davitz (ed.) *The Communication of Emotional Meaning.* New York: McGraw-Hill.

LEWIS, S. A. and W. R. FRY (1977) Effects of visual access and orientation on the discovery of integrative bargaining alternatives. *Behavior and Human Performance,* 20: 75-92.

LEYHAUSEN, P. (1967) The biology of expression and impression, in K. Lorenz and P. Leyhausen (eds.) *Motivation of Human and Animal Behavior.* New York: Van Nostrand Rheinhold.

LIBBY, W. L., Jr., B. LACEY, and J. I. LACEY (1968) Pupillary and cardiac activity during visual stimulation. Presented at the meeting of the Society for Psychophysiological Research, Washington, D.C.

LOCKHART, C. (1978) Flexibility and commitment in international conflicts. *International Studies Quarterly,* 22: 545-568.

LONDON, H. (1973) *Psychology of the Persuader.* Morristown, NJ: General Learning Press.

LOWENSTEIN, O. and I. LOEWENFELD (1970) The pupil, in M. H. Davson (ed.) *The Eye,* Vol. 3. New York: Academic.

LUFT, J. (1966) On nonverbal interaction. *Journal of Psychology,* 63: 261-268.

MAHL, G. F. (1956) Disturbances and silences in the patients' speech in psychotherapy. *Journal of Abnormal and Social Psychology,* 53: 1-15.

MAHONEY, R. and D. DRUCKMAN (1975) Simulation, experimentation, and context: Dimensions of design and inference. *Simulation and Games,* 6: 235-270.

MATARAZZO, J. D., M. WEITMAN, G. SASLOW, and A. N. WIENS (1961) Interviewer influence on durations of interviewee speech. *Journal of Verbal Learning and Verbal Behavior,* 1: 451-458.

MATARAZZO, J. D. and A. N. WIENS (1972) *The Interview: Research on Its Anatomy and Structure.* Chicago: Aldine.

MATARAZZO, J. D., A. N. WIENS, R. G. MATARAZZO, and G. SASLOW (1968) Speech and silence behavior in clinical psychotherapy and its laboratory correlates, pp. 347-394 in J. Shlien, H. Hunt, J. D. Matarazzo, and C. Savage (eds.) *Research in Psychotherapy,* Vol. 3. Washington, DC: American Psychological Association.

MAYO, C. and M. LaFRANCE (1973) Gaze direction in interracial dyadic communication. Presented at the meeting of the Eastern Psychological Association, Washington, D.C.

McCLINTOCK, C. C. and R. G. HUNT (1975) Nonverbal indicators of affect and deception. *Journal of Applied Social Psychology,* 1: 54-67.

McDOWELL, K. V. (1973) Accommodations of verbal and nonverbal behaviors as a function of the manipulations of interaction distance and eye contact. Summary in *Proceedings of the American Psychological Association,* 8: 207-208.

McGINLEY, H., R. LeFEVRE, and P. McGINLEY (1975) The influence of a communicator's body position on opinion change in others. *Journal of Personality and Social Psychology,* 31: 686-690.

MEHRABIAN, A. (1972) *Nonverbal Communication.* Chicago: Aldine.

––– (1971a) Nonverbal betrayal of feeling. *Journal of Experimental Research in Personality,* 5: 64-73.

––– (1971b) Verbal and nonverbal interaction of strangers in a waiting situation. *Journal of Experimental Research in Personality,* 5: 127-138.

––– (1968a) Inference of attitudes from the posture orientation, and distance of a communicator. *Journal of Consulting and Clinical Psychology,* 32: 296-308.

––– (1968b) Relationship of attitude to seated posture, orientation, and distance. *Journal of Personality and Social Psychology,* 10: 26-30.

MEHRABIAN, A. and S. G. DIAMOND (1971) Seating arrangement and conversation. *Sociometry,* 34: 281-289.

MEHRABIAN, A. and S. R. FERRIS (1967) Inference of attitudes from nonverbal communication in two channels. *Journal of Consulting Psychology,* 31: 248-252.

MEHRABIAN, A. and J. T. FRIAR (1969) Encoding of attitude by a seated communicator via posture and position cues. *Journal of Consulting and Clinical Psychology,* 33: 330-336.

MEHRABIAN, A. and S. KSIONZKY (1972) Categories of social behavior. *Comparative Group Studies,* 3: 425-436.

MEHRABIAN, A. and M. WIENER (1967) Decoding of inconsistent communications, *Journal of Personality and Social Psychology,* 6: 109-114.

MEHRABIAN, A. and M. WILLIAMS (1969) Nonverbal concomitants of perceived and intended persuasiveness. *Journal of Personality and Social Psychology,* 13: 37-58.

MEISELS, M. and M. A. DOSEY (1971) Personal space, anger-arousal, and psychological defense. *Journal of Personality*, 39: 333-344.

MIDDLEMIST, R. D., E. S. KNOWLES, and C. F. MATTER (1975) Personal space invasions in the lavatory: Suggestive evidence for arousal. *Journal of Personality and Social Psychology*, 33: 541-546.

MILBURN, T. W. (1977) The nature of threat. *Journal of Social Issues*, 33: 126-139.

MONSON, T. C. and M. SNYDER (1977) Actors, observers, and the attribution process: Toward a reconceptualization. *Journal of Experimental Social Psychology*, 13: 89-111.

MURRAY, D. C. (1971) Talk, silence, and anxiety. *Psychological Bulletin*, 75: 244-260.

NICHOLS, K. A. and B. G. CHAMPNESS (1971) Eye gaze and the GSR. *Journal of Experimental Social Psychology*, 7: 623-626.

NIERENBERG, G. I. (1971) *How to Read a Person Like a Book*. New York: Hawthorne Books.

NISBETT, R., C. CAPUTO, P. LEGANT, and J. MARECEK (1973) Behavior as seen by the actor and as seen by the observer. *Journal of Personality and Social Psychology*, 27: 154-164.

NISBETT, R. and L. ROSS (1980) *Human Inference: Strategies and Shortcomings of Social Judgment*. Englewood Cliffs, NJ: Prentice-Hall.

OSGOOD, C. E. (1966) Dimensionality of the semantic space for communication via facial expressions. *Scandinavian Journal of Psychology*, 7: 1-30.

OSMOND, H. (1959) The history and social development of mental hospitals. *Psychiatric Architecture*, pp. 7-9 in C. Goshen (ed.) Washington, DC: American Psychiatric Association.

PACKARD, V. (1957) *The Hidden Persuaders*. New York: David McKay.

PACKWOOD, W. T. (1974) Loudness as a variable in persuasion. *Journal of Counseling Psychology*, 21: 1-2.

PANEK, D. M. and B. MARTIN (1959) The relationship between GSR and speech disturbances in psychotherapy. *Journal of Abnormal and Social Psychology*, 58: 402-405.

PATTERSON, M. L. (1974) Factors affecting interpersonal spatial proximity. Presented at the meeting of the American Psychological Association, New Orleans.

––– (1973a) Compensation in nonverbal immediacy behaviors: A review. *Sociometry*, 36: 237-252.

––– (1973b) Stability of nonverbal immediacy behaviors. *Journal of Experimental Social Psychology*, 9: 97-109.

PATTERSON, M. L., S. MULLENS, and J. ROMANO (1971) Compensatory reactions to spatial intrusion. *Sociometry*, 34: 114-121.

PELLEGRINI, R. J., R. A. HICKS, and L. GORDON (1970) The effects of approval-seeking induction on eye-contact in dyads. *British Journal of Social and Clinical Psychology*, 9: 373-374.

PEPPER, S. (1942) *World Hypotheses*. Berkeley: University of California Press.

PETROVICH, S. B. and E. H. HESS (1978) An introduction to animal communication, in A. W. Siegman and S. Feldstein (eds.) *Nonverbal Behavior and Communication*. Hillsdale, NJ: Lawrence Erlbaum Associates.

POPE, B., T. BLASS, A. W. SIEGMAN, and J. RAHER (1970) Anxiety and depression in speech. *Journal of Consulting and Clinical Psychology*, 35: 128-133.

POPE, B., A. W. SIEGMAN, and T. BLASS (1970) Anxiety and speech in the initial interview. *Journal of Consulting and Clinical Psychology*, 32: 588-595.

PRIMEAU, C. C., J. A. HELTON, J. C. BAXTER, and R. M. ROZELLE (1975) An examination of the conception of the police officer held by several social groups. *Journal of Police Science and Administration*, 3: 189-196.

RAND, G. and S. WAPNER (1967) Postural status as a factor in memory. *Journal of Verbal Learning and Verbal Behavior*, 6: 268-271.

ROHNER, S. J. and J. R. AIELLO (1976) The relationship between the sex of interactants and other nonverbal behaviors. Presented at the meeting of the Eastern Psychological Association, New York.

ROSENFELD, H. M. (1966) Instrumental affiliative functions of facial and gestural expressions. *Journal of Personality and Social Psychology*, 4: 65-72.

ROSENTHAL, R. [ed.] (1979) *Skill in Nonverbal Communication*. Cambridge, MA: Oelgeschlager, Gunn & Hain.

ROZELLE, R. M. and J. C. BAXTER (1978) The interpretation of nonverbal behavior in a role-defined interaction sequence: The police citizen encounter. *Environmental Psychology and Nonverbal Behavior*, 2(3): 167-180.

——— (1975) Impression formation and danger recognition in experienced police officers. *Journal of Social Psychology*, 96: 53-63.

RUBIN, J. and B. BROWN (1975) *The Social Psychology of Bargaining and Negotiation*. New York: Academic.

SAUNDERS, D. A. (1970) On the statistical treatment of remarkable data. *Educational and Psychological Measurement*, 30: 533-545.

SCHEFLEN, A. E. (1968) Human communication: Behavioral programs and their integration in interaction. *Behavioral Science*, 13: 44-55.

SCHERER, K. R., J. KOIVUMAKI, and R. ROSENTHAL (1972) Minimal cues in the vocal communication of affect: Judging emotions from content-masked speech. *Journal of Psycholinguistic Research*, 1: 269-285.

SCHWARTZ, G. E. (1974) Facial expression and depression: An electromyogram study. *Psychosomatic Medicine*, 36: 458.

SCHWARTZ, G. E., P. L. FAIR, P. S. GREENBERG, M. R. MARDEL, and G. L. KLERMAN (1975) Facial expressions and depression. II. An electromyographic study. *Psychosomatic Medicine*, 37: 81-82.

SCRIVEN, M. (1965) An essential unpredictability in human behavior, in B. Wolman (ed.) *Scientific Psychology*. New York: Basic Books.

SIEGEL, S. (1956) *Nonparametric Statistics for the Behavioral Sciences*. New York: McGraw-Hill.

SIEGMAN, A. W. (1976) Do noncontingent interviewer mm-hmms facilitate interviewee productivity? *Journal of Consulting and Clinical Psychology*, 44: 171-182.

SIEGMAN, A. W. and S. FELDSTEIN [eds.] (1978) *Nonverbal Behavior and Communication*. Hillsdale, NJ: Lawrence Erlbaum Associates.

SIEGMAN, A. W. and B. POPE [eds.] (1972) *Studies in Dyadic Communication*. New York: Pergamon.

——— (1965) Effects of question specificity and anxiety-producing messages on verbal fluency in the initial interview. *Journal of Personality and Social Psychology*, 2: 522-530.

SILVERMAN, A. F., E. PRESSMAN, and H. W. BARTEL (1973) Self-esteem and tactile communication. *Journal of Humanistic Psychology*, 13: 73-77.

SIMPSON, H. M. and S. M. HALE (1969) Pupillary changes during a decision-making task. *Perceptual and Motor Skills*, 29: 495-498.

SKOLNICK, J. (1967) *Justice Without Trial*. New York: John Wiley.

SLOVIC, P. (1976) Toward understanding and improving decisions, in E. I. Salkovitz (ed.) *Science, Technology and the Modern Navy: Thirtieth Anniversary, 1946-1976*. Arlington, VA: Office of Naval Research.

SNOW, P. A. (1972) Verbal content and affective response in an interview as a function of experimenter gaze direction. Master's thesis, Lakehead University, Thunder Bay, Ontario, Canada.

SNYDER, G. H. and P. DIESING (1977) *Conflict Among Nations*. Princeton, NJ: Princeton University Press.

SNYDER, M. (1974) Self-monitoring of expressive behavior. *Journal of Personality and Social Psychology*, 30: 526-537.

SODIKOFF, C. L., I. J. FIRESTONE, and K. J. KAPLAN (1974) Distance matching and distance equilibrium in the interview dyad. Presented at the meeting of the American Psychological Association, New Orleans.

SOMMER, R. (1968) Intimacy ratings in five countries. *International Journal of Psychology*, 3: 109-114.

——— (1967) Small group ecology. *Psychological Bulletin*, 67: 145-152.

SORRENTINO, R. M. and R. G. BOUTILLIER (1975) The effect of quantity and quality of verbal interaction on ratings of leadership ability. *Journal of Experimental Research in Personality*, 11: 403-411.

STANG, D. J. (1973) Effect of interaction rate on ratings of leadership and liking. *Journal of Personality and Social Psychology*, 27: 405-408.

STEINZOR, B. (1950) The spatial factor in face-to-face discussion groups. *Journal of Abnormal and Social Psychology*, 45: 552-555.

STONE, G. L. and C. J. MORDEN (1976) Effect of distance on verbal productivity. *Journal of Counseling Psychology*, 23: 486-488.

STORMS, M. D. (1973) Videotape and the attribution process: Reversing actors' and observers' points of view. *Journal of Personality and Social Psychology*, 27: 165-175.

STREETER, L. A., R. M. KRAUSS, V. GELLER, C. OLSON, and W. APPLE (1977) Pitch changes during attempted deception. *Journal of Personality and Social Psychology*, 35: 345-350.

STRONG, S. R., R. G. TAYLOR, J. C. BRATTON, and R. G. LOPER (1971) Nonverbal behavior and perceived counselor characteristics. *Journal of Counseling Psychology*, 18: 554-561.

TERHUNE, K. W. (1968) Motives, situation, and interpersonal conflict within Prisoner's Dilemma. *Journal of Personality and Social Psychology Monograph Supplement 8*, 3: Part 2.

THAYER, S. (1969) The effect of interpersonal looking duration on dominance judgments. *Journal of Social Psychology*, 79: 285-286.

THAYER, S. and W. SCHIFF (1969) Stimulus factors in observer judgment of social interaction: Facial expression and motion pattern. *American Journal of Psychology*, 82: 73-85.

THOMPSON, D. F. and L. MELTZER (1964) Communication of emotional intent by facial expression. *Journal of Abnormal and Social Psychology*, 68: 129-135.

THOMPSON, D. J. and J. C. BAXTER (1973) Interpersonal spacing in two-person cross-cultural interactions. *Man-Environment Systems*, 3: 115-117.

TOMKINS, S. S. (1962) *Affect, Imagery, Consciousness, Vol. 1: The Positive Affects*. New York: Springer.

VINE, I. (1971) Judgment of direction of gaze: An interpretation of discrepant results. *British Journal of Social and Clinical Psychology*, 10: 320-331.

von CRANACH, M. (1971) The role of orienting behavior in human interaction, in A. H. Esser (ed.) *Behavior and Environment: The Use of Space by Animals and Men.* New York: Plenum Press.

WASHBURN, P. V. and M. D. HAKEL (1973) Visual cues and verbal content as influences on impressions formed after simulated employment interviews. *Journal of Applied Psychology,* 58: 137-141.

WATSON, O. M. (1970) *Proxemic Behavior: A Cross-Cultural Study.* The Hague: Mouton.

WATSON, O. M. and T. D. GRAVES (1966) Quantitative research in proxemic behavior. *American Anthropologist,* 68: 971-985.

WATSON, S. E. (1972) Judgment of emotion from facial and contextual cue combinations. *Journal of Personality and Social Psychology,* 24: 334-342.

WAXER, P. H. (1979) *Nonverbal Aspects of Psychotherapy.* New York: Praeger.

WEITZ, S. [ed.] (1974) *Nonverbal Communication: Readings with Commentary.* New York: Oxford University Press.

WIEGELE, T. C. (1978) The psychophysiology of elite stress in five international crises: A preliminary test of a voice measurement technique. *International Studies Quarterly,* 22: 467-512.

WIENER, M., S. DEVOE, S. RUBINOW, and J. GELLER (1972) Nonverbal behavior and nonverbal communication. *Psychological Review,* 79: 185-214.

WIENER, M. and A. MEHRABIAN (1968) *Language Within Language: Immediacy, A Channel in Verbal Communication.* New York: Appleton-Century-Crofts.

WIENS, T. B. (1979) ECON User's Manual: Version 1.0. Report prepared for Mathtech, Inc.

WILLIAMS, J. L. (1971) Personal space and its relation to extraversion-introversion. *Canadian Journal of Behavioral Science,* 3: 156-160.

WILLIS, F. N. (1966) Initial speaking distance as a function of speakers' relationship. *Psychonomic Science,* 5: 221-222.

WOLFF, C. (1948) *A Psychology of Gesture.* London: Methuen.

WOLFF, P. and J. GUTSTEIN (1972) Effects of induced motor gestures on vocal output. *Journal of Communications,* 22: 277-288.

WOODWORTH, R. S. (1938) *Experimental Psychology.* New York: Henry Holt.

WRIGHTSMAN, L. S. (1977) *Social Psychology* (2nd Ed.). Monterey, CA: Brooks/ Cole.

ZECHMEISTER, K. and D. DRUCKMAN (1973) Determinants of resolving a conflict of interest: A simulation of political decision making. *Journal of Conflict Resolution,* 17: 63-88.

ZUCKERMAN, M. (1979) Attribution of success and failure revisited, or: The motivational bias is alive and well in attribution theory. *Journal of Personality,* 47: 245-287.

ZUCKERMAN, M., R. S. DeFRANK, J. A. HALL, D. T. LARRANCE, and R. ROSENTHAL (1979) Facial and vocal cues of deception and honesty. *Journal of Experimental Social Psychology,* 15: 378-396.

ZUCKERMAN, M., M. S. LIPETS, J. H. KOIVUMAKI, and R. ROSENTHAL (1975) Encoding and decoding nonverbal cues of emotion. *Journal of Personality and Social Psychology,* 32: 1068-1076.

ZUNIN, L. with N. ZUNIN (1972) *Contact: The First Four Minutes.* Los Angeles: Nash.

REFERENCE INDEX

This index is designed to assist the reader in locating material relevant to each of the references cited in the text. It should be useful to the reader who has an interest in particular subjects or authors. The complete citation is to be found on the last page number listed for the reference. (It will be noted that some references appear only in the bibliography. While not cited in the text, these references were used in the work.)

AUTHORS' NOTE: Thanks go to Kathy Druckman for assistance in compiling this index.

ABOUT THE AUTHORS

DANIEL DRUCKMAN is the Mathtech Scientist at Mathematica, Inc. in Bethesda, Maryland. He received a Ph.D. in social psychology from Northwestern University. His primary interests are in the areas of interparty conflict resolution, policy decision-making, negotiations, coalition formation, and modeling methodologies, including simulation. Among his current concerns is the interface between behavioral science and political (including intergovernmental) decision-making.

RICHARD M. ROZELLE is Professor of Psychology and Director of Graduate Training in the Department of Psychology at the University of Houston. He received a Ph.D. in social psychology from Northwestern University. His research interests include impression formation and management, attitude-behavior change, bargaining behavior, behavioral medicine, and program evaluation.

JAMES C. BAXTER is Professor of Psychology at the University of Houston. He received a Ph.D. in clinical psychology from the University of Texas at Austin. His primary research interests are in person perception, self-presentation, personality theory, proxemics, and statistical methodologies.